USING YOUR MONEY WISELY

USING YOUR YOUR MONEY WISELY

LARRY BURKETT

MOODY PRESS
CHICAGO

© 1985 by
CHRISTIAN FINANCIAL CONCEPTS

Moody Press Trade Paper Edition, 1990

Original title: *Principles Under Scrutiny*

All Scripture quotations in this book are from the *New American Standard Bible,* © 1960, 1962, 1963, 1968, 1971, 1972, 1973, 1975, and 1977 by The Lockman Foundation, and are used by permission.

Christian Financial Concepts, Inc., is a nonprofit, nondenominational ministry dedicated to teaching God's principles of finances. CFC offers teaching and training materials in the area of finances for youth, family, business, and education. All materials are available in video, audio, and written format.

Library of Congress Cataloging in Publication Data

Burkett, Larry.
   Using your money wisely.

   Rev. ed. of: Principles under scrutiny. c1985.
   1. Stewardship, Christian. 2. Finance, Personal
I. Burkett, Larry. Principles under scrutiny.
II. Title.
BV772.B79 1986   332.024'2   86-8664
ISBN 0-8024-3425-8 (pbk.)

5 7 9 10 8 6

Printed in the Unites States of America

My wife, Judy, and I dedicate this book
to the supporters of Christian Financial Concepts,
who make this work possible.

Contents

Part 3: Insurance and Investing

Part 4: Borrowing and Lending

Part 5: Business

Part 6: Family

Part 7: Ministries and Scriptural Highlights

Dear Christian friends,

Finances are an integral part of daily living today and can affect us either positively or negatively. Through His Word, God gave us specific guidelines to direct our lives so that we can enjoy the blessings He promises us. There are more than sixteen hundred verses in the Bible that deal directly with financial situations. Only love is discussed more often than money in the New Testament, which says something about the importance of finances.

Using Your Money Wisely presents the financial principles found in the Bible and applies them to daily life in the home, business, and church. These simple principles will forever change the way you think about finances. I pray they will be used as a guide for making financial decisions in accordance with God's Word.

Because of Christ,
Larry Burkett

Part 1:

Attitude

Fear of the Future

Many of the decisions that God's people make on a day-by-day basis are motivated not by trust in God but rather by fear of the future. That is most often true with financial decisions. For example, many people stay with jobs they fear changing. That is particularly true with those who are forty and older. Society has convinced us to large degree that those over forty are past their prime. That is nonsense and runs totally contrary to God's intention.

Fear of the future causes Christian families to scrimp and sacrifice for retirement. Often the total focus of the earlier years is toward the eventful day when "we can relax and really enjoy ourselves." Unfortunately, the same fear that necessitated the hoarding for the latter years then forces further sacrifices "just in case."

I don't mean to imply that some planning is not God's will; obviously it is. But when a Christian looks inside and finds primary attitudes of fear and worry, bondage has occurred.

"WOULD A MAN ROB GOD?"

Many families literally rob God and their families because of that underlying fear. They start a savings or insurance plan initially with an eye toward family provision but then more contingencies must be provided for. Finally there are so many contingencies that no amount of protection is adequate, and fear pervades all decisions about money. Some are willing to give a tithe from regular income, but any invasion of their surplus prompts resentment and alarm.

The net result of this life-style is bitterness, conflict within the family, and growing separation from God.

My heartfelt concern for this spiritual illness is that it is increasing among dedicated believers and is being rationalized as good planning for the future. That is an absolute lie. Any action that is not done from faith is done from sin (Romans 14:23). The growing mania for buffering ourselves against any possible future event is straight from the deceiver. When our sand castle of affluence comes tumbling down—and it will—our faith had better be founded in the person of Jesus Christ and not in material security (Matthew 7:24-27).

FAITH CONQUERS FEAR

The opposite of fear is faith. Therefore, when dealing with fear, one must first understand faith. In Hebrews, faith is described as things that we hope for and things that we do not presently have. Therefore, if we have no needs, we have no need of faith.

It is God's plan that we have some needs in order that we may develop faith in Him. It is vital that we view these future needs as opportunities to exercise and develop our faith.

In Hebrews 11:6 we are told that God is a "a rewarder of those who seek Him." Each Christian must decide, "Do I really believe that?" No Christian can truly serve God and live in fear. Christ says that it is a black-and-white choice: either you choose to serve God or you choose to serve money (Matthew 6:24).

CAN YOU REALLY TRUST GOD?

We live in a materialistic generation. Priorities are established based on desires, not needs. That is not limited to unbelievers. When we see how much confidence other Christians place in money, including those in the pastorate, it's easy to lose sight of the mark. Problems seem to erode our faith when it seems that some who truly trust God suffer financially and physically. Finally, we yield to the impulse and get caught up in the mad rush to protect against the future. We are guilty of attempting to counsel God rather than accepting His counsel.

We will never know with certainty why God allows problems to come into the lives of some godly people. But we can look back upon the lives of the apostles and see that God allowed them to suffer for their maturity and His glory.

Have you ever asked God for something and when it didn't happen you thought God had failed you? Isn't it strange that we usually expect God's answer to be a "yes" rather than a "no"? There are many reasons why God would not respond the way we desire:

1. We ask with the wrong motives (James 4:3).
2. It is the wrong time according to God's plan (Luke 11:3-10).
3. It is contrary to God's greater plan (Acts 21:13-14).
4. We are here to serve God, not for God to serve us (Job 41:11).

HOW TO TRUST GOD

1. Find God's direction for YOUR life. Most of the frustrations experienced by Christians come as the result of patterning their lives after someone else's. Even the most devout believer can drift off of God's path by trying to match assets with another. Remember that God's successes are not graded by accumulated savings.

Accept God's provision as His plan for your life, and find contentment in the source rather than the supply (1 Timothy 6:7-8).

2. Make a conscious act of trusting God. The method of doing that will vary from family to family. For one, it will mean actually withdrawing some of their stored resource and sharing it as God directs them. For another, it means taking the step of faith to leave that fruitless job. For another it may mean being content without that new, bigger home. The ways to practice putting our faith into motion are as different as God's plan for each of us. I would challenge you to find a way to express your faith through a material commitment.

3. Develop a long-range viewpoint. Since God rarely works on the same timetable that we do, it is important that we learn what patience is—waiting. Just because you don't understand what is going on in your life, don't begin to doubt God's direction. I don't think that Joseph really understood God's long-range plan as he sat in the Egyptian jail. He did understand what God expected of him each day and was faithful to do what God asked him.

"Therefore do not be anxious for tomorrow; for tomorrow will care for itself. Each day has enough trouble of its own" (Matthew 6:34).

4. Pray diligently. It has been said that prayer is God's secret weapon. It's time we let the secret out and begin to exercise the most powerful tool that God has given us. Prayer is the key to unlocking God's blessings and power. It is the most neglected part of most Christians' lives. Faith is not possible outside of prayer, and with prayer all things are possible.

"Pray without ceasing; in everything give thanks; for this is God's will for you in Christ Jesus'" (1 Thessalonians 5:17-18).

14

Brokenness—God's Best

Perhaps no principle in God's Word is less understood than that of brokenness. Brokenness does not mean being broke financially. It is a condition in which God allows circumstances to control our lives to the point that we must depend totally upon God.

It would seem that the greater God's plan for a person, the greater the brokenness. The life of the apostle Paul reflects both great power and great brokenness. Yet Paul never considered his personal circumstances punishment. He consistently asserted that his sufferings were a direct result of service to Christ.

"For just as the sufferings of Christ are ours in abundance, so also our comfort is abundant through Christ" (2 Corinthians 1:5).

THE PURPOSE OF BROKENNESS

In God's wisdom He realizes what it takes to keep us attuned to His direction. He then allows problems to occur that will break our will and keep us dependent upon Him. Once a Christian makes a total surrender of that old self to God, then (and only then) God can begin to use him. Since "self" continues to surface, God must allow testing to continue in order to "kill" the old self.

Many times we pray, "God mold me into a vessel You can use," and then when God's work begins, we want to run.

James 1:2-3 says, *"Consider it all joy, my brethen, when you encounter various trials, knowing that the testing of your faith produces endurance."* If you want the perfecting of your faith, it comes by way of testing.

THE EVIDENCE OF SERVICE

The principle of brokenness is easier to teach than to live. The teaching is very clear in the lives of those whom God has chosen to use throughout the Bible. The greater the service to God, the greater the potential for ego and self-centeredness. Thus, the greater the necessity for maintaining a "God first" spirit. Brokenness is an apt term for those being molded into Christ's image.

Clearly the purpose of brokenness is to make a Christian totally dependent on God and separate from this world.

"And in all this, they are surprised that you do not run with them into the same excess of dissipation, and they malign you; but they shall give account to Him who is ready to judge the living and dead" (1 Peter 4:4-5).

HOW IS BROKENNESS ACCOMPLISHED?

Since finances is one of the most often discussed topics in the New Testament, it would seem obvious that God would use that area to test our obedience to Him. In our society we have a value rating system that is based upon material worth. That is just as true within Christianity as it is in the unbelieving world. Fortunately, God's value system is based on spiritual worth and is measured by our willingness to accept *His* direction.

The conflict between materialism and Christianty is addressed directly by the Lord in Matthew 6:24, *"No one can serve two masters; for either he will hate the one and love the other, or he will hold to one and despise the other. You cannot serve God and mammon."*

Many Christians have had their egos

shattered by financial setbacks. Some respond by panicking to the point that they abandon their Christian principles and cheat and lie to protect their security. Others fall back in defeat and lose their trust in God. Some live a life of fear, and as a result they lose their witness. Others accept God's authority over their lives and use this as an opportunity to trust God more fully and to demonstrate to others that they serve God. As was said of Job, *"Through all this Job did not sin nor did he blame God"* (Job 1:22).

Until a Christian is broken to the point of *total* dependence on God, he is not really useful in God's plan. *"But whatever things were gain to me, those things I have counted as loss for the sake of Christ"* (Philippians 3:7).

EGO: GOD'S ENEMY

Few Christians are willing to share an experience with brokenness. So often we equate problems with sin and illogically conclude that those who have problems are being punished by God. If that's so, then Paul was the worst sinner in the history of Christianity. He was flogged five times, beaten, stoned, shipwrecked, imprisoned, and deserted. And yet he said that he was in God's will and was comforted by God.

"Therefore we do not lose heart, but though our outer man is decaying, yet our inner man is being renewed day by day" (2 Corinthians 4:16).

God desires to break our ego and pride—*not* our spirit. Indeed, in the spirit we should grow stronger under affliction. The purpose is to strip us of all self-gratification. *"But he who boasts, let him boast in the Lord. For not he who commends himself is approved, but whom the Lord commends"* (2 Corinthians 10:17-18). A man can accomplish a great deal in his own strength and ability, but the lasting effect is minimal.

RUN OR RELAX?

Our first reaction to the pressures that accompany brokenness is to run. It's simply easier to withdraw and feel sorry for ourselves than it is to stand against the enemy. No one can question Elijah's courage or commitment to God. He regularly risked his life to deliver God's messages. And yet right after he had called down God's fire from heaven and had destroyed the prophets of Baal, he ran when Jezebel threatened him. In 1 Kings 19:4, he is found under a juniper tree asking God to let him die; instead, God comforts him, feeds him, and tells him to relax and rest. Later, when Elijah was refreshed, God sent him back into the battle.

There are times in all of our lives when we feel defeated and would like to simply get away from it all. If that happens to those between forty and fifty years of age, we usually label it a mid-life crisis. In reality such crises come at every stage of life. It's just that at mid-life they are amplified by doubts about the future.

Paul must have had some real doubts about the difficulties he faced throughout his service to the Lord. But the overwhelming characteristic we see in Paul's letters is the ability to relax and enjoy life regardless of his external circumstances. Paul was truly a broken man but not a defeated one.

"For the sorrow that is according to the will of God produces a repentance without regret, leading to salvation; but the sorrow of the world produces death" (2 Corinthians 7:10).

16

THE LESSON OF BROKENNESS

Brokenness, whether it is financial, physical, emotional, or all three, has at its center the purpose of teaching us to trust in God. Paul knew that his tribulations were the result of constantly stepping on Satan's toes. They were neither pleasant nor enjoyable to Paul, but he knew they were necessary in order to build the courage of others.

"Therefore I ask you not to lose heart at my tribulations on your behalf, for they are your glory" (Ephesians 3:13).

FINANCIAL BROKENNESS

God is in control. If we are serving Him, then nothing can befall us except that He allows it. It will rarely seem beneficial at the time, but if we believe God's Word, then we must believe He will ultimately receive the glory.

"And we know that God causes all things to work together for good to those who love God, to those who are called according to His purpose" (Romans 8:28).

An important aspect of God's work in our lives is to teach God's people to love and care about each other. When Christians are suffering from a financial disaster, the last thing they need is an accusation.

In fact, they need help. So the testing of our faith through brokenness extends over to the testing of the faith of others through compassion. No message in God's Word is clearer than that of John's on this subject: *"But whoever has the world's goods, and beholds his brother in need and closes his heart against him, how does the love of God abide in him? Little children, let us not love with word or with tongue, but in deed and truth"* (1 John 3:17-18).

We are admonished to love with deeds. That is a prerequisite to having God answer our requests (1 John 3:22-24).

If you're going through a period of trials and testing, don't get discouraged. Share your struggle honestly with those around you, and get the prayer support and other support that God has already provided. Remember that God does not want to break you spiritually. He desires that you and I conform to His Son's image. To do that we must have our ego and pride broken.

17

Being Content

One of the great mysteries of Christianity is contentment. At least one must presume it is a mystery because so few people have found it. Actually, contentment is an attitude.

EXTREMES

There are many people who seemingly have little or no regard for material possessions. They accept poverty as a normal living condition, and their major concern is which doorway to sleep in. Are they living a life of contentment? Hardly so, because that description aptly fits the winos found in the Bowery of New York. In contrast are the affluent who have the best our society has to offer at their disposal. Their homes are the community showplaces, their summer cottages are more like small hotels, and their automobiles cost more than most families' houses. Does their abundance guarantee contentment? Considering the amount of alcohol and tranquilizers many of them consume, it's hard to imagine that this group is any more content than the previous one.

BALANCE

If money can't buy it and poverty doesn't provide it, what is contentment? Contentment, contrary to popular opinion, is *not* being satisfied where you are. It is knowing God's plan for your life, having the conviction to live it, and believing that God's peace is greater than the world's problems.

But often we get so involved in the day-to-day activities of earning a living and raising a family that we forget our real purpose: to serve God. Consequently, the trivial problems such as buying a new car or attaining a higher position begin to crowd our conscious mind, and God's plan becomes an abstract goal rather than our focus.

"And others are the ones on whom seed was sown among the thorns; these are the ones who have heard the word, and the worries of the world, and the deceitfulness of riches, and the desires for other things enter in and choke the word , and it becomes unfruitful" (Mark 4:18-19).

SOCIAL GOALS

Christians get trapped into a discontent life by adopting worldly goals. These goals always boil down to: more, bigger, best. Scripture defines that as indulgence, greed, and pride. Often a successful man comes to the Lord out of desperation when he realizes that his whole life is characterized by fear and anxiety, and the accumulation of assets has not alleviated the fear. For a while after accepting Christ as Savior, there is a peace and a real desire to commit everything to God. Unfortunately, since most other Christians are living "natural" lives, the tendency is to fall back into the same old routine, only now rationalizing that it is "serving the Lord." The evidence to the contrary is a lack of peace, a lack of spiritual growth, and a growing doubt about God. Satan's ploy is to use the riches of the world to keep people away from God's salvation. If that fails he simply uses it to steer them away from God's path.

REGRESSION

In our society it is not normal to step down. Once a certain level of income or spending has been attained, it is considered a sign of failure to step down. Even in the face of certain disaster, the image must be maintained. Families that suffer a job loss will continue to maintain their style of living through debt rather than risk the stigma of failure. Others who have felt God's leading to reduce their living style fail to respond because of social status pressure.

Is the concept of conservation and moderation really a loser's attitude? Not according to biblical standards. Contentment cannot be achieved without personal discipline.

"No servant can serve two masters; for either he will hate the one, and love the other, or else he will hold to one, and despise the other. You cannot serve God and mammon. Now the Pharisees, who were lovers of money, were listening to all these things, and they were scoffing at Him" (Luke 16:13-14).

"And He said to them, 'Beware, and be on your guard against every form of greed; for not even when one has an abundance does his life consist of his possessions'" (Luke 12:15).

THE DANGER OF ABUNDANCE

The majority of warnings in Christ's messages were to the wealthy, not the poor. In poverty, the issue is usually black and white—honesty or dishonesty. In affluence, it is much more subtle. In America I believe nearly everyone would be graded as wealthy by any biblical standard. Our anxieties and worries are not related to the *lack* of things but rather to the *loss* of things. Many, if not most, Christians inwardly fear they might lose the material goods they have acquired. Therefore, they compromise God's best for their lives to hang on to the very way of life that brought so much worry and turmoil before they met the Lord. This does not necessarily mean surrendering the assets. It means being willing to.

GOD'S PLAN FOR CONTENTMENT

Although many Scriptures teach about the dangers of material riches, God's Word does not teach that poverty is the alternative. God wants us to understand that money is a tool to use in accomplishing His plan through us. If we are to find true contentment we must establish some basic guidelines.

1. *Establish a reasonable standard of living.* Having a surplus does not mean that it's there for us to use as we want. *"So is the man who lays up treasure for himself, and is not rich toward God"* (Luke 12:21). It is important to develop a life-style based on conviction—not circumstances. *"Since all these things are to be destroyed in this way, what sort of people ought you to be in holy conduct and godliness"* (2 Peter 3:11).

Since there is no universal plan suitable for everyone, this must be a standard established among husband, wife, and God. Obviously, God will assign Christians at every economic tier. If God's plan for you is at the upper tier, there will be a purpose for the abundance and a ministry through it. Just having an abundance is not a sign of God's blessings. Satan can easily duplicate any worldly riches. God's riches are without sorrow and are for bringing others to salvation. A disciplined life-style with an abundance is greater witness than the abundance could ever be.

2. *Establish a habit of giving.* Above the tithe God wants Christians to be involved with the needs of others. *"And the King will answer and say to them, 'Truly I say to you, to the extent that you did it to one of these brothers of Mine, even the least of them, you did it to Me'"* (Matthew 25:40). There is no better way to appreciate what we

have than to observe those who truly have needs. Every Christian should be directly involved with the needs of another. There are many Christian organizations that act as a funnel for such funds. If you can't be personally involved, this is the best alternative. With millions of people literally starving in the world today, the rewards are saved lives as well as souls.

"At this present time your abundance being a supply for their want, that their abundance also may become a supply for your want, that there may be equality; as it is written, 'He who gathered much did not have too much, and he who gathered little had no lack'" (2 Corinthians 8:14-15).

3. *Establish priorities.* Many Christians are discontented—not because they aren't doing well but because others are doing better. *"Let your character be free from the love of money, being content with what you have; for He Himself has said, 'I will never desert you, nor will I ever forsake you'"* (Hebrews 13:5). Too often we let the urgent things take priority over the important things. Virtually every get-rich-quick scheme is directed at those who have not established firm priorities. They imply that more money is the way to glorify God and that it is a sign of failure not to have every desire met.

That is the same attitude that Paul admonished in 1 Corinthians 4:7-21. Paul's priorities were established according to God's plan for his life, and that didn't happen to include the accumulation of money. If spiritual and family priorities were considerd before financial desires, few Christians would get involved with "free time" money schemes. Most of the free time is actually robbed from the Lord and the family.

4. *Develop a thankful attitude.* It is remarkable that in America we could ever think that God has failed us materi-ally. That attitude is possible only when we allow Satan to convince us to compare ourselves to others.

"But if you have bitter jealousy and selfish ambition in your heart, do not be arrogant and so lie against the truth. This wisdom is not that which comes down from above, but is earthly, natural, demonic" (James 3:14-15).

The primary defense against this attitude is praise to God. Satan uses lavishness and waste to create discontent and selfish ambition. Why else would a man drive himself to acquire more than he needs or can logically use and in the process destroy his health, family, and usefulness to God? Thankfulness is a state of mind, not an accumulation of assets. Until a Chistian can truly thank God for what he has and be willing to accept that as God's provision for his life, contentment will never be possible.

5. *Reject a fearful spirit.* Another tool of Satan is the question, "What if?" Dedicated Christians get trapped into hoarding because they fear the "What if?" of retirement, disability, unemployment, economic collapse, and so on. Obviously, God wants us to consider these things and even plan for them—within reason. But when fear dictates to the point that giving to God's work is hindered, foolish risks are assumed, and worry becomes the norm rather than the exception—contentment is impossible. A Christian must consciously reject the attitude of fear. It may be necessary to face the fear to claim God's victory. If the fear is a lack of surplus, it may be necessary to live without it in order to conquer it.

6. *Seek God's will for you.* "More than that, I count all things to be loss in view of the surpassing value of knowing Christ Jesus my Lord, for whom I have suffered the loss of all things, and count them but rubbish in order*

that I may gain Christ" (Philippians 3:8).

7. *Stand up to the fear.* "*I can do all things through Him who strengthens me*" (Philippians 4:13).

8. *Trust God's promise.* "*And the peace of God, which surpasses all comprehension, shall guard your hearts and your minds in Christ Jesus*" (Philippians 4:7).

Love Your Enemies

Recently a close friend whom I will call Bill called to discuss a difficult situation he was facing. Several months before, Bill had released a key employee because of his belligerent attitude. Now that employee was going into competition with him with one of his clients.

Obviously, it was his right to start a new business, except that to do so he had to sub-contract his business to Bill until he could get his equiptment functioning. Also, the ex-employee was calling on Bill's customers and casually dropping degrading remarks about his former employer.

The questions Bill asked were honest and difficult ones: How far do I go as a Christian in aiding my competitors? Is it really my responsibility to carry him with my business until he develops his and competes for my customers? and, Should I tell my customers what is going on to combat the innuendos of the ex-employee?

BEWARE OF FEELINGS

Generally, our initial impression is a purely emotional one, and unless we are controlled primarily by God's Word, that first impression is rarely the correct one. In fact, I have discovered that many initial impressions run opposite to God's direction. Therefore, we must turn to His Word.

BIBLICAL BALANCE

The Scriptures present an interesting perspective of strength and compassion when dealing with enemies (I stretch that term to include deceitful competitors). The account of David's confrontation with Nabal is given in 1 Samuel 25. It seems that in spite of David's noble gesture to protect Nabal's property, when David needed help Nabal refused even to acknowledge him. That obvious affront infuriated David.

In anger David decided to take matters into his own hands and destroy Nabal. God used Abigail, Nabal's wife, to stop David from taking vengeance. In the face of godly counsel, David cooled off and withdrew. His withdrawal could well have been interpreted as weakness by others—even his own men. However, the result was that God executed judgment in His own time. Thus, the use of restraint was more effective than the use of strength.

WHAT IS STRENGTH ?

Even a cursory review of Scripture reveals that strength does not always mean the exercise of power. More often it means the relinquishing of personal rights to God. That may also mean relinquishing the "right" to retribution or revenge.

The opposite of strength is cowardice. Those who flee from any confrontation display cowardice. What is the difference then? Whether or not God receives honor from the action.

A person who allows others to cheat and abuse him because he is fearful of any conflict is a coward. Cowardice is generally motivated by self-preservation, not compassion. The classic example of that is found in Numbers 13 and 14 where God's people refuse to occupy their Promised Land because of the giants living there. Were they demonstrating compassion for their enemies? Hardly so—they were clearly self-motivated.

Strength, then, is the proper use of power to acomplish God's assigned task.

HATE THE ENEMY?

In our society, it appears acceptable to conform to the Old Testament law of "an eye for an eye." In truth, such retribution was always limited to an action of the community—the government. Its purpose was to maintain order by punishment.

A Christian must decide early in his spiritual life that surrendering to God necessitates giving up some personal rights, one of which is retaliation.

"You have heard that it was said, 'You shall love your neighbor, and hate your enemy.' But I say to you, love your enemies, and pray for those who persecute you" (Matthew 5:43-44).

AID THE ENEMY?

Loving your enemies is different from aiding them. Christ loved the Pharisees as He loved everyone, but He certainly did not help them. To the contrary, He opposed them often and warned His disciples to stay away from them (Matthew 16:6). They represented a counterforce that was anti-Christian.

That is not meant to imply that all competitors fall into the same classification as the Pharisees. But when a competitor purposely sets himself against your and God's interests, he certainly cannot be classified as a friend.

God would have us love competitors both prayerfully and spiritually, but that does not mean aiding them. There can be occasions when God directs us to aid a competitor, but only because it provides a witness for Him.

LOVE YOUR ENEMIES

Even a survey of this subject would be incomplete without discussing Proverbs 25:21. *"If your enemy is hungry, give him food to eat; and if he is thirsty, give him water to drink."* Paul makes reference to that proverb in Romans 12. The context in which it is used dispels any idea that a Christian has a right to revenge.

A common misconception is that you must hand your enemy a cup of water while he beats upon your head. Clearly that is not so. Rather, we are to forgive our enemy and acknowledge his needs as we would a friend's.

SUMMARY

A Christian is instructed to love his enemies (I stretched this principle to include business competitors). However, we are not asked to aid an enemy in our defeat. The only motivation for doing so would be a personal revelation from the Lord that He was using us to accomplish a greater work.

God instructs a believer to forgive an offense, not to seek revenge. Before taking any action, a Christian must evaluate the motivation.

In the situation that generated this study, a Christian businessman was faced with a decision about aiding his competitors. What was the conclusion? He decided not to do so. He requested that they take their business elsewhere or do it themselves. The motivation was not to punish them but to be the best possible steward of God's business. He determined that he had a greater responsibility to his stockholders and employees than to his competitors.

To be as fair as possible, he gave them adequate notice so that they could transfer their business. He did not inform his customers of any of the events but left the matter in the Lord's hands.

Suffering for Christ vs. Living Like a King

Some time ago, I had the opportunity to view the misapplication of a scriptural principle in the lives of two people. The first was a believer working in a full-time Christian ministry. Along with his commitment to serve others, he had dedicated himself and his family to a life of virtual poverty. He sincerely felt that in order to serve Christ, one had to relinquish all ownership of worldly goods and look poor. He decided to sell his family's home, most of their furniture, and the majority of their other possessions.

SCRIPTURAL CLUB

His scriptural justification was based on Luke 9:3: *"And He said to them, 'Take nothing for your journey, neither a staff, nor a bag, nor bread, nor money; and do not even have two tunics apiece.'"*

Christ was teaching His disciples a simple truth: trust God—He is sufficient. There is no doubt that each of us needs to act in accordance with this principle. All through Scripture, God teaches that words without corresponding actions mean absolutely nothing. In a generation in which most people live by fear, God expects His people to live by faith.

This passage leaves no doubt that Christ directed His disciples to take no provisions with them. They were to live by faith; those to whom they were ministering would supply their needs. There is also no doubt that Christ has since directed many others to do the same thing. Most notable among them was George Mueller. However, one thing that identifies those who are chosen by God from those who impose such hardships on themselves is an attitude of peace and joy.

That was certainly not so with the individual I met. He was egotistical about his commitment and openly critical of other Christians who were living "carnal, worldly" lives. He was on the verge of bitterness and had rebellion in his home. His wife was resentful about the abrupt change in their life-style. She said his response to every material request by her or the children was, "God doesn't want us to have that." The more we discussed these inconsistencies with what he was doing, the more he rationalized them as sufferings for the Lord. I pointed out that another group had felt the same way.

LEGALISMS

The Pharisees of Christ's day did what they thought were great things for God, and most of the things they did were even the right things. They prayed, they fasted, they tithed. Christ never challenged their actions—He challenged their motives.

"But woe to you Pharisees! For you pay tithe of mint and rue and every kind of garden herb, and yet disregard justice and the love of God; but these are the things you should have done without neglecting the others" (Luke 11:42).

They were so blinded by their own self-righteousness they couldn't see God's true promises. He confronted them with this truth in Matthew 12:7. *"But if you had known what this means, 'I desire compassion, and not a sacrifice,' you would not have condemned the innocent.*" Some were prideful in their poverty, while others required the best of everything. But in God's eyes they suffered from a common malady: ego.

BALANCE

It's interesting that Bible-believing Christians will sometimes focus on a single Scripture to justify their actions while ignoring other references contrary to their personal "revelation." That is not to discredit a believer's uniqueness from the world. God calls each of us to a radical life-style—total commitment to Him—but rarely does the Lord call one of His to voluntary poverty. And He never singles out an individual to such a life-style without other verifications of this calling. The least of these verifications will be love, compassion, and acceptance that God doesn't call everyone to sacrifice similarly.

That truth is evidenced in Scripture when Peter proclaims to Christ that he is ready to go to prison and die for his faith. Christ responded by telling him that he would deny his faith three times before morning. Then He reminded His disciples of the time earlier when they had been instructed to go out taking along no provisions, only this time He gave them new instructions.

"*And He said to them, 'When I sent you out without purse and bag and sandals, you did not lack anything, did you?' And they said, 'No, nothing.' And He said to them, 'But now, let him who has a purse take it along, likewise also a bag, and let him who has no sword sell his robe and buy one'*" (Luke 22:35-36).

The possession or absence of material things is not an issue with serving Christ—the attitude about them is.

It is important for us not to assume the role of God's advisor in the area of sacrifice. God knows what each of us is called to do, and He equips us to do it. In the case of this Christian, the evidence was conclusive that a lot more prayer would be needed before he could make a decision to "suffer" for Christ in this way.

LIVING LIKE A KING

Shortly after the "poverty syndrome" situation, I came in contact with another Christian who was also in full-time Christian work. But he presented the opposite and far more popular extreme. "I'm a child of the King," he said, "and I'm going to live like it." To emphasize his point, he told me about his $40,000 car, his son's private school, the new house, pool, and so on. With a little prompting, he told me how God had directed him into a home sales company with a pyramid marketing system, and how he was one of its leading new distributors. It was a great opportunity to help others in a more practical way, he said. I soon learned from his comments that he was prospecting for additional people to "help."

He went on to declare that God really wants to bless His people, and unless a Christian is materially successful, God isn't blessing him.

SELFISHNESS

The theology of selfishness is an easy one to promote because most of us were raised with it, and today it virtually dominates our society. It's the philosophy called "get all you can out of life today, live with all the gusto you can get."

That is certainly not a new philosophy. Solomon described it very well in the book of Ecclesiastes. "*I said to myself,*

'Come now, I will test you with pleasure. So enjoy yourself.' And behold, it too was futility" (Ecclesiates 2:1).

It is important to discern the difference between the pride of wealth and the wealth itself. Christ never condemned the wealth—it belongs to God. He condemned the wealthy-minded of this world. God has made many people wealthy both spiritually and materially, but wealth was never a sign of God's blessing (1 Corinthians 4:9, 11). Overwhelmingly, those selected by God to manage a large surplus to feed His sheep manifest humility, not pride.

A SEPARATED LIFE

One of the evidences of Christianity is that we desire to keep and obey God's statutes and commandments (1 John 3:22) and do what is pleasing to Him. We are called lights and God's people. Nowhere does God say that to follow Him we are to live like a king. In fact, He says that the tug of this world and its pleasures will be the greatest threat to our walk with Him.

"Do not love the world, nor the things in the world. If anyone loves the world, the love of the Father is not in him" (1 John 2:15).

Certainly, it is initially easy to attract people to Christianity by a show of wealth, but the evidence in the world around tells us that the effect in changed lives is very temporary. A Christian whose witness is based on a supply of material things will quickly find that people are interested only if God will promise to do the same thing for them. If He won't or doesn't, then they look elsewhere. Give them a little truth about what Christ really expects in the way of commitment, and most would say, "It's not for me."

"Sell your possessions and give to char- ity; make yourselves purses which do not wear out, an unfailing treasure in heaven, where no thief comes near, nor moth destroys. For where your treasure is, there will your heart be also"* (Luke 12:33-34).

A BALANCED LIFE

It's clear that neither a voluntary rejection of all wealth nor a display of material success are part of a balanced Christian walk. Obviously, God will have Christians at each end of the material spectrum. It is God's right to determine how we are to be used.

"On the contrary, who are you, O man, who answers back to God? The thing molded will not say to the molder, 'Why did you make me like this,' will it?" (Romans 9:20).

There is little danger that the imbalance of self-enforced sacrifice will catch on in our society. Sacrifice to most of us means driving a standard shift car without air conditioning. However, there is a growing emphasis in Christianity toward a materialistic life-style. That is reflected in a de-emphasis on caring for the needs of others. Once that attitude catches on within our churches, the priorities shift from caring for the poor, invalid, and elderly to building bigger and better buildings.

Obviously, we need buildings in which to minister adequately, but we don't need palaces. The danger of affluence has been a real threat in every generation of Christians, but today it's becoming an epidemic.

Most Christians are familiar with the parable of the rich farmer in Luke 12:16-20, but it's also necessary to remember the preceding passage.

"And He said to them, 'Beware, and be on your guard against every form of greed; for not even when one has an abundance does his life consist of his possessions'" (Luke 12:15).

27

Without a surplus, little could be done in Gods work, so obviously some Christians must have an abundance. God allows us to use part of that abundance for ourselves and our families. That amount will vary according to God's unique plan for each of us. But when our attitudes become controlled by our possessions rather than by God's Word, we're no longer useful to God.

"Now He was also saying to the disciples, 'There was a certain rich man who had a steward, and this steward was reported to him as squandering his possessions. And he called him and said to him, "What is this I hear about you? Give an account of your stewardship, for you can no longer be steward"' " (Luke 16:1-2).

That warning is one that each Christian should consider well. What a shame it is to be deceived by Satan into trading an eternity of riches for a few shiny trinkets.

"And He said to them, 'You are those who justify yourselves in the sight of men, but God knows your hearts; for that which is highly esteemed among men is destestable in the sight of God'" (Luke 16:15).

Being Excellent
in a Mediocre World

"**D**o you see a man skilled in his work? He will stand before kings; he will not stand before obscure men" (Proverbs 22:29).

I guess that's why there aren't very many kings left; there are very few skilled men to stand before them.

We live in a society where average is exceptional, and slothful is normal. The trend today is to seek the path of least resistance, and when the going gets difficult, give up. In school, when the total grades are averaged together, it's called "grading on the curve." In our society, we Christians have allowed our standards to be graded on the curve of the world.

We are no longer "the lights in a world of darkness," particularly where excellence is concerned. We are not noted as the best in any area, including business, education, and work—or even in the area of faith. We have lowered our standards to those of the average around us. More Christians depend upon the governement than upon God. Why? Because we have found it easier to adjust to mediocrity than to the source of excellence—God's Word.

Therefore, it is vital that we walk according to God's Word. *"Trust in the Lord with all your heart, and do not lean on your own understanding. In all your ways acknowledge Him, and He will make your paths straight"* (Proverbs 3:5-6). To do so there are some basic attitudes to reassess.

First, recognize that the world has not conformed to God's standards; we have conformed to Satan's.

Second, recognize that God's standards are not always pleasant because they require discipline. In the long run, discipline yields greater freedom because it frees us to serve God even more. God's boundaries are not there to test or punish us. They are established because God made us and knows what truly gives us peace. In order to establish God's excellence, we must recognize the fallacy of the world's standards.

IOU VS. YOU-OWE-ME

The common attitude today is "somebody owes me something." Many Americans think that a lifetime job with good pay and a guaranteed retirement plan at sixty-five comes with being born; promotion is just a matter of time; forty hours a week is the maximum endurance for any worker; the last hour of each day is there to make the transition to home easier; a ten-minute coffee break should take at least half-an-hour; a half-hour lunch should take at least an hour-an-a-half; and an equal share of company profits belongs to the workers.

Honestly consider whether Christian employees act as if they believe differently from the you-owe-me attitude found in industry today. What does God require? *"Whatever you do, do your work heartily, as for the Lord rather than for men"* (Colossians 3:23).

God's principles demand that no matter what others are doing, we serve Him through every action we take.

OUR RIGHTS

The banner of nearly everyone in our society today is "we demand our rights." Exactly what are our rights as Christians? The rights of servants.

Being a servant is not a particularly appealing image to most Christians, but that is precisely what we are called to be. Perhaps one of the most common reasons many Christians are not useful to God is because of a proud, defiant attitude toward an employer, husband, or other person. But that attitude has its roots in a rebellious spirit toward God. When a person with a rebellious spirit is confronted with the principle of self-sacrifice from God's Word, the truth will become evident.

"Do nothing from selfishness or empty conceit, but with humility of mind let each of you regard one another as more important than himself" (Philippians 2:3).

WHY DO MORE THAN NECESSARY?

There is an old saying, "If you want someone to do a good job, find a busy man." The precept is that a man who is not busy probably doesn't want to be. Obviously, that's not always true, but in the long run, I have found a great deal of truth in it. Many people do no more than is necessary to meet the minimum standards set for them. They will continually belittle others who work to capacity and will demand more and more protection for their position. Solomon described them well.

"Poor is he who works with a negligent hand, but the hand of the diligent makes rich" (Proverbs 10:4).

GOAL SETTING

To avoid the trap of "curve grading" each of us must establish some minimum, godly goals. It means that we cannot be content to "get by." That does not justify swinging to the opposite extreme and exhibiting a perfectionist attitude or abandoning God and family in the pursuit of success. It means balance. Excellence is *not* extreme; it should be normal.

A wife and mother must become so skilled at homemaking that she is noted by others for her excellence. What a great opportunity for witness when the secular world comes to a Christian woman for counsel on how to live on a budget or how to economize in the home.

"An excellent wife, who can find? For her worth is far above jewels" (Proverbs 31:10).

A husband and father must have standards that do not get eroded by slothfulness. It is important that the image a child perceives of his father is not of one who sits in front of a TV demanding silence from everybody. Many men who are excellent at work seem to feel that the same standard is not applicable to the home.

An employee must be willing to go far beyond the minimum demands to retain a job. That means adopting a steward's attitude about everything he does. If the jobs is sweeping the floors, it should be done with such thoroughness and excellence that it would be known even to the president of the company.

SUMMARY

Obviously, we could go on and on reviewing the positives of excellence and negatives of mediocrity. It should be sufficient to say that God established excellence as our norm. *"Whether, then, you eat or drink or whatever you do, do all to the glory of God"* (1 Corinthians 10:31). To accept less is dishonoring to God and demoralizing to us. The result will be a loss of credibility in the eyes of others—especially the slothful—and the chastening of the Lord.

Finances and Your Relationship with God

Without a doubt, there is a great need in Christianity to get back to the basics of God's Word. That is true whether we're talking about salvation, sanctification, service, or finances.

In reality, we have only one purpose for anything we do in this lifetime—to glorify God. If our day-to-day lives don't reflect that service, then we're not serving God.

There is a great deal of false service by many who profess to serve God but actually want God to serve them. They will give, but they always expect to be repaid. They will help the needy, but it's to keep God from allowing some tragedy to befall them. The list could go on and on and would eventually touch every one of us. Why? Because I believe so few really understand the function that finances play in our spiritual lives.

The financial principles given throughout God's Word are not there to see if we're strong enough to live by them—they're given because God knows that they are the *best* for us. God's principles of finances are not an arbitrary set of rules by which to govern us—they are a loving Father's wisdom to those who will listen and trust Him.

We have built an affluent society based upon a sand foundation of future debt. All that we have is in danger of being wiped out by any financial crisis, even a relatively minor one. Not so with those who observe and obey God's financial wisdom. God's financial wisdom builds to last, not to impress others.

WHY DID CHRIST TEACH ON FINANCES?

It surprises many Christians to learn that approximately two-thirds of the parables that Christ used in teaching deal specifically with finances. The reason for that is very simple—He chose a topic with which everyone could identify. A parable is a form of teaching in which a well-known topic is used to explain a relatively unknown topic. Christ was describing a spiritual kingdom that is actually more real than this material kingdom. But in order to relate to worldly people, He had to use a worldly example—money.

Christ never said money or material things were problems. He said that they were *symptoms* of the real problems. He constantly warned us to guard our hearts against greed, covetousness, ego, and pride, because those are the tools that Satan uses to control and manipulate this world. Christ warned us a great deal more about materialism than He did any other sin.

"And He said to them, `Beware, and be on your guard against every form of greed; for not even when one has an abundance does his life consist of his possessions'" (Luke 12:15). In fact, in the parable about salvation in Matthew 13:18-23, "the deceitfulness of riches" is given as a cause for unfruitfulness.

Satan has taken the very riches provided by God to enhance our lives and bring others to salvation and has diverted them for his use. Today, even Christians evaluate others on the basis of how much they have and how successful they are in

31

worldly terms. The poor are thought to be losers—less spiritual than the winners.

IS IT WRONG TO BE RICH?

Rich is a very subjective term, but here it's used in context with having enough money to meet all of your reasonable needs and still have funds left over. Clearly, God's Word teaches that many of His people will fit into that category. They will not only be able to meet their needs, but they will also be able to help others who have needs.

Obviously, in God's economy, He must either provide a material surplus to some Christians to meet the needs of others, or He must provide manna from heaven. God's plan is clearly stated in 2 Corinthians 8:14-15—that our abundance at the present time will meet the needs of others, and later their abundance will meet our needs—a good alternative to welfare within the church.

Christ warned those who are rich to always be on their guard (Luke 12:15-21). There is a great temptation to trust in the security that a surplus can provide. The greater the surplus, the greater the temptation. That's why those who are rich (most of American Christianity) must guard their hearts and minds with the principles from God's Word.

FINANCES: OUR SPIRITUAL BAROMETER

A definition of *faith*, according to Hebrews 11, is trusting God *totally*. It means trusting God for things you cannot see or manipulate into happening. Most of us truly desire to be able to exercise this faith. But the world around us tells us to do just the opposite. If you don't have the money for what you need, borrow to get it.

God's Word tells us to learn to be content and dedicate ourselves to serving God. In Hebrews 12:1 we are told, *"Let us also lay aside every encumbrance, and the sin which so easily entangles us, and let us run with endurance the race that is set before us."*

Instead, we encumber ourselves by following the worldly advice that says bigger and more are better. Just about the time most of our children are grown and leaving home, we can afford a big home and more cars, so we expand our lifestyles rather than simplify them.

One of the surest signs of worldly values in Christianity is the love of money. That is manifested in fear of the future. This fear dominates the attitudes of most believers today. The evidence of that is the mania over guaranteed incomes and retirement plans. Neither of these is necessarily wrong in itself. Obviously, most Christians would like a steady income to provide for their family's needs, and that's not unscriptural, except when they compromise God's Word for fear of losing their tenure in an education job or when they fear speaking out against obvious sin.

Retirement planning so dominates the thinking of Christians who have sizeable incomes that they overkill in this area enormously. The fear of doing without in the future causes many Christians to rob God's work of the very funds He has provided. These monies are tucked away in retirement accounts for twenty to forty years. God's Word does *not* prohibit but rather encourages saving for the future, including retirement (Proverbs 6:6-11; 21:20), but the example of the rich fool, given by the Lord in Luke 12:16-20, should be a clear direction that God's balance is "when in doubt—give; don't hoard."

THE GREATEST NEED

The greatest need in our generation is for God's undiluted Word to be taught clearly. The next greatest need is for Christians who will demonstrate that it works. In Romans 10:14, we are told that for the unsaved to believe, someone must tell them about Jesus. The book of James tells us that we are the walking, talking evidence before the unsaved world that God's Word is true. As I think about our witness before the unsaved, it would appear to be evident that in our most visible area, finances, we don't have much of a witness.

In great part, that is because Christians just haven't been taught what God's Word says. A few examples from the Word should clearly point this out.

Borrowing. We are told to borrow very modestly and cautiously, always repaying what is owed (Psalm 37:21; Proverbs 3:27-28).

Lending. Christians are to lend to one another without interest and are not to engage in lawsuits to recover losses (Deuteronomy 23:19-20; 1 Corinthians 6:1-7).

Sharing. Christians should provide for every legitimate need within their own fellowships. That would include funds for illnesses, unemployment, and old age (2 Corinthians 8:14-15).

WHAT SHOULD WE DO?

It would be negligent to conclude this study of ways finances reflect our faith without pointing out some simple steps to start applying God's wisdom.

First, study the available materials on God's principles for managing finances. You could glean all of the principles out of the Bible yourself—many Christians have. However, an organized study can reduce the time involved and give additional insights from others who have applied the principles.

Second, apply godly discipline to your life-style. It's clear that God doesn't demand the same life-style for any two families. Each of us is to witness to those whom God has placed around us. So there will be Christians at every level of income and society. But God's Word makes it *very* clear that lavishness and waste are worldly, not godly, values. Each Christian family must look at their spending habits, and particularly their waste, and give an account for their stewardship to God.

Third, teach your children God's principles. The toll that worldly financial values place on young families today is enormous. More than one-half of their marriages will fail because of unnecessary financial pressures. The vast majority of these problems could be avoided and marriages salvaged if families were taught early how to anticipate and avoid such problems. When a young couple is required to develop a budget prior to marriage, and then another couple works with them and monitors the budget for the first year, the financial problems are reduced dramatically. Christian parents should never let their children leave home without equipping them with the fundamental knowledge of finances that they will need to survive in a materialistically insane society.

Fourth, teach your neighbors. There are now several hundred Christian couples who regularly teach courses on God's principles of finances and basic budgeting in homes and churches around the country. Those who feared they would meet with indifference or disinterest found themselves swamped with requests for counseling and advice. Millions of people are hurting and don't know where to go for help. They will respond, not only to the financial advice, but also to the gospel message that always must go with it.

How to Be a Success

Ads in many national magazines promise to reveal the secrets of being a success today. Naturally, the ads are obscure enough that they don't reveal these "secrets" unless you respond. But the implication is clear enough—success today is related to money, power, and position.

It's really not much different today from how it has always been. We look first at someone's material accumulation to determine if he is successful. The admiration of society is carried one step further because even those who earn their wealth by deceit, extortion, or pornography are elevated to a platform of success today. That seems odd even in worldly terms because the evidence doesn't support the idea that material accumulation is the same as success.

A successful person is one who accomplishes goals and is able to enjoy the fruits of them. Most of those we call successful today are frustrated and miserable people with terrible family lives. Many "successful" people terminate their own lives because they have nothing to live for. Sometimes the worst thing that can happen to those without Christ is for them to accomplish their goals, because they turn out to be so worthless.

THE CHRISTIAN'S VIEW OF SUCCESS

Obviously, Christians don't fall into the same traps set by Satan, do they? We have our guard up so thoroughly that we recognize the dangers: if you spend too much time building security, the family grows up without proper guidance; when material priorities are substituted for spiritual priorities, children are spoiled by things and, thus, have an indifferent attitude; and so on and so on.

Unfortunately, Christians do fall into these traps. Why? Because the lies are so convincing that we believe they have to be true. From the outside, big homes, new cars, and private schools seem great. However, what had to be surrendered in the pursuit of them may have been greater—family relationships and the like. Remarkably, God's Word says that the things aren't the problem at all.

In fact, God promises His people the things that the unbeliever has: *"For all these things the Gentiles eagerly seek; for your heavenly Father knows that you need all these things. But seek first His kingdom and His righteousness; and all these things shall be added to you"* (Matthew 6:32-33). It is the desire that causes the grief, not the material possessions.

Poverty syndrome. Since the world puts so much store in material success, many Christians have naturally concluded that the opposite extreme is God's way, and Christians should be poor. Or if they aren't poor, at least they ought to look that way. Satan is tricky. Those that he can't trap into his plan, he tries to drive through and out the other side. He perverts one of God's blessings so that God's people will be careful to avoid it. Poverty is a reality in Scripture, but it certainly is not a promise. God said there would always be poor in the land, but He never said they would be His people. When God chose someone to live on limited resources, it was either to teach that person a lesson or to use him as an example.

The norm taught in God's Word is either enough or an abundance for those who believe and follow (Psalm 37:25;

Proverbs 3:18; 10:3; 13:22; Matthew 13:12; Mark 11:24; Luke 6:38). Many Christians believe that giving up something makes them spiritual. Although they may not believe they "earned" their salvation, they now believe that by self-sacrifice they must earn God's acceptance.

Paul laid this deception to rest once and for all in his letter to the Corinthians. *"And if I give all my possessions to feed the poor, and if I deliver my body to be burned, but do not have love, it profits me nothing"* (1 Corinthians 13:3). God is not looking for martyrs but for believers (literally, "doers").

Riches syndrome. Many Christians have concluded that since poverty isn't normal, then riches must be. They, therefore, have assumed that God must make them wealthy to protect His image. Most then set about in a totally secular way to accumulate what is supposed to be a Christian testimony.

If God doesn't provide according to their preconceived plan, they rationalize that the end justifies the means and help Him out. So what if they don't have a personal prayer or study life? After all, just think what a witness God will get from their success. And even though their children don't get much parental direction, they do get the best possible advantages.

Others try to manipulate God to work for them. They give, but usually to get. They continually demand more and the best, while fervently trying to convince others that this is normal. Rarely, if ever, do they stop to consider God's plan for fear that it won't coincide with their concept of prosperity.

"On the contrary, who are you, O man, who answers back to God? The thing molded will not say to the molder, 'Why did you make me like this,' will it?" (Romans 9:20).

There is a great danger in seeing God only from worldly eyes. Then all riches and all blessings are measured in terms of what God can do for us, rather than what we can do for God.

"But a natural man does not accept the things of the Spirit of God; for they are foolishness to him, and he cannot understand them, because they are spiritually appraised" (1 Corinthians 2:14).

God's plan may not always provide the best or the most but always enough. To be a spiritual success, a Christian must be willing to relinquish all rights and accept God's plan. Of necessity, God will place believers at every tier in society to minister to those around them.

"So then it does not depend on the man who wills or the man who runs, but on God who has mercy" (Romans 9:16).

GOD'S VIEW OF SUCCESS

A look into God's Word quickly reveals that material blessings were given because God loved His people, not because they deserved them. They were withdrawn from those who used them foolishly and transferred to a more faithful steward. *"You ask and do not receive, because you ask with wrong motives, so that you may spend it on your pleasures"* (James 4:3).

To be a success from a biblical perspective, some prerequisites must be met:

1. *Surrender.* Every successful servant of the Lord who was entrusted with material and spiritual rewards first demonstrated an acceptance of God's lordship. The list extends throughout the Scripture: Abraham, Noah, Nehemiah, David, and Paul. Even Solomon, who later strayed because of material riches, first demonstrated a surrender to God's authority.

2. *Obedience.* Those who are truly blessed by God have demonstrated a

willingness to use their material resources for God. Literally, the more they let God, the more God is able to glorify Himself through them. An unwavering dedication to God's way is the mark of a true steward.

"Because of the proof given by this ministry they will glorify God for your obedience to your confession of the gospel of Christ, and for the liberality of your contribution to them and to all" (2 Corinthians 9:13).

3. *Persistency.* One attribute of a successful person is persistency in the face of problems. God wants Christians who don't give up easily. Too often today Christians who live by the "open door" doctrine give up whenever an obstacle is encountered. If all the doors were to be open and waiting, there would not be so many Scriptures directing us to knock (Luke 11:10; 18:5). If God's people give up easily when faced with difficulties, the world will consider us losers. Nothing and nobody can shake a true believer from doing God's will once it is understood. The evidence of that can be observed in the lives of every servant who was ever used by God (Esther 4:16; Nehemiah 6:11; Acts 21:13).

RECOGNIZING GOD'S WILL

It seems evident that many Christians fall prey to worldly success motivation. They have a lot of drive and ambition but fail to recognize God's will for them and thus fall dupe to the world's will. Often they spend too much time asking someone else about God's will for their lives when it is *God* they should be asking. Ask anyone who is truly living God's plan for his life how he found it,

and usually he will say, "God just revealed it to me." Many times others helped to point him in the right direction, but usually just as many tried to talk him out of God's will. God will reveal His plan to those who seek Him diligently.

"Trust in the Lord with all your heart, and do not lean on your own understanding. In all your ways acknowledge Him, and He will make your paths straight" (Proverbs 3:5-6).

The difficulty is that, although Christians may sense God's will, if it doesn't agree with what they had in mind, particularly in regard to income and ego, they may rationalize themselves out of it. For a while there is a feeling of loss, but with time it passes. The next time the direction is not quite so strong, and it's easier to ignore. Eventually, God's call just fades away, and the thorns choke out any further direction.

"And the one on whom seed was sown among the thorns, this is the man who hears the word, and the worry of the world, and the deceitfulness of riches choke the word, and it becomes unfruitful" (Matthew 13:22).

Once a Christian examines his life and discovers that the fruitfulness is gone—regardless of the income—it is certain that God's will has been bypassed, and another master has become Lord.

"No one can serve two masters; for either he will hate the one and love the other, or he will hold to one and despise the other. You cannot serve God and mammon" (Matthew 6:24).

There are no quick, simple solutions to resolving this condition. Only earnest, honest prayer and petition will restore that sensitivity to the Holy Spirit's guidance.

How to Handle a Surplus

A Christian businessman asked a very pertinent question: "I have a surplus of money each year. What am I to do with it: give it away, invest it, put it into a retirement plan, or what?" On the surface, the Scriptures would seem to be confusing on this issue. One proverb says a wise man has a surplus in his home, while a fool has bare cupboards. However, another says that a poor man has God's blessings, and a rich man is a fool. Even the parables of Christ would appear somewhat confusing. In one parable He rebuked a rich fool who built larger barns to store his surplus, and in another he rebuked the man who failed to invest a large surplus wisely.

There is one absolute that helps to answer confusing questions: God's Word is always right and is never in conflict. God is always dealing with heart attitudes. We would call them motives. In each situation the motives must be analyzed. For one person, a surplus of money represents a trust from God that can be used for current and future needs. For another, it represents a trap of Satan to lead him out of God's path. The certainty is that Scripture warns that there is a greater danger in having a surplus than in having a need.

"And Jesus looked at him and said, `How hard it is for those who are wealthy to enter the kingdom of God! For it is easier for a camel to go through the eye of a needle, than for a rich man to enter the kingdom of God'" (Luke 18:24-25).

For those Christians with a surplus of money provided by God to meet future needs, good stewardship of that surplus requires that some or all of it must be invested. It is a fact that God has provided a great surplus to many Christians today.

CREATING A SURPLUS

The first investment can be found in Genesis 3:23. Adam was cast out of the garden and told to cultivate the soil for his food. To do so he had to risk seeds that could have been eaten; thus, he became an investor. Every farmer understands the principle of investing. Each year he is faced with a choice of eating all the seeds, selling all the seeds, or retaining some to replant. It would be a very short-sighted farmer who would either eat or sell his entire harvest. A wise farmer not only holds back some seed for replanting, but he also sorts out some of the best seed to insure a greater harvest. By doing so he exercises self-discipline to achieve greater prosperity.

Contrary to what many people believe, God is not against prosperity. The Scriptures give evidence that prosperity is one of God's blessings to those who love and obey Him (2 Chronicles 16:9; Psalm 37:4; Proverbs 8:21). The attitudes that God dislikes are greed, covetousness, and pride. Investing for selfish reasons breeds these attitudes.

JUSTIFICATION FOR "INVESTING"

The scriptural justification for investing is to multiply current assets to meet future needs. *"And the one who had received the five talents came up and brought five more talents, saying, `Master, you entrusted five talents to me; see, I have gained five more talents'"* (Matthew 25:20). A talent, as described here, would be worth nearly $400,000 in our economy today. So it was not an insignificant sum of money that the Lord was discussing. It required investing a sizeable surplus of money.

Many Christians firmly believe that there is no scriptural justification for investing while others have a lack. That simply is not true. The justification for anyone's investing is that he has given what God asked him to give. He has met the *reasonable* needs of his family, and he still has a surplus.

PREREQUISITES FOR INVESTING

The number one prerequisite for investing is attitude. Why are you investing, and how will the surplus be used? If a Christian wants God to entrust greater riches to him, he must be found faithful in the smaller amount first.

"He who is faithful in a very little thing is faithful also in much; and he who is unrighteous in a very little thing is unrighteous also in much. If therefore you have not been faithful in the use of unrighteous mammon, who will entrust the true riches to you?" (Luke 16:10-11).

To protect against the infectious diseases of greed and pride, the best weapon is a specific plan for returning the excess to God's kingdom. I find that once a commitment has been made to a disciplined lifestyle, regardless of the available income, the dangers of greed and self-indulgence are significantly reduced. The term used throughout Paul's writings is contentment.

"But godliness actually is a means of great gain, when accompanied by contentment" (1 Timothy 6:6).

SCRIPTURAL MOTIVE FOR INVESTING

There are several scriptural motives for investing.

To further God's work. Some Christians have received a gift of giving (Romans 12:8). To them the multiplication of material worth is an extension of their basic ministry within the Body of Christ. Even to those who do not have a gift of giving, investments are a way to preserve and multiply a surplus that has been provided for a later time. In Acts 4:34, the believers sold their assets and surrendered the proceeds to meet the needs of other believers. God blesses some with an earlier surplus to be used at a later date.

Family responsibility. We are admonished to provide for those within our own households (1 Timothy 5:8). That provision was never limited to the life span of a father. It extended to providing for— not protecting—the family even after the father's death.

Future needs. If parents believe God wants their children to go to college, is it more spiritual to expect the government to educate them than to store for the eventual need? The parable of the ant in Proverbs 6:6 says to "observe her ways and be wise." One of her ways is to plan ahead by storing. In an inflationary economy, even storing requires investing to maintain value.

WORLDLY MOTIVES FOR INVESTING

There are also several worldly motives for investing. Unfortunately, these represent the most common motives of investors, both Christian and non-Christian, because Satan has so thoroughly dominated our attitudes about money.

Greed. The continual desire to have more and demand only the best. *"But those who want to get rich fall into temptation and a snare and many foolish and harmful desires which plunge men into ruin and destruction"* (1 Timothy 6:9).

Pride. The desire to be elevated

because of material achievements. *"Instruct those who are rich in this present world not to be conceited or to fix their hope on the uncertainty of riches, but on God, who richly supplies us with all things to enjoy"* (1 Timothy 6:17).

Ignorance. Following the counsel of other misguided people because of a lack of discernment. *"Leave the presence of a fool, or you will not discern words of knowledge"* (Proverbs 14:7).

Envy. The desire to achieve based on observation of other people's success. *"For I was envious of the arrogant, as I saw the prosperity of the wicked"* (Psalm 73:3).

The bottom line is: worldly motives reflect worldly values. The result is anxiety, frustration, and eventually a deadening of spiritual values. Thus, as our Lord says, *"No servant can serve two masters; for either he will hate the one and love the other, or else he will hold to one, and despise the other. You cannot serve God and mammon"* (Luke 16:13).

HOW MUCH TO INVEST?

Once a Christian has accepted the purpose of investing to serve God better, the crucial decision is: how much to invest? Obviously, there is no absolute answer. It is an individual decision made by a Christian after much prayer. With earnest prayer the decision is difficult—without it, impossible. There are some initial choices to be made that will greatly simplify the decision about how much to invest.

1. *Give to God's work.* Give until you know that all the needs God has placed on your heart are satisfied. Don't be misled by thinking that means there will be no more needs in the world. There will always be needs, but God doesn't place every need on every heart. Giving, like spiritual discernment, is a matter of

growth and practice. One suggestion is, "when in doubt, give." It is better to be wrong and give too much than to ignore God's direction and give too little. The spirit is never dampened by being too sensitive, only by developing calluses.

"Therefore openly before the churches show them the proof of your love and of our reason for boasting about you" (2 Corinthians 8:24).

2. *Control personal spending.* Settle on a level of family needs that is God's plan for you. Too much spending by a family can rob surplus funds as surely as bad investments. Each Christian family must decide on the level God has planned for them and stick to it in spite of available surpluses. Remember that balance is essential. Too much spending breeds indulgence; too little is self-punishment.

"And whatever we ask we receive from Him, because we keep His commandments and do the things that are pleasing in His sight" (1 John 3:22).

3. *Develop a written plan.* Have a plan for the use of your potential surpluses. One interesting characteristic about humans is that we can rationalize nearly anything, including reinvesting God's portion or saving it for Him. Therefore, it is important to settle on a plan for distributing the profits from investments before they arrive. Decide what portion is to be reinvested. Clearly, the greatest danger is to continually reinvest the profits and rationalize it because of tax planning, lack of discernable needs, or a fear of the future. Do your planning before the money becomes available. One good way to do that is to give away a large percentage of the investment before it appreciates.

"Because of the proof given by this ministry they will glorify God for your obedience to your confession of the gospel of Christ, and for the liberality of your contribution to them and to all" (2 Corinthians 9:13).

How to Prosper from Problems

Discouragement is only one of many symptoms associated with problems. During today's economy we counsel a great many Christians who are discouraged over their problems. Many are discouraged to the point of suicide. Satan knows where we're vulnerable, and in America it's usually in our self-esteem about material things.

Discouragement abounds today because of unemployment or underemployment. When everyone is poor, it seems that most people can adjust to that. But when someone has lost a job and most of his friends still have theirs, it's hard to handle. High debt loads and creditor pressures simply add to the feelings of inadequacy and failure.

CAUSES OF DISCOURAGEMENT

In a land of plenty like ours, even those who are poor are better off than the majority of the world. So why do we feel despair and discouragement? Because we have adjusted our expectations and made them relative to everyone else around us. It's the same symptom that causes despair in a multimillionaire whose assets have shrunk to a few hundred thousand.

CONTENTMENT

Most of us suffer from unrealistic expectations of what God promised us. And as Christians we sometimes fear that our problems will make others think of us as less spiritual. We have actually come full circle from those Christians of the first and second century who believed that problems were evidence of spiritual depth. Actually, neither extreme is scripturally correct, but the case for Christians undergoing problems is more scriptural. *"Consider it all joy, my brethren, when you encounter various trials"* (James 1:2).

But the trials that James is addressing are a consequence of serving God uncompromisingly. Most of our current problems are the result of violating biblical principles, particularly those relating to money.

Certainly the most common cause of discouragement has finances at its roots. We grade people by their finances in America today, and it's no different within Christianity. We put subtle pressures on each other to achieve success as a testimony to the Lord. Therefore, the failure to do so must represent spiritual failure.

When Paul wrote in 1 Timothy 5:8 that a Christian is to provide, he didn't realize how much provision it would take for us. Therefore, when a man can't provide as much as those around him, discouragement sets in. That reaches its peak around Christmas. With all the giving and receiving during the holidays, those who are unable to participate often feel despair and even guilt. In fact, the incidence of suicide increases significantly during this period.

CHRISTIAN CONCERN

Perhaps the number one cause of discouragement for Christians with problems is lack of support on the part of other Christians. Children are often cruel to someone who is different, and I sometimes wonder if Christians have reverted back to their childhood. What most people with problems don't need is for someone to point them out or "counsel" them on the "sin" in their lives that is causing the problems. That is not to imply that those who are sinning should not be confronted—they should be—but blatant sin is rarely the case. The majority of people who are discouraged already recognize that they have erred—if they have—and have more than adequately condemned themselves. What they usually need is support and love.

"A friend loves at all times, and a brother is born for adversity" (Proverbs 17:17).

The lack of loyalty to Christians undergoing problems is not new. All through Paul's letters there is evidence that his problems caused others to doubt his calling and to avoid him. *"At my first defense no one supported me, but all deserted me; may it not be counted against them"* (2 Timothy 4:16).

Looking further back in time, the record of Job's friends stands as a testimony to disloyalty. *"For the despairing man there should be kindness from his friend; lest he forsake the fear of the Almighty"* (Job 6:14).

UNREASONABLE EXPECTATIONS

As stated before, unreasonable expectations often create discouragement. The pastor obviously should be a Christian of very high character (Titus 1), but where in that description does it imply that he is perfect? Unfortunately, according to many Christians' opinions, pastors shouldn't have problems. So those who have trouble communicating with their wives or managing to live on half of what others live on often fall victim to discouragement. It would shock many Christians to find out that even their pastors doubt God from time to time and that their problems get so overwhelming they may suffer depres-

sion. *"For we do not want you to be unaware, brethren, of our affliction which came to us in Asia, that we were burdened excessively, beyond our strength, so that we despaired even of life"* (2 Corinthians 1:8).

Another area than can discourage Christians is spiritual expectations about children. That often means that if Mom and Dad have missionary zeal, the kids must too. I believe that nothing exposes our egos like our children. Even the most humble Christian is quick to brag about an achievement by his child, particularly if it's something in the Lord's work. It's as though we want to validate our commitment through our children. If we are elevated spiritually by the achievements of our children, then we are also demoralized by their failures—only more so.

It's probably time that we, as Christians, realize that God doesn't have grandchildren or stepchildren. Everyone decides individually to follow or not to follow the Lord. That does not mean that we shouldn't lead our children, correct them, or encourage them, but we must recognize their right to choose, just as we did. We must also support and encourage those who have children who learn by failure. It would be great if all children were as smart as most parents and could learn without any personal difficulties, just as we did—right? A good way to start this change is to share a few failures you have had with your own children and allow others to observe that Christians haven't totally arrived—we're still on the way.

I experienced such an event when one of my sons came home from college to ask me to help him clear up his checking account. It seems that he had about eight checks overdrawn and some seventy dollars in over-draft charges. Well, needless to say, I was discouraged. The only thing worse for a Christian financial counselor would be for his own account to be overdrawn (that happened one summer when I forgot to make a deposit). God used my son's problem to help me realize that just because I teach financial discipline doesn't mean that my children understand it. It gave me an opportunity to share why these principles are in God's Word.

"Like apples of gold in settings of silver is a word spoken in right circumstances" (Proverbs 25:11).

Perhaps the most consistent area of discouragement for most people is financial failure. Not only are our egos involved with our ability to provide, but our security is also threatened. Quite often the demonstration of a Christian's stewardship is not how much he gives but how he reacts when there is not much to give. With many, if not most Christians, their faith at any given time seems proportional to their material resources. Not for all, obviously. Some Christians find that in the midst of their most difficult times their faith grows and matures, which is exactly what James says it will do if we abide in Christ.

God's Word teaches that it is impossible for a Christian to divide loyalties. We will serve but one God.

"No one can serve two masters; for either he will hate the one and love the other, or he will hold to one and despise the other. You cannot serve God and mammon" (Matthew 6:24).

The greatest threat to our service to God is being sidetracked into a preoccupation about success. Therefore, God will allow financial crises to come into many of our lives to give us the opportunity to decide whom we *really* serve.

We signed a contract with God when we made Christ Lord over our lives and gave God the right to do whatever is necessary to keep us on His path.

"When you make a vow to God, do not be late in paying it, for He takes no delight in fools. Pay what you vow!" (Ecclesiastes 5:4).

So rather than immediately seeking to escape a financial difficulty, first determine what faults can be corrected by turning to God in your time of need.

HOW TO DEFEAT DISCOURAGEMENT

There is an old cliché that summarizes this area, "Keep on keeping on." You must decide what you believe and trust God regardless of the outside circumstances. Also, your response to any situation should be determined *in advance.* If anyone, Christian or otherwise, waits until a problem occurs to decide how he'll handle it, he will be controlled by the events, not God's Word. God gave us many examples of people who faced difficult situations. Some collapsed into despair and self-pity, while others grew stronger. Those who grew stronger could be categorized, as James said, as "doers" of the Word, not merely "hearers" who delude themselves.

Examples of doers would be Abraham, Nehemiah, Daniel, and Paul. It's pretty clear that they weren't perfect, but they were obedient. In their times of difficulty they did not panic or get depressed. They turned to the Lord. Some of them weren't rescued immediately, and some even died. But remember this—so did everyone else. If all we're looking for is what we can have in this world, then we're only slightly better off than the lost. God wants to bless us with peace in this life and eternal rewards in the next.

How Deceit Destroys

As I was reading a familiar passag in Matthew 13, I had to stop and reflect on what the Lord says in verse 22: that the deceitfulness of riches chokes out God's Word. As I pondered over that, I wondered, "Are the riches deceitful, or are they just a simple tool used in deception?" Obviously, the answer is that material possessions are not problems themselves; they are the reflection of problems. Deceit is an external, visible expression of inner spiritual flaws. It just happens that virtually every reference to deceit in God's Word is exemplified in materialism.

With believers, the most devastating loss associated with deceit is the dulling of our spiritual awareness. Guilt associated with a known deception will cause the Christian to withdraw from God's presence. Once withdrawn, subsequent deceptions become easier, and less conviction is felt. Often the pretense of spirituality remains (church, conferences, Bible studies, and so on), but the sensitivity and fellowship are gone. The believer no longer feels "worthy" and feels like he has failed God. If such an attitude is allowed to continue until a facade can be perfected, the result can easily be a life of defeat and frustration.

I have found that no one is immune to the temptation to deceive, particularly when money is concerned. Some people establish their responses prior to the situation and are able to resist, not on the basis of their own strength but on God's.

I can recall clearly that as an unsaved businessman, the temptation to deceive was a constantly nagging problem. Quite often it was not a desire to lie, but rather to just simply omit a few pertinent facts about a product to a potential buyer. After all, I would tell myself, what they don't know won't hurt them. Sometimes that old cliché is right, and sometimes it's wrong, but invariably I found the one that got hurt was me. I felt guilt and not just a little loss of honor each time I misled someone. After becoming a Christian, I just naturally assumed such weaknesses would never tempt me again, especially as I became more familiar with God's Word.

Allow me to share a personal observation here: the one way to fail is to deceive yourself into believing you're too strong to fail. Many times in our lives there are situations in which an undetected compromise to God's way could be made and in fact is made. Fortunately, God knew we wouldn't be perfect and made allowances for our weaknesses by a principle called confession. Those who practice this often find that confession is more difficult than honesty would have been originally, but it is absolutely necessary to restore fellowship with God.

"He who conceals his transgressions will not prosper, but he who confesses and forsakes them will find compassion" (Proverbs 28:13). When confession is so painful, total honesty looks a whole lot more attractive the next time.

DECEPTION DESTROYS TRUST

"The perverse in heart are an abomination to the Lord, but the blameless are His delight" (Proverbs 11:20). The Christian walk is not an academic exercise in Scripture memorization—it's a way of life. The purpose of God's Word is to give us guidelines for making decisions in

spite of our normal reactions. God wants us to be able to trust Him regardless of the circumstances around us. It is the physical evidence that we believe in a life greater than we now have and in the One who has ultimate authority over everything. Deception is not a problem. It is a testimony that we don't really believe God owns everything and has already considered the consequences. That is true whether we're taking a loss on a car, paying income taxes, or overcharging a travel expense.

DECEPTION LEADS TO HYPOCRISY

"A scoffer does not love one who reproves him, he will not go to the wise" (Proverbs 15:12). There is nothing more personally devastating to a believer than looking spiritual and living defeat. The immediate consequence is the loss of esteem in the eyes of family and close friends. Children are rarely attracted to a weak, watered down version of Christianity that says one thing and does another. If they see Mom and Dad put on their "church" faces on Sunday, they will believe that's what Christianity is all about.

DECEPTION LEADS TO A CRITICAL SPIRIT

"Put away from you a deceitful mouth, and put devious lips far from you" (Proverbs 4:24). When a believer is living a life-style that is contrary to God's way, the step from hypocrisy to a critical spirit is a short one. It is the desire to cut others down to his level that brings about the critical or judgmental attitude. Every small flaw in others will be amplified and expounded upon in an effort to justify the flaws in his own attitudes. Instead of accomplishing the desired result of hiding the deceptive spirit, usually the opposite occurs, and others who would not normally notice are even more aware.

THE EFFECT ON CHILDREN

"Train up a child in the way he should go, even when he is old he will not depart from it""(Proverbs 22:6). It is amazing how slowly children learn good habits and how quickly they pick up bad ones. The reason would seem to be that bad habits are more common and are in fact more enticing than good ones.

Children can easily be taught to deceive by parents. Young children want to please their parents, and if parents get very angry when they hear the truth, then a natural alternative would be to tell them a lie. Some parents would rather hear a lie, because they don't want to have to deal with a difficult situation. If childhood deceptions are allowed and reinforced by seeing Mom or Dad deceive, it can easily become a lifetime attitude. Perhaps more than anyone else, the father affects the attitudes of his offspring. He is the leader in the home, and as such is the authority.

If the children are made to fear being totally honest or are encouraged to develop pride in their parents, the result will often be deception. An attitude in the home that people do make mistakes, and as such need to be able to confess to each other, will go a long way in helping children to be honest rather than having to hide their initial lie by more lies.

CORRECTING DECEPTION

Be accountable. "Without consultation, plans are frustrated, but with many counselors they succeed" (Proverbs 15:22). All Christians need to be accountable to others, so that when we stray off the path, someone else will correct us. Unfortunately, many Christians are accountable to no one because they don't have to be. That is particularly true of whose who are materially successful, because they isolate themselves behind a wall of ego and pride.

The best accountability comes within the home, especially between husband and wife. With rare exception, one spouse is acutely aware of the other's strengths and weaknesses. If they have an open and honest relationship, one will detect the other's deceptions quickly. Correcting must be done gently and in love, or the result will be bitterness. Always remember that the purpose is to restore a loved one to the right relationship with God, not to accuse him.

Children will participate wholeheartedly in the detection and correction process. (Mine never fail to detect when I exceed the posted speed limit.) In addition to family, every Christian should become accountable to one or more other Christians who care enough to admonish and correct. Sometimes it's painful for both parties, but it is absolutely necessary for spiritual growth.

Quick confession. "*He who conceals his transgressions will not prosper, but he who confesses and forsakes them will find compassion*" (Proverbs 28:13). Whenever you detect a deception in your own life, large or small, stop what you're doing and con

fess it immediately. That means not only to God, but to the others who are involved as well. There are many rationalizations for not doing this but really only one reason: pride. You must resolve yourself to confess before the situation presents itself, or it will be impossible. You can't always assume that the others involved will understand or accept an apology, either. It is not necessary for them alone; it is also for you.

Restitution. "*If therefore you are presenting your offering at the altar, and there remember that your brother has something against you, leave your offering there before the altar, and go your way; first be reconciled to your brother, and then come and present your offering*" (Matthew 5:23-24).

That means that if you must suffer a financial loss to correct an earlier deception, then do what is necessary. The most important relationship is between you and God, and after all, everything belongs to Him anyway. If you have established an absolute standard that you will retain no personal benefit as a result of deception, it will precondition your response to any temptation. That is particularly true if you adopt the same restitution that Zaccheus did and repay 400 percent (Luke 19:8). It then becomes economically unprofitable to deceive; you know that ultimately even more must be repaid.

How "Things" Demand Attention

The affluence of the American way of life is a mixed blessing. On the positive side, our prosperity has made life much easier and has freed a great deal of money to spread God's Word. But on the negative side, prosperity requires a great deal of our time and attention. In fact, the urgency of our materialistic life-styles becomes a tyranny that demands most of our energies. It would seem that the labor cycle since the industrial revolution is reversing itself. Industrialization provided a higher standard of living with a shorter work week. In the early 1900s, it took every family member working sixty hours per week just to make ends meet. By the mid-twentieth century, the average work week was forty-eight hours, and in most families the husband was the primary wage earner. Now, in over 70 percent of American families two incomes are again necessary to support the family's life-style.

CONCERN ABOUT THE FUTURE

The American dream only a couple of decades ago was a good job, a comfortable home, and a nice car. Today, it has become guaranteed employment, retirement plans, a home, two cars, a summer cottage, and college educations for all the kids. The possession of "things" has become the scorecard to determine "success." The pressure to provide the luxuries that have now become commonplace causes many Christian families to encumber themselves with debts that eventually destroy their marriages. It's not surprising that many couples look back on their early years of marriage as the best, even though materially they were the leanest. Their lives were usually focused on the day-to-day events, and before the use of mass media advertising, most of us didn't even know what we were missing. It seems clear that the Lord would have all of us focus more on today and less on the uncertainty of the future.

"Therefore do not be anxious for tomorrow; for tomorrow will take care of itself. Each day has enough trouble of its own" (Matthew 6:34).

MAKING LIFE EASIER

The initial purpose of material things is to make our lives easier and more comfortable. But it's amazing how complicated they can become. A family wants to spend a relaxing vacation in the mountains or at the beach, so they buy a summer cottage in that area. Then they find they must spend most of their free time keeping it repaired or protecting it from vandals. Often the experience is so bad they end up loathing the very thing they thought would make life easier. Many times Christians get trapped into operating by the world's wisdom rather than God's.

The world says, "Whatever you see and desire, acquire." God's Word says, *"But seek for His kingdom, and these things shall be added to you"* (Luke 12:31).

THE REAL PURPOSE OF THINGS

A survey of the scriptural warnings about riches and their dangers might suggest that we should avoid all luxuries. That simply is not true. God does not prohibit us from enjoying the benefits of this world (after all, they are His). Rather, we are admonished not to get entangled in them to the point that we are no longer able to fulfill our primary purpose—to serve God. *"No soldier in active service entangles himself in the affairs of everyday life, so that he may please the one who enlisted him as a soldier"* (2 Timothy 2:4). Unfortunately, today that is exactly where most Christians are. Individual ownership is a biblical principle, but carried to the extreme it becomes greed.

The real purpose of our resources is to free us to do more for Christ, not less. When the pursuit of things becomes our focus in life, there can be no doubt about whom we serve.

"No one can serve two masters; for either he will hate the one and love the other, or he will hold to one and despise the other. You cannot serve God and mammon" (Matthew 6:24). It is more than just becoming enmeshed in this world. The real danger is that we will lose our first love and our only source of peace.

"Do not love the world, nor the things in the world. If anyone loves the world, the love of the Father is not in him" (1 John 2:15). Consistently, God's Word teaches that focusing on material things is the greatest danger we face. What makes it seem so normal today is that virtually everyone in America is doing it. Our great abundance has not made us more content; it has made us less content.

THE FIVE DANGERS OF THINGS

1. *Adjusting to a life of indulgence as normal.* It is amazing that in less than fifty years we have grown to accept guaranteed salaries, insurance for every contingency, retirement benefits, and two-car families as normal. When the economy couldn't supply those things quickly enough we simply mortgaged our future generations to pay for them. That selfishness is short-lived, because eventually we borrow more than can ever be repaid. But the real reason this debt-funded economy always fails is because it violates basic biblical principles.

"A faithful man will abound with blessings, but he who makes haste to be rich will not go unpunished" (Proverbs 28:20).

2. *Focusing on worldly success.* For people who have committed themselves to an eternity with God, it's amazing how worldly our value system has become. We give positions of authority in our churches and organizations most often on the basis of material success rather than spiritual maturity. Obviously, many Christians are materially and spiritually mature, but when we esteem people on the basis of material success, we begin to equate riches with spirituality. Thus, those who are not materially successful are deemed less spiritual. To be assured that God does not hold to the same value system, observe the apostles.

"To this present hour we are both hungry and thirsty, and are poorly clothed, and are roughly treated, and are homeless" (1 Corinthians 4:11).

3. *Dulling God's direction.* Nothing prohibits Christians from obeying God more than the tug of material comforts. Once we have adjusted to a life-style that includes many comforts, it is very difficult to surrender them to serve God. Obviously, God doesn't call everyone to leave his vocation and go into what is traditionally called "Christian work." God can and does use Christians everywhere. But in order to be used by God in any capacity, a Christian must be willing to serve God no matter what the costs.

"More than that, I count all things to be loss in view of the surpassing value of knowing Christ Jesus my Lord, for whom I have suffered the loss of all things, and count them but rubbish in order that I may gain Christ" (Philippians 3:8).

Whenever someone asked Christ about what would be expected of him as a follower, He always tested their willingness to surrender everything for God's sake. Without that attitude, we can't even be trusted with material riches because we would spend them on our own indulgences or build larger barns to store them in.

But God's Word says, *"And without faith it is impossible to please Him, for he who comes to God must believe that He is, and that He is a rewarder of those who seek Him"* (Hebrews 11:6).

We must believe that God wants to bless us, and until God individually convicts someone that His plan is otherwise, we are not to accept failure. Tribulation brings about proven character. Don't withdraw because of failure. Learn from it. Perseverance is a characteristic lacking in Christianity today. Some Christians who fail get defeated and feel like God has abandoned them. Some despair to the point of depression or suicide.

4. *Adopting an attitude of superiority.* You would think that knowing everything belongs to God would make even the wealthiest among us humble. But it's sad what a little bit of material success will do to our ego and pride. Very few Christians can really handle success well. Some of the most devoted men of God have been sorely tested when they became known well enough to be a celebrity. Those who have been given responsibility in this life must be very careful to exercise it with great caution, lest they give up their eternal rewards for some temporary ones.

"Do nothing from selfishness or empty conceit, but with humility of mind let each of you regard one another as more important than himself" (Philippians 2:3).

5. *Indifference toward the needs of others.* A real danger of material affluence is that we begin to think everybody has it. But that's simply not true. The vast majority of people in this world go to bed hungry and wake up hungry. They love their children as much as we do ours, and every day they die a little bit more because they cannot provide even the little food it takes to keep them alive. Let me assure you that most of them aren't lazy or evil—they are poor. They are the ones that Christ describes in Matthew 25:45:

"Then He will answer them, saying, 'Truly I say to you, to the extent that you did not do it to one of the least of these, you did not do it to Me.'"

Most often our indifference is passive. It isn't that Christians don't care; we do. It's just that we don't personally know any really poor people, and we're wary of the give-away plans of many ministries. But let me assure you, there are many really poor people and legitimate ministries who care for them, one on one. Giving to feed the poor and homeless is a command, not a request. This area would seem to be the biggest lack of Christianity today and is a direct result of our great affluence. It's unfortunate that those in need are the most sensitive to the needs of others.

ESTABLISH A BALANCE

There must always be a balance in the area of material "things." God does not have an identical plan for any of us, and what one family spends is different from another. The common measure for all of us is to reach that balance between using material things and being controlled by them. To do this, a Christian must establish that he serves Christ first and all other considerations come after that. That means that all of our actions should be heavily weighted to Christ's service first. Our giving should reflect this commitment, and a tithe should not be our goal but rather our minimum. Each increase in our income should increase our outreach before it does our life-styles, and we should be known primarily for our commitment to God's work rather than our display of material things.

Dealing with Pride

Once a Christian is trapped by his pride, he is no service to God. Without a change and a commitment to accountability, he will not be aware of his attitude of pride.

God will give us plenty of opportunity to recognize and correct the attitude of pride. The difficulty most times is admitting that we actually have a problem. Recently, God gave me the opportunity to assess myself about pride. I was working on some important material, and a deadline was approaching when I received a phone call from a widow I was counseling. I was a little irritated because she had been in several times previously with relatively trivial problems. She asked if she could come in right away because she had a crisis in her budget—her checking account didn't balance. I explained that I really didn't have any time available and suggested another counselor we had trained. A short time later I received a call from a businessman who wanted to bring by a celebrity who was in town working on a movie. I knew it was a rare opportunity, and I said yes.

As soon as I hung up the phone the words of James came ringing in my ears. *"But if you show partiality, you are committing sin and are convicted by the law as transgressors"* (James 2:9).

I found myself trapped by the most devious snare that Satan lays: pride. I also found that God's correction system is very painful sometimes. I had to call the businessman back and tell him I couldn't meet with them until later and call my counselee back and ask her forgiveness. By the way, the celebrity never did come in. He was too miffed by being put off.

Pride is so deceptive because it's so normal today. Christians are told to achieve and be the best so they can be an effective witness. Then somewhere along the way the goal of achieving takes a higher priority than the witnessing. By the time most Christians should have the greatest witness they become boastful and indulgent. They believe it's better to live their witness, so they surround themselves with enough indulgence to prove that God really blesses the faithful. He does, but not for the purpose of building our egos.

"Because you say, `I am rich, and have become wealthy, and have need of nothing,' and you do not know that you are wretched and miserable and poor and blind and naked" (Revelation 3:17).

SYMPTOMS OF PRIDE

In order to cure a disease, we must first be able to recognize its symptoms. They are the visible, outside indicators. Although we may not always recognize them in ourselves, others will. So it becomes vital for us to stay open to criticism, particularly from those who are spiritually discerning. Those most consistent in discerning our faults are usually our spouses. God has placed them in our lives as a balance, and they will help to offset our extremes if we will listen. That works both ways because we are also their balance. But more often than not it is the husband who refuses to take counsel from his wife. Why? Pride.

BE A LEADER

"For who regards you as superior? And what do you have that you did not receive?

But if you did receive it, why do you boast as if you had not received it?" (1 Corinthians 4:7).

Nothing points more clearly to a pride problem than an aloof leader. When Christians find that they only want to associate with the "right" people and look down at others because they're less educated, less intelligent, or less successful, then they are no longer useful to God's work. A businessman who looks down at his employees and other contacts will not be a witness on the job. He will have to go outside his company environment in order to share his faith. If you are in authority, it is important that you care as much about the least significant person in the company as you do the most important.

It is easy to be nice to those who can benefit you, but Christ said that anyone would do that. He said to give to those who can never repay you and you will be rewarded.

"For if you love those who love you, what reward have you? Do not even the tax gatherers do the same? And if you greet your brothers only, what do you do more than others? Do not even the Gentiles do the same? Therefore you are to be perfect, as your heavenly Father is perfect" (Matthew 5:46-48).

That requires an attitude change on our part. We must actually demonstrate that no one person is more or less important than another. One might have the ability to make money, and another to teach, or write, or pray. But which is more important from God's perspective?

One businessman I know has made a concerted effort to step out of his executive mold and serve others first. He directed his efforts toward getting to know his lowest level employees. When he did, he found they had many financial problems he had long since forgotten even existed. The net result was that he substantially increased most of their wages. One employee had tremendous medical bills for a child with cancer. He paid the majority of the bills himself and raised the rest through friends. Initially, not one of the employees was a Christian, but today, over half are. Two have even left for full-time service. You can't grade that kind of commitment financially, but on an eternal scale it's a ten-plus.

"Do nothing from selfishness or empty conceit, but with humility of mind let each of you regard one another as more important than himself" (Philippians 2:3).

SELFISHNESS

It is easy to rationalize an indulgent life-style in a society where most people indulge themselves. In order to get the right balance, we must go back to God's Word. Obviously, it is not necessary to live poorly to serve the Lord. The only people who think poverty is spiritual are those who haven't tried it. But just as certainly, it is clear from God's Word that affluence presents the greatest threat to our walk with the Lord.

"For where your treasure is, there will your heart be also": (Matthew 6:21).

It is a rare individual who can actually handle much wealth and keep his priorities straight. One wealthy man rationalized his need for a $2 million airplane because he had to wait two hours in an airport one day. It is easy to gratify every whim or indulgence simply because we can afford to. Today the cliché is, "Live like the King's kids." But I don't see anything in Christ's teachings that directs us to do so. I truly believe that poverty is not God's norm, but neither is lavishness.

"But those who want to get rich fall into temptation and a snare and many foolish and harmful desires which plunge men into ruin

and destruction" (1 Timothy 6:9).

A Christian must learn self-discipline in money to be able to teach others. Our affluence has distorted our priorities. While we go to sleep disturbed over whether or not to buy a big screen TV, over half the world's kids go to bed hungry and cold. Communism is taking over the world with its false promises, but Christianity isn't even making promises anymore. Many of the world's governments care more for human needs than the church does. Obviously, we can't give away all of our goods, but we've stopped even giving a fair share.

Everything starts with a first step, and that first step is to get involved with the needs of others. That will help focus more clearly on what your actual needs are. One businessman determined to help where he could. He and several other businessmen started buying run-down houses, repairing them, and making them available to the elderly at whatever they could afford. Several times they pooled their funds and purchased a small home outright for elderly widows. The homes were usually inner city houses that could be purchased and repaired for $20,000 or less. With twenty businessmen involved, the expense was not prohibitive.

ACCOUNTABILITY

If you have a problem with pride, it's doubtful that anyone will point it out to you. Most of those with whom you have daily contact are people who won't say anything (at least to you), and besides, many people who are egotistical enough to show their pride are too proud to accept counsel from another. Once a Christian is trapped by his pride, he is not of service to God.

How do you break out of the pride trap? First, vow to serve God and God's people, and then make yourself accountable to others. Too often Christian leaders, including ministry heads, are not accountable to anyone. Consequently, they have little or no feedback from those who can recognize the symptoms associated with pride.

First and foremost, a husband and wife must be accountable to each other. Major decisions should be discussed together and opinions and insights exchanged. If a wife has the liberty to be honest, she will usually detect and expose her husband's pride, and vice versa.

Second, a Christian businessman should be accountable to a peer or someone he respects who is strong enough to be totally honest. Those I know who practice accountability find they must meet regularly and learn each other's basic flaws. They must both be studying God's Word and be seeking to truly serve God, or it won't work. The rules I use for those I have helped get started are: (1) The criticism must be honest and based on God's Word. (2) The person pointing out the problem must suggest a way to change the attitude and must testify how the change helped in his own life.

Assuming God's Will

Have you ever witnessed a Christian who was obviously doing something rather dumb but rationalizing it to all dissenters by saying, "God told me to do it?" For most of us, that's a hard argument to overcome because by merely challenging it you feel as though you're doubting God. Later, when the whole thing falls apart, most Christians wish they had had the courage to speak up.

Why won't we speak up when we see another Christian who is obviously wrong? Because most of us are timid about applying biblical truth to a real-life situation and challenging anything contrary to God's Word. Sometimes the person in question is a notable Christian in the community. Let me assure you of this: no one has a perfect insight into God's will. The soundest, most mature believers can and do make mistakes about God's will. Usually, when confronted by either a loving but firm challenge from another Christian or the resulting problems, they will change direction.

Apparently, such was the case when Paul opposed Peter at Antioch. *"But when Cephas came to Antioch, I opposed him to his face, because he stood condemned"* (Galatians 2:11).

Paul knew the truth, and Peter's actions didn't conform to the truth, so he confronted the leader of the Christian church. Judging from the fact that Paul never mentions that incident again, Peter changed direction.

However, some Christians simply refuse to believe they could be wrong and cloak themselves in spirituality by saying, "I know God wants me to do this." Those who consistently do that confirm an old cliché, "Often wrong, but never in doubt."

OPEN DOOR PHILOSOPHY

Many Christians make decisions on major issues based on what is called the "open door" philosophy. In other words, God would never let anyone do something wrong and therefore, if the door is open, I should go through it. I often think of this as the "open mine shaft" philosophy because a lot of Christians stumble down open shafts thinking God wouldn't let them fail. Clearly, God has given us the authority to do dumb things. A brief review of those whom God chose to use, beginning with Adam, will attest to that. There is ample direction in God's Word to avert most errors. Unfortunately, too often Christians feel like God is dealing with them in a new and unique dispensation, especially where money is concerned.

I know of a Christian businessman who was involved in deception and rationalized it. It seems his business had failed when the economy dipped and interest rates didn't. Excessive debt load wiped out his capital and ultimately forced him out of business. His first personal revelation was that God told him to go bankrupt. That was confirmed by a Christian lawyer on a television program who said that bankruptcy was a modern-day form of "the year of remission" (Deuteronomy 15:1). Unfortunately, he forgot to mention that debt remission was always an option of the lender, not the borrower. God demands repayment of debt (Psalm 37:21), so the businessman filed bankruptcy, with the stated intent of repaying the debts later.

Since he needed a large amount of money to get started again, he approached several other Christians he had met while in business and got them to invest in a new venture, without any mention of the previous bankruptcy. Being rather persuasive, he raised enough capital to open a new office and hire some people. He then applied for and received a sizable government new-business loan. This he believed had to be from God because his previous bankruptcy didn't show up in the loan check. Further confirmation came when a major supplier shipped him tens of thousands of dollars worth of inventory on a 120 days' payment basis. He said God must have blinded them to let him get started again.

During that time, several Christians in his church felt his actions were contrary to good Christian conduct, and one even approached him about it. The reply was always the same, "God wants me to do this. I'm believing Him for a great success, and I won't listen to any negative talk." The success of such ventures won't be measured in dollars and cents. Even if such a venture succeeds, it's a failure according to God's Word. God does not work through guile and unspoken deceit.

"He who walks in integrity walks securely, but he who perverts his ways will be found out" (Proverbs 10:9).

In this particular case, the unspoken deceit resulted in a fraud conviction and prison sentence. He had to default on the government loan when the business failed.

CONFIRMED BY SUCCESS

It's worth repeating that material success does not necessarily constitute God's endorsement of our actions. That applies to businesses and ministries alike. Every decision we make should meet two criteria. First, it must be compatible with God's written Word. Some decisions are objective enough to be eliminated on the basis of direct contradiction to God's Word.

For instance, a short time ago, a friend told me that he received a notice from a Christian organization saying they would accept a gift of $100 or more through the month of January and receipt the donor in the previous year—a great tax planning help. I counseled my friend to contact the head of that organization and inform him that their proposed action was illegal. He did so and was told that this procedure was used every year and had proved to be very successful. The ministry head said he was sure it was legal as God wouldn't bless something illegal. A few calls to the I.R.S. absolutely confirmed its illegality. Unraveling the mess created over the last several years will probably destroy the effectiveness of that group. No, God won't bless something illegal, but He will let us do it and suffer the consequences.

Second, each decision must be compatible with our personal convictions. Paul wrote, *"The faith which you have, have as your own conviction before God. Happy is he who does not condemn himself in what he approves"* (Romans 14:22).

The Christian life is not just a set of rules that can be obeyed to the letter and thus satisfy our commitment. We are held to an even higher standard that requires constant input from the Holy Spirit to keep our direction straight. It means that we are accountable if we defile our conscience by doing something we feel is wrong. That feeling must be based on a firm conviction from God. How do you know? You just *know*. I usually know by a lack of inner peace.

A businessman called recently with such a doubt. He said he had a strong conviction from the Lord to get involved with helping unemployed people in his community. To do so he had provided jobs for three of them in his plant and had involved them in various community service projects. Then his accountant discovered that their employment qualified his business for the government "jobs" program and an associated grant. The grant provided more funds than their actual salaries and would have allowed him to hire more unemployed. But he had a lack of peace about accepting the grant—in stark contrast to the original peace he had felt about the work program. The grant was legal, and the funds could be put to good use; but for him it was wrong.

After much prayer and a great deal of searching, he found his answer in 1 Chronicles 21:24: *"But King David said to Ornan, `No, but I will surely buy it for the full price; for I will not take what is yours for the Lord, or offer a burnt offering which costs me nothing.'"*

The project was to be God's project, not the government's. As a result of his stand, several other businessmen have joined with him in providing more jobs. Certainly, with the government involved the project might be bigger, but God's best is not always manifested in "bigness."

FAILING GRACEFULLY

There are many Christians who are "graceful failures." They don't demand anything of God and, in fact, expect nothing. Usually, they get what they expect—nothing. Just because manipulating God's Word for self-benefit if wrong, that doesn't mean that we shouldn't ask and expect. Many Christians accept failure as "God's will" when it is not at all. Scrip-

ture says that God wants to bless us and wants us to ask of Him. It's why we ask that's important. *"You ask and do not receive, because you ask with wrong motives, so that you may spend it on your pleasures"* (James 4:3). We have God's authority to ask and expect to receive when the motives are correct.

But God's Word says, *"And without faith it is impossible to please Him, for he who comes to God must believe that He is, and that He is a rewarder of those who seek Him"* (Hebrews 11:6).

We must believe that God wants to bless us, and until God individually convicts someone that His plan is otherwise, we are not to accept failure. Tribulation brings about proven character. Don't withdraw because of failure. Learn from it. Perseverance is a characteristic much lacking in Christianity today. Some Christians who fail get defeated and feel like God has abandoned them. Some despair to the point of depression or suicide.

Those who believe you should accept failure as a "no" from God or as some kind of punishment need to reread Christ's parables in Luke 11:5-13 and Luke 18:1-8. One of God's principles is persistence in the face of discouragement. Anyone would do God's will if God would prove Himself first. But do we trust God or just say we do?

BALANCE

Even with the best discernment it's possible, and even probable, that we will do things that are out of God's will. Paul said that now we see dimly, as through a mirror, and therefore our spiritual vision will be imperfect. The key is not to let pride get in the way and say, "Well, it's just God's will." That imbalance is usually a rationalization for slothfulness or an inner doubt about God. Our attitude should be to thank God for showing us what doesn't work and get back to the task of discovering what does.

On the other side, a sure way to step out of God's path is to compromise His Word or His will for us and justify it by the obvious "success" it brings. Satan is quite willing and able to "bless" any plan that serves his purpose rather than God's.

Only by staying in God's Word and seeking strong godly counsel can you avoid these traps. If you find yourself outside of God's will and are experiencing a lack of peace you must be willing to abandon everything and seek God's path again.

"Brethren, I do not regard myself as having laid hold of it yet; but one thing I do: forgetting what lies behind and reaching forward to what lies ahead" (Philippians 3:13).

Christian Commitment— What Is It?

If most Christians in the West were as dedicated to Christian activities, such as Bible study, prayer, and evangelism, as they are to sports, we would truly have a spiritual revival today. As Christ taught, Christians are always confronted with a conflict between God's way and the world's attractions.

This came to mind some time back when I received a call from a pastor asking if we could change the date of a seminar that had been scheduled for over a year. When I asked why, he said that at a recent deacon's meeting it was noted that the seminar was being held on the same weekend as the traditional college football game. Unfortunately, he said, several of the church leaders had "conflicts" that weekend.

One pastor of a large dynamic church confided that he had come under severe criticism for allowing the Sunday morning services to go beyond twelve o'clock when the local professional football team had home games. Obviously, it is not sports, recreation, or other activities that are the problems. It is a lack of vital, dynamic commitments to God's way. The other things are merely outside indicators of an inside condition.

The non-Christian world will try to test our commitment to see if it's real. If it's not, they will reject our message as just another philosophy. Quite often, the testing ground will be on the job or in our own neighborhood. Many Christians have lost their witness because they weren't really "doers of the Word."

"*But prove yourselves doers of the word,*

and not merely hearers who delude themselves" (James 1:22).

COMMITMENT TO SELF

There are many dedicated Chris-tians who are willing to accept God's direction at any moment and surrender their jobs, home, and comforts to accomplish their assigned tasks. However, they do not represent a majority within the Christian community. We have a standard for Christian service that requires very little of us. It yields a sizeable body of believers who never really mature. It would seem in God's discipleship plan that some adversity and self-denial are necessary ingredients for spiritual maturity.

"*Consider it all joy, my brethren, when you encounter various trials, knowing that the testing of your faith produces endurance. And let endurance have its perfect result, that you may be perfect and complete, lacking in nothing*" (James 1:2-4).

One has to wonder what Bible it is that some Christians claim promises them perfect health, unlimited success, and permanent residence at the location of their choice. Certainly, it's not the same one that says, "*Whoever does not carry his own cross and come after Me cannot be My disciple*" (Luke 14:27).

A commitment to the lordship of Christ means that we must be willing to go where God determines we can best beutilized. Paul describes us as soldiers in God's army, and we are admonished not to get so caught up in the everyday affairs of this life that we take ourselves out of the battle.

58

PRIORITIES: GOD, FAMILY, WORK

Most Christians know that in God's priority system He must come first, family second, and work, recreation, and so on should assume lower priorities. However, it is possible to confuse this priority system and step out of God's will. Putting God first means the active, daily process of knowing and being known by God. It starts with a thorough understanding of God's handbook for life, the Bible. It requires a heartfelt desire to please God and a willingness to accept God's authority over us.

Many times in the pursuit of this first priority, conflicts will arise in the lower priorities. For instance, what happens when a husband's call to serve God requires relocating, which causes family conflicts? Usually, it's a conflict because of family ties to a particular area. It seems that through the years, those who were willing to be used by God have faced the same conflicts but have determined that the first priority lasts for eternity—all others cease at death.

CHRIST'S REQUIRED COMMITMENT

A review of Christ's ministry on earth demonstrates pretty clearly that He was seeking those who would commit everything to the service of God's kingdom. Even as He walked and taught, many people were attracted to Him because of the miracles He was performing. Each time someone asked Him if they could join His disciples, He directed them to lay aside their own desires and follow Him unreservedly.

"But Jesus said to him, `No one, after putting his hand to the plow, and looking back, is fit for the kingdom of God'" (Luke 9:62).

With few exceptions, they turned back to whatever they had been doing before; the price was simply too high for them.

The lesson for Christians today should be overwhelmingly clear: All of those who are too busy for Christ will regret it. All that truly matters then is what we can do for the kingdom of God. The things we accumulate are not important. They are tools for us to use in accomplishing God's work. Some will need a great resource and some only a little. God owns it all, anyway. Christ said we must make a choice about our commitment and there are only two choices.

"No servant can serve two masters; for either he will hate the one, and love the other, or else he will hold to one, and despise the other. You cannot serve God and mammon" (Luke 16:13).

COMMITTING OUR TIME, TALENT, AND TREASURES

Sometimes it is easier to commit money than it is to commit our time and talent. Consistently, I find that a stewardship commitment involves all three. Perhaps the simplest truth about commitment ever written can be found in Matthew 6:21, *"For where your treasure is, there will your heart be also."* You can determine a great deal about a Christian's spiritual commitment by what he treasures.

Treasures. The way a Christian uses money is the clearest outside indicator of what the inside commitment is really like. The passage in Matthew 6:21 is a spiritual truth being reflected in a material way. *"For where your treasure is, there will your heart be also."* The opposite is also true that where your heart is, your treasure will follow.

In reality, it is the sowing and reaping principle taught by Paul in 2 Corinthians

9:6. *"Now this I say, he who sows sparingly shall also reap sparingly; and he who sows bountifully shall also reap bountifully."* The commitment of material resources to God's work is a proof that the spiritual seeds sown found good soil and matured.

Talent. Many Christians waste the intellect and abilities God has given by dedicating their entire lives to the pursuit of material success. There is obviously nothing wrong with success, as long as it is a by-product of a fruitful life dedicated to God's service. But it's time we realize that a sizeable portion of our talent must be utilized in serving Him too.

Time. I suspect that not many Christians would want to stand before the Lord today and give an account of their daily activities. For instance, if we look at our available day (less sleeping time, eating time, bathing, and so on) as equal to 100 percent, what percentage is spent in the first priority, seeking God? Most surveys show that less than two percent of the average Christian's day is spent in personal Bible study and prayer.

SERVING THE MASTER

The commitment of our treasures goes far beyond just giving money to the Lord's work. It encompasses our motives about earning a living. Many times a commitment will break down when it requires a sacrifice that may include a career change. Some time ago, I met a Christian who was an executive with a national hotel chain. He was faced with just such a decision. The company he worked for had made a decision to include a pornographic cable system in their rooms. After speaking as loudly as he could against it, he determined that he, as a Christian, could no longer be associated with them. At almost sixty years of age, he knew his decision was clearly one of deciding which master he must serve. Today, he is a successful real estate salesman who seeks to put the Lord first in everything.

"But seek for His kingdom, and these things shall be added to you" (Luke 12:31).

The decision of choosing which master to follow is one that each of us must make every day. Are we willing to weigh every decision against God's Word and follow the narrow path God requires?

Is Gambling Wrong?

At first glance, most Christians would respond to the question, "Is gambling wrong?" with a hearty yes. But is gambling *spiritually* wrong? It would appear that the apostles gambled, according to Luke's historical record in Acts 1:26, when they drew lots to determine who was to replace Judas Iscariot. Quite correctly you might say, "But they didn't risk money." The issue, though, is not what the risk or reward was, but rather the action itself. But we'll leave that discussion until later.

Does the fact that the secular world has greatly abused a concept like gambling necessarily make the activity wrong? If so, then we must expand our list to include sex, money, education, and so on. All of these areas have been greatly abused by our secular society. Indeed, today the list might include nearly every human activity. No, we're on shaky ground, spiritually, to exclude an activity on the basis of misuse in our society.

Perhaps we could approach gambling from the perspective of the harm it causes. After all, it attracts a very greedy element of society and robs families of needed resources. But couldn't we say the same thing about credit? We know it robs many more families of needed resources than does gambling, and it has long been associated with organized crime. Even a cursory review of God's Word reveals that all harmful practices aren't eliminated or prohibited—they are controlled. Again, the classic example from Scripture is debt. Even though a man could lose his freedom and family through debt, the practice was discouraged but allowed in both the Old and the New Testaments.

WHY GAMBLE?

Before reviewing the principle of gambling, let's take a look at why most people gamble. Many people gamble because they have needs that cannot be met through earned income. They barely make ends meet, and gambling represents their opportunity to acquire material comforts. In the past, these were the people who played the two-dollar window at the race track. Today, they play the lotteries that many states now offer to attract more funds for the public coffers.

Another group gambles just for the fun of it. They say it doesn't matter if they win or lose. But let them start winning, and you find out that's not so. These are the social gamblers, and they represent most of the people found at Las Vegas or Atlantic City. They go on vacation with a set amount of money. Once it's gone, they pack up and go home, often living conservative lives that require disciplined budgeting.

One last group gambles compulsively. Gambling, to them, is a disease that wrecks their finances, families, and careers. The compulsive gamblers will lie, steal, cheat, and use virtually everyone around them. A game of chance to them is what alcohol is to the alcoholic. Often, they are successful professionals with promising careers. One compulsive gambler I counseled maintained a successful career for several years while flying to Las Vegas twice a month without his wife's even knowing about it. His dual life ended when he owed over $200,000 in gambling debts to underworld lenders and had embezzled over $100,000 from trust funds in his care.

At first glance, each of these types of gamblers would appear to have different motives for gambling, but, in reality, they all suffer from the same basic problem—materialism.The one who gambles when in need is looking for the "big hit" just like the social gambler or the compulsive gambler.

James described the symptom very well in James 4:1. *"What is the source of quarrels and conflicts among you? Is not the source your pleasures that wage war in your members?"*

WHAT IS GAMBLING?

In order to evaluate gambling scripturally, we must first determine what it is. If it's labor, then it has scriptural value. *"In all labor there is profit, but mere talk leads only to poverty"* (Proverbs 14:23).

Well, gambling may be labor for a pit boss in Vegas, but for the gamblers, it's a scheme to escape labor, at least in most instances. Gambling is perhaps the ultimate in get-rich-quick schemes. It satisfies every element of get-rich-quick: (1) The participants are encouraged to risk money they usually can't afford to lose. (2) They know little or nothing about what they are doing. (3) They're forced to make hasty decisions. (4) The whole idea is to operate on the "greater sucker" theory. In other words, when you dump money into the slot machine, you believe there was a greater sucker who risked his money and then quit just before the big jackpot.

Any get-rich-quick scheme is developed to entrap the weak and especially the poor. After all, what does a wealthy man need with a get-rich-quick scheme? Gambling is an almost irresistible enticement to someone who desires to meet the wants and desires of his family but finds that he cannot. That's why the state lotteries are so popular. We don't have to wonder about the state of our society when governments resort to enticing their citizens to gamble to raise funds.

"Even so, every good tree bears good fruit; but the bad tree bears bad fruit" (Matthew 7:17).

IS GAMBLING A SIN?

Gambling, in the strictest sense, is as much a sin as having a false weight in your bag. To entice someone to gain money at the certain loss of another violates virtually every principle taught by Christ. It breeds and promotes selfishness, greed, and covetousness.

"For many walk, of whom I often told you, and now tell you even weeping, that they are enemies of the cross of Christ, whose end is destruction, whose god is their appetite, and whose glory is in their shame, who set their minds on earthly things" (Philippians 3:18-19).

A sin, according to God's Word, means missing the mark. Regardless of how socially acceptable the practice of gambling has become, it is still preying upon the weaknesses of others. It does *not* help to expand the gospel and, therefore, is a sin to a follower of Jesus Christ.

"So that you may walk in a manner worthy of the Lord, to please Him in all respects, bearing fruit in every good work and increasing in the knowledge of God" (Colossians 1:10).

To preempt the question about this conclusion's being legalism rather than a principle, you need only do a survey of Paul's letters. We are first told, as believers, to live by a standard higher than the world's (Romans 12:2). Also, we are told to do nothing that would give cause for offense or that might discredit our ministry (2 Corinthians 6:3). Even if a Christian believes that he is free to gamble, the truth is it will cause others to stumble. We are clearly directed in 1 Corinthians 8:13 to avoid anything that would cause a weaker brother to stumble.

COMPULSIVE GAMBLING

Many people are compulsive gamblers. A compulsive gambler is as addicted to risk taking as a dope addict is to drugs. He will bet on virtually anything and will rob his kid's piggy bank if necessary. Every church has at least one compulsive gambler, and some churches have several. All too often, they are supported out of a church benevolence fund without the benevolence group's even knowing about the gambling. The way to overcome this is to *require* counseling for any benevolence fund recipient and *absolutely* require that both husband and wife attend.

Having counseled several gamblers, I have found several common characteristics to look for. First, there is an unusually high debt load with little or no logical explanation for it. Second, there will be a history of borrowing from virtually every friend and family member. Third, you will find a vehement denial of anything to do with gambling. It is often in response to a direct question about gambling that the spouse will usually reveal the truth. A compulsive gambler may hide his secret from the outside world but not from a spouse.

Any gambler needs love and acceptance, but it must be accompanied by accountability. He needs to be held accountable to pay his debts, tell the truth, and stay away from *all* gambling. If God's people don't hold to this same standard, it's rather hard to give good counsel to a compulsive gambler.

SATAN'S LIE

In our society, sin is being spread under the guise of innocence. In the case of gambling, we are being fed the lie that legalized gambling doesn`t promote crime and will lower taxes when, in fact, the evidence shows just the opposite. Gambling promotes other vices that attract the criminal element. That results in higher, not lower, taxes.

Many Christians are guilty of supporting lotteries, bingo, and racing all under the assumption that gambling doesn't really hurt anyone. That's exactly what Satan would have us believe. We pass our value system along to those around us—first, to our own families, then to our friends and neighbors.

If our value system is no better than the world's, then truly we have been conformed to the image of this world.

"Whether, then, you eat or drink or whatever you do, do all to the glory of God. Give no offense either to Jews or to Greeks or to the church of God; just as I also please all men in all things, not seeking my own profit, but the profit of the many, that they may be saved" (1 Corinthians 10:31-33).

Christian Compromise

Few Christians would willfully violate the Ten Commandments. Most appear to be basically moral. But what about inward doubts, temptations, and failures—are these sin?

The actual violations of many of God's commandments involve attitudes more than actions: lustful thoughts, anger, and pride. These attitudes develop over a period of time and are very difficult to guard against. Most of us simply find ourselves doing them without realizing how or when they started. It is apparent from God's Word that He also recognizes that and has provided an objective means for us to measure our internal attitudes. That measure is how we respond to the smaller temptations involving money (Luke 16:10). Knowing and using this truth can be a key to becoming a truly Spirit-controlled Christian.

GOD'S ABSOLUTES

God's *minimum* acceptable attitudes basically boil down to two: to love God totally and to love others as ourselves (Matthew 22:37-39). Christ said that loving God more than anything else was a prerequisite to receiving God's best. *"But seek for His kingdom, and these things shall be added to you"* (Luke 12:31). John repeated this command as a condition for expecting answers from God. *"And whatever we ask we receive from Him, because we keep His commandments and do the things that are pleasing to His sight"* (1 John 3:22).

That explains in great part why so few people are willing and able to totally trust God for material needs. It is not that they don't desire to obey and trust God—

they just are not willing to stand without compromise, regardless of the situation.

TEMPTATIONS TO COMPROMISE

Compared to overt sins, compromises don't seem so bad. If God was merely an accountant weighing good against bad, and one person against another, there would be no problem. However, God deals in absolutes, not comparisons, and each individual is totally responsible and accountable for his actions regardless of what others do. Compromises of God's Word are simply outside material symptoms of inside spiritual problems. Quite often in financial situations, the urge to compromise is evident. It may be the tendency to cheat on income taxes or to take bankruptcy in the face of overwhelming debts. It may be a white lie to sell a product or a padded expense account. The Lord said that the desire for money would lead to the worship of money and the violation of the first commandment.

"No one can serve two masters; for either he will hate the one and love the other, or he will hold to one and despise the other. You cannot serve God and mammon" (Matthew 6:24).

The accumulation of money is a major deterrent to a humble spirit. The tendency is to desire to be served rather than to serve: *"It is not so among you, but whoever wishes to be first among you shall be your slave"* (Matthew 20:26-27).

Obviously, money is *not* the problem, it is only the symptom. Many temptations associated with materialism are so common today that most Christians accept them as a normal way of life. Fear of the future is so great in our society that millions of Christians have been persuaded to squirrel away literally billions of dollars without any real plans for its future use, even though it requires a direct compromise to God's instructions.

"But seek first His kingdom and His righteousness; and all these things shall be added to you. Therefore do not be anxious for tomorrow; for tomorrow will care for itself. Each day has enough trouble of its own" (Matthew 6:33-34).

Greed has become such an accepted attitude that most major advertisements for luxury products are built around it. Many committed believers are convinced (often by other believers) that it is God's absolute responsibility to make them wealthy and successful. Just to help Him out (in case God neglects His responsibility), they are willing to borrow large amounts of money to invest in get-rich-quick schemes, abandon their families to provide the "good life" for them, rob God of His tithes and offerings, and rationalize all of it as serving Him.

God does have a plan for success. Although it is unique for each individual, it is common in the following ways: (1) God never provides success at the expense of serving Him first. *"But those who want to get rich fall into temptation and a snare and many foolish and harmful desires which plunge men into ruin and destruction"* (1 Timothy 6:9). (2) God never provides success at the expense of our peace. *"Peace I leave with you; My peace I give to you; not as the world gives, do I give to you. Let not your heart be troubled, nor let it be fearful"* (John 14:27). (3) God never provides success at the expense of the family. *"It is vain for you to rise up early, to retire late, to eat the bread of painful labors; for He gives to His beloved even in His sleep"* (Psalm 127:2).

GOD'S WAY: OPTIONAL OR MANDATORY?

It seems abundantly clear from God's Word that those who accept Christ as their Lord are to live by a much higher standard than the rest of the world, not because Christians are to be pious or super-spiritual but simply because they are to be normal. It is God's way that is normal and the world's way that is abnormal. Christians are to be lights to lead others to God in a dark world. What we say is not enough. God requires that we show and tell.

"That you may prove yourselves to be blameless and innocent, children of God above reproach in the midst of a crooked and perverse generation, among whom you appear as lights in the world" (Philippians 2:15).

As Christians, we learn a great deal about discipline and dedication from the secular world. It is interesting that those in the secular business world are almost always more punctual and reliable in their work than Christians are in serving God. Usually, Christians apply a degree of excellence and dedication to their business careers that is woefully lacking in their walk with the Lord.

The secular business world practices what is called "preconditioned response." For instance, the airlines have found that it is not feasible to wait until an inflight emergency occurs to acquaint the pilot with emergency procedures. Therefore, they attempt to precondition his response. The techniques for responding to every kind of emergency are practiced again and again. Obviously, some pilots won't ever be faced with such emergencies, and most won't be faced with more than one or two. But having the knowledge makes them more relaxed and confident and better pilots.

Many Christians have been duped

into believing that no emergencies will ever occur in their lives, and even if they do, they can handle them by instinct. Thus they are ill-prepared and out of condition to handle problems and temptations. When faced with a potentially compromising situation, they lack the basic tools to make the choice God's way.

Even a cursory scan of Scripture will reveal that the truly successful servants of the Lord made decisions on the preconditioned belief that God's way wasn't just the best way—it was the *only* way. The consequences of not obeying God were so dreadful that any earthly consequences were considered trivial. The worldly consequences of making decisions God's way might be less income, no sale, the loss of a job, or overpayment of taxes. However, the consequences of compromising God's way are:

- Lack of peace (James 4:4)
- Cooling toward God (James 4:17)
- Critical spirit (James 3:16)
- Uselessness to God (Titus 1:16)

Just as Nehemiah did (Nehemiah 6:11) when he refused to compromise God's way even to save his own life, a Christian must precondition all responses to temptations and problems on the basis of what God says, *not* what is normal and acceptable. God promises that He will prosper us and protect us so that He may receive the glory (Palm 50:14-15). It also makes life a whole lot simpler when facing decisions that many face every day about suing, borrowing, lending, co-signing, bankruptcy, and paying taxes.

God's Word challenges us to look beyond the temporary rewards of being a conformist to the eternal rewards of being a "light."

"More than that, I count all things to be loss in view of the surpassing value of knowing Christ Jesus my Lord, for whom I have suffered the loss of all things, and count them but rubbish in order that I may gain Christ" (Philippians 3:8).

Part 2:

Church and Sharing

Financial Needs of Divorcees

There is perhaps no more emotionally charged area of Christianity today than that of divorce. Approximately one-half of all current marriages fail in the first six years of marriage, including couples who profess to be Christians. Failed marriages within the church leave us with a great many divorcees. But recent statistics also indicate that a great many divorcees become Christians and, thus, find their way into a local church. It is estimated that if the trend continues into the twenty-first century, a typical local church would be made up of from 40 to 60 percent divorced members. At least half of these would be single, divorced parents—primarily women.

THE ISSUE OF DIVORCE

To teach that God condones divorce is to make God's Word conditional. In other words, if you keep your word, God will keep His. If that's so, then we're all in big trouble. I count on God being faithful and never changing, no matter what anyone else might do. If I have vowed to remain with my wife for life, then that vow is unconditional. If it's conditional, then it's not a vow—it's an option.

"It is better that you should not vow than that you should vow and not pay" (Ecclesiastes 5:5).

NEEDS OF SINGLE PARENTS

Because of limited space, I would like to focus on the largest and most needy group of single parents—divorced mothers. Obviously, there are divorced men raising families and divorced singles with no families. They have the same emotional and spiritual needs as divorced women who are raising families. But few people understand the financial needs of these mothers.

The estimated average income for a North American family of three (husband, wife, and one child) is about $22,000 a year. The minimum need level is about $16,000 a year, and the official poverty level is about $13,000. For a typical divorcee with one child, her income is about $11,000, including Aid to Dependent Children. Her life-style is one of surviving from check to check, hoping that nothing breaks down, because there's no money to fix it. She will typically spend 30 percent of her net take home pay on child care (usually inadequate). Her housing is usually a small apartment that takes 40 percent of her pay. The 30 percent that is left over has to cover food, clothing, transportation, medical, dental, and so on. It just won't stretch far enough. If she has more than one child and is over thirty, her problems of finding a job are compounded.

Of course, we can take the position that she's reaping what she sowed, but so far that hasn't done much to reverse the trend, so I would discount that as being God's attitude. I have counseled enough divorced parents to know that quite often the divorce was not their option.

A young woman I'll call Sherri is a typical case. Her ex-husband was a chronic gambler who divorced her for another woman and left her with $6,000 in credit card bills because her name was on the accounts also. She lives in a small apartment with two children, owns a seven-year-old car, and makes about five dollars an hour as a steno-typist. She is a

Christian and attends a major denominational church. When she appealed to the benevolence committee for help, they sent her to the state welfare department for assistance. Her financial needs are at least $300 a month more than she makes, with no foreseeable end to this need over the next several years. She desperately desires fellowship for herself and her children but no longer fits into a family unit. She feels like an outcast and feels betrayed by a church where she has tithed regularly for several years. Sherri's financial needs fit into a typical pattern for young divorcees with children:

1. *Child care.* She has a four-year-old son and an eight-year-old son. The four-year-old is in a day care center (at a monthly cost of $250). The eight-year-old is home by himself for about two hours a day after school. He wanted to play Little League baseball, but his mother couldn't arrange transportation.

2. *Repairs.* Her seven-year-old car has need of brakes, tires, and a tune-up. Even a minor repair of $100 strips her of any surplus funds for two to three months. Appliances are simply left broken for the lack of any mechanical skill to fix them and no budgeted funds available.

3. *Male influence.* She is particularly concerned that her two boys are growing up without a good role model for becoming young men. Her ex-husband lives out of state and refuses to take the children for even a short period.

4. *Low income.* She knows that she is basically peaked out on her job as a steno-typist and would like to go to school for computer training. She lacks the funds for child care or school. The credit card company is threatening to attach Sherri's wages for $100 a month. That would literally destroy her ability to provide for her family.

WHAT CAN WE DO?

We could choose from any of nearly twenty references to helping those within the Body of Christ. By doing so, we're not condoning divorce or raising the divorced to some "official status"—we're merely following Christ's example of showing our love, rather than just talking about it. Consider Christianity from Sherri's eyes when she is told that the church can't meet her needs, but the government can. She knows that by accepting government aid she must also accept government supervision over her children. Yet it must seem inconsistent to Sherri that the very same church is in the midst of an expensive program to build a youth center to attract young people and their families to the church.

That is not to imply that a building program itself is wrong—but that we are guilty of having the form without the substance of Christianity. I wonder when we will wake up and recognize that more programs and buildings don't attract the lost to God. The lost are attracted by the love and dedication that they see. If a program can attract them to the church, then a bigger program can attract them away again.

"But whoever has the world's goods, and beholds his brother in need and closes his heart against him, how does the love of God abide in him? Little children, let us not love with word or with tongue, but in deed and truth" (1 John 3:17-18).

There are several programs that any fellowship can start to minister to the singles within their midst.

1. *Helps program.* "Beloved, let us love one another, for love is from God" (1 John 4:7a). Any church can organize a program to help single women in the area of repair and maintenance of machines. For example, several churches can organize a joint

joint effort to assist single women in repairing their cars. I'm aware of several churches that have done this. One Saturday (usually every other month), the men of these churches who have any mechanical ability meet in one of the church parking lots. The single women who have need for minor repairs on their cars can bring them to be fixed or serviced for only the cost of parts, or nothing at all.

Obviously, there must be controls and supervision, but that is normally done by a trained layman. The work is scheduled through a church counselor, and to participate, a woman must be actively attending church and counseling. Other churches also have appliance repair centers where single women can drop off appliances for repair without cost. Some churches even offer volunteer repair crews for work on homes, such as painting, roofing, and yard work.

2. *Counseling.* Churches with "helps" programs should always operate under the guidance of a singles' counseling center. The purpose is to work at restoring the family unit if possible and to share Christ with those who are lost. The singles who are involved with the helps programs should be discipled and encouraged to work in other service for the church, such as babysitting, visitation, and health care.

This counseling center *must* be under the guidance and supervision of the church leadership, and all rules for singles' counseling should be observed. This is especially true of men counseling singled or divorced women.

3. *Child care centers.* Even if an individual church cannot afford to operate a child care center, certainly several churches (or businesses) working together could. There are several churches now doing this as a ministry— not a business. These centers are provided as an outreach to single parents in the church and are operated on a donation basis. The purpose is not to just babysit children, but to nurture them in the Lord. If you really want to reach single parents for the Lord, start ministering to them through their children. They will respond. Helping in a child care center can be an excellent ministry for mothers within the church who have child care and educational training skills but need to be with their own children during the day.

"By this is My Father glorified, that you bear much fruit, and so prove to be My disciples" (John 15:8).

4. *Clothes closets.* Within every church there are both needs and surpluses. God's Word indicates that they will nearly always offset one another. The difficulty is in getting those with a surplus together with those who have needs. A "clothes closet" is a way to do this. This is a common location in the church that is used to hold goods that one family no longer needs, until that need surfaces in another family.

Is Welfare Scriptural?

The Bible's stand on welfare is very clear: we are to help those in need. There may be a disagreements about how much help is necessary and who should receive it, but there should be no disagreement on the necessity to feed, clothe, and shelter the poor. Yet the church is no longer the prime mover in meeting the needs of the poor—the government is. And there can be no doubt that government welfare has helped produce a society where many families live in permanent poverty. Because of that, many Christians have developed resentment and indifference to the real poor. But the fact that the government has assumed the function of caring for the poor does not negate our responsibility. Welfare for the poor is biblical and necessary.

THE PURPOSE OF WELFARE

"For the poor will never cease to be in the land; therefore I command you, saying, 'You shall freely open your hand to your brother, to your needy and poor in your land'" (Deuteronomy 15:11).

God's Word says that there will always be needs in the world around us. The purpose is twofold: one, to test our commitment to obedience (Matthew 25:40); and two, to create an attitude of interdependence (2 Corinthians 8:14). We are admonished to meet the needs of the widows and orphans because they are unable to meet their own needs. But does welfare stop with the elderly widows and orphans? Unfortunately, in most of Christianity, it doesn't even include them. Simply because Satan has misused welfare for his purpose does not make welfare wrong.

It is impossible to read the epistles of James and John without recognizing the requirement to help others in need. John uses the lack of concern for the needs of others as evidence of lack of love (1 John 3:17-18). Therefore, we know that the true purpose of *welfare* (meeting the needs of others) is to demonstrate God's love through us. An outside observer would have to conclude that there is little evidence of God's love in America. That is exactly the conclusion many unsaved come to. The church is more interested in buildings, programs, and promotions than in caring.

EFFECTS OF WELFARE

It is interesting to see the contrasting objectives of biblical welfare and government welfare. Sharing with others in need out of God's love should produce three results: one, a sense of fellowship and belonging (2 Corinthians 9:13); two, a stronger family unit (1 Timothy 5:8); and three, a high standard for work, which prohibits laziness (2 Thessalonians 3:9-10).

Unfortunately, the effects of social or government welfare are almost the opposite. Why is that? It is because the motivation is not love but pity or, even worse, guilt. When society tries to make up for previous wrongs by providing government welfare, the results will be permanent dependence and poverty. With the best of intentions, our welfare system traps people at the lowest economic level through indiscriminate giving. To qualify for support, most recipients must show only that they are not working, not that they cannot work.

Additionally, most welfare recipients resent the system and ultimately the society that supports them. Why? Because of the degrading method in which the funds are distributed and the stigma attached to "taking someone else's money." Government welfare recipients must adopt an attitude of "you owe it to me" to justify receiving the money even if they have legitimate needs. After only one generation, a welfare mentality and permanent dependence develops. The temptation of "free" money attracts more and more recipients until finally there are fewer givers than takers.

BIBLICAL ABSOLUTES

Christians are given clear and absolute direction about welfare in God's Word. Fortunately, the standards for welfare are also given. Indiscriminate welfare traps the recipients by making them dependent. Biblical welfare meets needs and always looks toward restoring the individual back to a position of productivity.

QUALIFICATIONS FOR WELFARE

Those who qualify for welfare are:

1. *The poor.* In Scripture, being poor literally meant being unable to meet even the most basic needs. Those who were poor—not lazy—were worthy of support (Deuteronomy 15:7-11; 2 Samuel 12:1-5; Proverbs 19:17).

2. *The diligent.* There are many people who are lazy by nature. They do not qualify for support and, in fact, require a good swift kick for motivation. Supporting such people is just as unscriptural as not supporting those with legitimate needs. *"A worker's appetite works for him, for his hunger urges him on"* (Proverbs 16:26; see also 19:15; 20:4; 24:33; 2 Thessalonians 3:10).

3. *The widows.* A qualified widow is defined as a woman sixty years or older whose only husband has died (1 Timothy 5:3-10). In the first century it was acknowledged that families took care of their own widows. In our generation, the qualification could well be extended to those who cannot get help from their own families—divorcees included.

4. *The orphans.* It would seem evident that children who are parentless are dependent on others for help. All children belong to God's family. If Christians fulfilled their function, every child would have parents. Even if we can't adopt them all, we most assuredly can help care for their needs, both material and emotional.

5. *Those with immediate needs.* Long-term needs require welfare; immediate needs require benevolence. In James 2:15-16, we are admonished to help those in need. They do not have to qualify as "poor" or "widows" but only as "lacking of the daily food." Such temporary needs can easily be the result of illness, imprisonment, and unemployment. Benevolence means giving to the obvious needs of another.

6. *Those with legitimate needs.* Many Christians ask what constitutes a "legitimate need" in another's life. *"For this is not for the ease of others and for your affliction, but by way of equality"* (2 Corinthians 8:13). Reason would indicate that a need is relative to the society and times. A Cambodian's needs probably do not include an automobile. But for many, a car is necessary for earning a livelihood. Since there are no absolutes on this issue, it would seem that God allows individual discernment. However, the need for food, shelter, and clothing to survive are absolutes, and, unfortunately, there are many people in our world

who are dying for the lack of these things.

CHRISTIAN RESPONSIBILITY

The truth is that Christians are doing a miserable job of caring for the physical needs of the poor. If we can't meet the needs of those around us, we won't meet the needs of those in other countries. Few churches today have any organized program for helping the poor of their own fellowship or community. Some have a benevolence fund to help meet some emergencies but nothing to meet continuing needs. Obviously, vision and leadership come from the top down. If the church doesn't practice the "body" concept of Christianity, it is a certainty that it will never reach the unsaved community.

At present, the governments of the world supply nearly 95 percent of all the care to the aged, ill, and impoverished, and the evidence shows they are using it as a tool to spread atheism. Is it any wonder that the unsaved are rejecting Christianity? Obviously, there are exceptions, and many Christian organizations do a great job of meeting the physical and spiritual needs of others, but they are few in comparison. It is not a question of ability or direction. Christians in North America have the resources to do at least ten times what we are presently doing for the poor, with little or no alteration of life-styles. Many Christians are going to be very ashamed to face the Lord and explain why they hoarded money for indulgences while others went hungry.

"And he said, 'This is what I will do: I will tear down my barns and build larger ones, and there I will store all my grain and my goods.'" . . . *"But God said to him, 'You fool! This very night your soul is required of you; and now who will own what you have prepared?'"* (Luke 12:18, 20).

WHAT CAN WE DO?

Welfare was transferred from the church because the church neglected it. It can be recovered, and the church can become a leader in caring about personal needs. That is not an option from God— it is an imperative. *"He who gives to the poor will never want, but he who shuts his eyes will have many curses"* (Proverbs 28:27).

Committed Christians should encourage their church leaders to establish a body life ministry. A portion of every church's budget should be designated for needs in the fellowship and in the community. There should also be an outreach to starving people in other countries. If your denomination doesn't have a care program, then support a good, independent ministry that feeds the hungry. Each church should have a resource committee set up to counsel families in need and to determine who does and does not qualify for help.

There should be such an atmosphere of sharing and caring that members would feel as free to share a financial burden as they would a physical burden. Ultimately, within the Christian community there should be health and child care centers, vocational training centers, and employment agencies so that when faced with needs from within the Christian community or the secular community, we could respond without relying on government help.

Fleecing the Flock

There are few things that really rile me as a Christian. But one thing that does is Christians who "fleece" other Christians. That can be done in a variety of subtle ways, from selling get-rich-quick schemes to selling soap. Fleecing is probably a pretty accurate analogy, because when you fleece sheep you don't really want to hurt them, you just shear them of a little extra wool. Most groups that fleece God's sheep simply want to sell them a product, not rob them. The products may even be good ones, although usually they are high priced. It is because they are higher priced that a personal marketing system is attractive. If most people were evaluating the products on a purely competitive basis, they would usually find a better deal.

Almost without exception, the real clincher in a "Christian" marketing scheme is the idea that you can sell to your friends and "help" them as well. After you've accepted that, objectivity disappears, and the plan or product becomes incidental to the profit motive.

One of the best marketing method within Christian circles is assumed credibility. That is when the sales group assumes someone else's credibility. Allow me to use a personal example. One thing I realized from the earliest stages when organizing Christian Financial Concepts was that a lot of wrong had been done to many Christians under the guise of "Christian finances." Many groups that had sprung up claiming to teach and counsel on biblical principles of finances were really sales companies in disguise. Many taught good concepts, but their intent was to sell a product or service, and the teaching was usually a gimmick

to gather a group. As a result, many pastors were justifiably cautious about any financial "ministry."

From the beginning, CFC determined to operate as a ministry and sell no products or services, nor endorse any other group's product or services for a fee. Many times when funds were short it was truly tempting to compromise. As the ministry grew, we got offers from dozens of sales groups that would virtually underwrite the ministry if we would just send them people who needed products. I believed then, as now, that to do so would be to use God's Word for gain and would be deceptive.

"But those who want to get rich fall into temptation and a snare and many foolish and harmful desires which plunge men into ruin and destruction" (1 Timothy 6:9).

Because of that stand, we earned the trust of those we taught and counseled and have been able to cross denominational and doctrinal boundaries to share God's principles. Most pastors who know of the ministry know that they can trust what we teach and say even though we may not always agree on exact interpretations.

Quite often over the last few years, various groups have sprung up teaching biblical finances in the local church and selling a product as well. Many have implied that CFC endorses them, and lately one group even said that we asked them to call on a pastor (we did not). In many cases one of our staff may use a product or service offered by a group. If that group assumes blanket endorsement, that is deceptive and wrong. Very few groups can meet our standards for recommendation, and we never accept a fee or commission. Any staff member who endorses a group without our approval is subject to dismissal. That is not to tout CFC; we have made errors and will again, I'm sure. But I want to demonstrate that when a sales group wants to assume someone else's credibility, watch out; it is usually because they can't assume their own.

There is an old secular cliché that says, "If you walk like a duck, and talk like a duck, and stay in the presence of ducks, maybe people will think you're a duck." In Christianity, that would seem to hold true. If a nonbeliever knows the words and hangs out in church a lot, quite often he will go undetected. By the same principle, if a business hires mostly Christians, has them tell everybody they're in a ministry, and uses mostly Christian terms, then others will think they are a "ministry." Please don't misunderstand this. Any business can and should be used to minister. Business is an excellent tool through which to share Christ. But a business sells a product and hopes to make a profit. A ministry serves a function that cannot be done at a profit. For instance, you cannot provide counsel to families in financial trouble profitably.

One of the keys to detecting a business being disguised as a ministry is to see how the funds are generated. If it's through the sale of products and services (including Christian products and services), it is a business and should be evaluated with a very critical eye. If a group uses "buzz words" to gain an entry, beware.

"I would like to come by and share our *ministry*." This is a common buzz word. If the business offers a legitimate product or service, then it ought to stand on its own merit. It should not require a spiritual endorsement to get in the door. My concern would be if someone would mislead about one part of the business, what else might he mislead about?

"*Pastor*, we have something that will help your people." When a group orients its sales pitch to pastors be on guard. If it's a product for pastors or a program for the local church, then pastors are the group to call on. But if it's a product, diet plan, insurance, wills, trusts, gold mines, and so on, and it is directed toward pastors, then be aware that the group is trying to ride in on his credibility.

Unfortunately, since many pastors are not well paid, they also fall into the finder's fee trap. Often the group will offer the pastor a fee for anyone he recommends who buys the products. There are many pastors who have lost their personal credibility by endorsing a company to their people. Integrity is won over a long time and can be lost all too quickly.

"You can *help* other Christians." Without a doubt this is the real clincher in fleecing the flock. If a company can convince its sales people that the end results of their efforts is to help others, then the methods can be justified. It's the old "the end justifies the means" syndrome. In other words, you're not really hurting them by deceiving them; after all, it's for their own good. The real test of motives is whether or not the salesman is willing to forgo all profit to "help" others. I personally know many honest, ethical Christian salespeople who refuse to profit when dealing with pastors or Christians encountered through their church. It's not that selling to Christian contacts is necessarily wrong. It's just that they believe the temptation to compromise is too strong. "*For where jealousy and selfish ambition exist, there is disorder and every evil thing*" (James 3:16). With certainty, God knows what our needs are, including our business needs. He will provide those who need the products without having to use

use the Christian community.

Matthew 21:12 describes the event when Christ ran the moneychangers out of the Temple. Why did He do that when obviously they were meeting a need of the people coming to the Temple to worship? The law gave the Jews the right to sell an animal designated for sacrifice if they had a long journey, then use the money to buy another animal for sacrifice. The moneychangers served this need and most of the people seemed satisfied. So why get so upset when both sides benefited? Because Christ knew that the motive of the moneychangers was to "fleece the flock." They bought low and sold high with the endorsement of the Temple priests and religious leaders. If the people wanted their sacrifices blessed, they had to use "blessed" animals.

Obviously, it didn't start out that way. It probably started with a moneychanger who showed a priest how he could *help* a lot of people and make a little profit for himself. Later it became how he could make a lot of profit and help the people a little. Why do you suppose this event was reported in the Scriptures? One reason may well be that Jesus wanted His disciples to understand exactly how He felt about "fleecing the flock."

If we, as Christians, are to do business with each other, we must follow fundamental biblical principles to avoid the "fleecing" trap.

1. *Don't develop a sales program exclusively for the church.* Obviously, Christian teaching materials are created for a Christian market, but other products are not. Most programs aimed almost exclusively at the Christian market are really secular products with some Christian terms sprinkled in.

Recently, a Christian called to ask for an opinion about a ministry (for profit company) that wanted to sell him a "Christian" will and trust. Since we function under secular law in our country, I was interested to see what a Christian will and trust was.

It turned out to be a fairly standard will and trust with several Christian words sprinkled throughout. It seemed to be a fairly good document with a pretty good testimony, at about twice the price of a standard will and trust. Its real benefit was that the client could get his money back if four friends would sign up, and he could make a profit if more than four signed up.

"And in their greed they will exploit you with false words; their judgment from long ago is not idle, and their destruction is not asleep" (2 Peter 2:3).

2. *Don't practice deception.* If you have a product to sell that you honestly believe will benefit other Christians, let it be known. But don't promote it as a "ministry" or as a spiritual "happening." Let your yes be yes and your no be no. In other words, let people know what the company is and what the product is. If there is a referral or finder's fee paid to another person for a lead, let that be known, too. If you're afraid of losing a sale because of total honesty, then the program is dishonest.

Church Borrowing

Church borrowing is an emotional and controversial topic. It is difficult to teach on the subject directly because it is primarily an attitude rather than an absolute. However, anything taken to excess is destructive, and most certainly that is true of debt.

Debt defined. For the sake of simplicity, we will define church debt as any borrowing by a church that carries with it a contingent liability. That means that the lender *expects* the money to be repaid—no matter what. That would include building loans and bonds. A debt would be defined scripturally as "surety." Definition: "to deposit a pledge, either in money, goods, or part payment as security for a bargain."

Normal use. It is no more abnormal for a church to finance a building program today than for a business to do so. Approximately 90 percent of all church building programs carry with them indebtedness ranging from one to twenty years.

The use of debt to build or expand the outreach of a church is so common a practice today that to even challenge the idea can create an air of animosity. However, just because a practice is normal does not mean it is scriptural or best. It should be noted that most churches repay their indebtedness according to contract. So the discussion is not whether a church can repay; it is whether or not churches should borrow, even if they can repay.

SCRIPTURAL GUIDELINES

Borrowing is not prohibited in Scripture. It is *discouraged*. There are no positive references to borrowing, and, in fact, there are explicit warnings to avoid it. *"The rich rules over the poor, and the borrower becomes the lender's slave"* (Proverbs 22:7). Thus the Word indicates that an unnecessary authority is created by borrowing. The question is often asked, "If borrowing is allowable for individuals, why shouldn't churches also be able to borrow?" The answer is twofold. One, churches *can* borrow. The evidence is abundant around us. Second, just because they can doesn't mean they *should*. The church as an entity comes under a more stringent judgment from God's Word because of its visible position.

"Let not many of you become teachers, my brethren, knowing that as such we shall incure a stricter judgment" (James 3:1). I would infer this condition to mean the visible church as well.

The church as a physical entity exists for just one purpose: to glorify God. It stands as the visible image of God's best, not subject to worldly compromise. It seems contradictory to profess the belief that God can heal the sick, feed the poor, and even transform the very heart of a corrupt man, but He can't supply the funds in advance with which to do these things. *"And my God shall supply all your needs according to His riches in glory in Christ Jesus"* (Philippians 4:19). Money is no different from any other promise that God gives us, except that it is physical, visible, and measurable. Many of the other promises are subject to feelings and interpretations, but money is a rare absolute; you either have it or you don't.

The argument that if individual Christians can borrow money, so should the church is not valid. In the first place, much of the borrowing that individual Christians do is, in itself, unscriptural because it is done in excess. That can be witnessed in the current level of divorce and bankruptcy, both of which are primarily motivated by the excessive use of credit. It is clear that the standards for leaders in the church are more stringent than for the individual members (1 Timothy 3:1-2). If that is so, then it would seem obvious that the standards of the church organization must be higher than that of its individual members.

SCRIPTURAL PRECEDENT

In doing a survey of this subject, I tried to be as objective as possible, knowing that I rarely observe the good side of credit. Few families or churches share with us the great successes they have made using credit, but many share their failures. However, the mere fact that others have misused credit does not necessarily make it wrong. Only Scripture has the guidelines we are to follow—not opinion, no matter how normal it may seem.

After reviewing the references to borrowing in Scripture, I came to several conclusions:

1. Borrowing is always presented in the negative (Proverbs 17:18).

2. God never once made a promise to anyone and fulfilled it through a loan (Luke 6:38).

3. God promised His people that if they would obey His commandment, they would not have to borrow (Deuteronomy 28:12).

4. God had worship structures built at least three times in the Bible, and no credit was used.

"Then the Lord spoke to Moses, saying, 'Tell the sons of Israel to raise a contribution
for Me; from every man whose heart moves him you shall raise My contribution'" (Exodus 25:1-2). *"O Lord God, all this abundance that we have provided to build Thee a house for Thy holy name, it is from Thy hand, and all is Thine"* (1 Chronicles 29:16; 1 Kings 6; 2 Kings 12).

It might be said that these aren't valid examples because borrowing was not a normal practice during these times. If not, then Solomon wasted a great many parables dealing with the dangers of too much credit.

In the New Testament, there are no direct references to church buildings or their funding. It would seem very out of character that the leaders of the first-century church who risked their very lives to deliver God's Word would have condoned or even permitted their churches to borrow. The basic attitudes reflected in Acts 4 and 2 Corinthians 8 would indicate a commitment to giving whatever was needed.

WHY NOT BORROW?

"If a church borrows money to do God's work and it is repaid on time, then what's the harm?" This question is logical and is frequently asked. There is no single answer but rather a series of them.

1. Each church leader and member must search God's Word with an open mind and heart and determine if God does or does not desire churches to be fundd with debt. If it is determined that to borrow is a compromise to God's will, then to do so is to sin.

"Therefore, to one who knows the right thing to do, and does not do it, to him it is sin" (James 4:17).

2. Borrowing denies God's people the opportunity to experience His overwhelming blessings in response to giving what is clearly within God's will (2

Corinthians 9:10). We are told in 1 John 3:22 that we can ask of God and expect to receive. Certainly, this would be true of the needs of the church. The experience of seeing God provide through His people is a witness to those within the church and to those looking at us.

3. A debt within the church restricts its ability to serve God. Quite often, controlling decisions are based on the need to meet debt payments rather than on God's redirection of funds to current needs.

4. Often, the ability to repay the debt is dependent on the ability of the pastor to preach. In many instances, lenders have required a signed contract from the pastor that he would not leave while the debt exists and would maintain an insurance policy to pay off the debt in the event of his death.

"Come now, you who say, 'Today or tomorrow, we shall go to such and such a city, and spend a year there and engage in business and make a profit'" (James 4:13).

5. Huge sums of God's people's money go to meet interest payments. That money could otherwise be used to further God's kingdom rather than Satan's. Many major denominations spend more on interest payments than on foreign missions.

OTHER CHRISTIAN MINISTRIES

There can certainly be no distinction between churches borrowing and other ministries borrowing. If an organization holds itself out to be an instrument of Jesus Christ, then it must be striving to meet God's standards. Certainly, there are no perfect ministries or churches, and try as we might, we will continue to fall below God's measure. Borrowing is not the only area of laxness; it just happens to be one of the most visible (and correctable).

Having faced the same choices in a ministry, I find the need to wait upon God's provision in advance to be confining. However, it is also tremendously freeing. If God can direct us by providing, then He can also direct by withholding. Many ministries have borrowed to do things God never intended they do. Others have borrowed to do God's will but have missed one of God's greatest areas of testimony. Very few nonbelievers could be convinced that there is anything supernatural or miraculous about a loan. Few would deny that there is something at least unique about a debt-free ministry.

CONCLUSION

I trust that this brief survey will not be viewed as any kind of indictment of churches or other ministries, because it is not. The purpose is to challenge church and ministry leaders, as well as their members, that God can and will provide through His people that which is *necessary* to do His will. One of our greatest assets is that God doesn't have a whole lot of talent with which to work down here. God will work with anyone willing to totally trust Him. Obviously, overnight changes are rarely possible, but God's people should always be aiming toward the "mark."

It is not a lack of funds that requires a church's borrowing. It is a lack of commitment on the part of God's people to give and trust.

"So Moses issued a command, and a proclamation was circulated throughout the camp, saying, 'Let neither man nor woman any longer perform work for the contributions of the sanctuary.' Thus the people were restrained from bringing any more. For the material they had was sufficient and more than enough for all the work, to perform it" (Exodus 36:6-7).

The Church and Money

Recently while I was speaking at a conference, a man asked, "Why bother with teaching money in the church? God promises to supply what we need, doesn't He?" His question was actually more of a statement than a question. What he actually meant was that he didn't believe the church should be involved with teaching about money. One of his comments was, "It's best to leave the teaching on money to the experts." In actuality, it is *because* we have left the teaching to the "experts" that we have strayed so far from God's path.

Scripture does *not* support the premise that the church should stay out of the area of money. In fact, it teaches that wisdom comes from God (Proverbs 3:13; 3:19; 8:10-11). Thus, true wisdom in finances comes *only* by studying and teaching God's Word. Jesus says in Luke 16:10-12 that good stewardship of money is a prerequisite to being used by God for greater things. The way we handle finances is not so much a test as a reflection of what we *really* believe.

Do we Christians really believe that God owns everything? If we do, then we must manage according to *His* principles. We will be accountable for our stewardship and for the positive or negative witness it provides. Also, God's Word promises that slothfulness will result in loss, but diligence results in gain.

"The soul of the sluggard craves and gets nothing, but the soul of the diligent is made fat" (Proverbs 13:4).

Thus, if God's church is to prosper materially and spiritually, its funds must be managed well. However, there must be a balance, because too much attention to money will divert the church and make it servant to materialism.

"No servant can serve two masters; for either he will hate the one, and love the other, or else he will hold to one, and despise the other. You cannot serve God and mammon" (Luke 16:13).

THE CHURCH AS AN EXAMPLE

The church in this case refers to the traditional institution, as opposed to the general Body of Christ. Any church should be the best possible example of good money management. Satan has been effective within the church, diverting God's people away from sound biblical principles.

ISSUES ABOUT MONEY

Budgeting. Should a church have an annual budget? One side says no, a budget removes the element of faith and brings the church down to a worldly level. However, quite often a church's creditors feel the absence of a budget puts the burden of faith on them. The other side of the budget issue is voiced by those who would operate the church just like a business, right down to eliminating the "nonproductive" benevolence program.

Both extremes are wrong biblically. A budget in itself does not reflect a lack of faith, but rather good planning (Luke 14:28-30). But it must not override the spiritual goals of God's church.

Savings account. One common question asked is, "Should our church maintain a savings account?" It's not the savings that really matters, but the purpose and attitude. There are many references to saving in God's Word (Proverbs 6:6;

21:20). In fact, a surplus should be normal to a church serving God; after all, God has promised to provide for every good work. But too often the money is hoarded rather than saved. It is not allocated to any needs, present or future, and represents a lack of trust, just as in the case of the rich fool in Luke 12:16-20.

Debt free. Perhaps no single issue about the church and money is more controversial than church debt. On one side it is argued that if borrowing is allowable for Christians, and it is within limits, then it must be allowable for the church too. And that would seem to be biblically correct; it is allowable. But does the church settle for the allowable, or the best? We know that God holds Christian teachers to a higher standard (James 3:1), and deacons and elders are held to a higher standard (1 Timothy 3). Since each of these is under the authority of the church, shouldn't we assume that the church is held to an even higher standard?

The church, as an institution, is to be a light of God's truth in a world of darkness. Our world is out of sync with God's Word on borrowing. The evidence is reflected in bankruptcy and divorce, and the sad truth is that the evangelical church has followed the lead of the secular world regarding debt.

Too often, building programs that should be a testimony of God's faithfulness and provision are more nearly a copy of the world's system called O.P.M. (other people's money). That is not to condemn or judge the leadership in churches that borrow. They are doing what they have been taught. But it's time we taught the truth: God can and *will* provide what He ordains by providing the surpluses to His people at the appointed time.

It's not a lack of money that necessitates church borrowing. It's lack of commitment to giving. Remember, the only source of true wisdom is God's Word, and you will not find a single instance of God manifesting Himself through a loan.

"And my God shall supply all your needs according to His riches in glory in Christ Jesus" (Philippians 4:19).

Reveal needs. Many church leaders believe they should never let a material need be known to the congregation. Sometimes this is a deep conviction and is God's will. More often it is the reflection of a misguided notion that sharing needs openly is unspiritual. If that's true, then we would have to count the apostle Paul among the unspiritual. In 1 Corinthians 9:1-14 Paul voices his "right" to share in the material rewards of the church.

If the church never lets material needs be known, then the members will also be trapped in that same restraint. The way to determine if this is a conviction from the Lord is that the needs will be met without asking.

The common principle delivered in God's Word is expressed by Paul in 2 Corinthians 8:14, *"At this present time your abundance being a supply for their want, that their abundance also may become a supply for your want, that there may be equality."*

CARING PROGRAMS IN THE CHURCH

Every church seeking to serve the Lord should have caring programs established to help its own needy, the needy in the community, and the needy in the world. The first step in any church is to teach God's people what His Word says about its own finances.

The surpluses that the church must have in order to minister to the needy are always available. Too often, Christians are consuming or wasting their funds.

Every church needs a regular program for sharing the biblical principles of managing money in the home and practical courses on planning (budgeting, insurance, housing, and so on). Once God's people learn God's plan for their finances, the funds will be available to meet legitimate needs.

Statistics prove that in the average evangelical church, about 20 percent of the people tithe. In the churches we have surveyed where a consistent program of teaching God's principles of finances has been established, the percentage is over 80 percent. The average American family spends over $2,000 a year on interest payments alone. If they were shown how to live debt-free and offered that money to the church instead, a church of one hundred families would have an additional $200,000 a year available for other programs.

Benevolence. Every church should have a benevolence program to help those who have legitimate financial needs. But a benevolence program should not be a "give away" program. There are definite biblical guidelines for those whom we are to help. Members of any local church should be able to look to the fellowship they attend as an extension of God's provision. They should feel the freedom to stand up and share their financial needs as freely as they would physical or spiritual needs.

Too often a local church's benevolence program amounts to the pastor directing the secretary to write someone a check for food, gas, or rent. That is usually the worst thing they could do. Without any controls or follow-up, giving away money is like pouring gasoline on a fire. Also, the system doesn't help those who have long-term needs due to illness, layoff, age, and so on. Benevolence is not an *event*, it is a vital part of ministering within the body of believers and requires several coordinated ministries:

1. *Benevolence committee.* This committee is primarily made up of lay people who will meet and evaluate needs presented within the church. Often that requires emergency action by one or two members to evaluate needs that result from "drop-ins" at the church office or parsonage. A well-coordinated committee will free the pastor from the pressures of some emotional appeals. The most effective benevolence committees usually have members with varied spiritual temperaments.

2. *Resource ministry.* To meet the needs of families, resources must be accumulated in advance. That might include food and clothing for a church in the inner city, but it should not stop there. The church should have contact with businesses that can provide part-time or temporary work. One of the most effective ways to test the spirit of someone who can't find work is to help him find it.

Many times I have heard someone say, "He doesn't want to work or he would have found a job by now." What they don't grasp is that when a normally productive man is suddenly unemployed, especially late in life, it often results in depression that paralyzes him. He needs sound biblical counsel and a helping hand, but not a handout.

Other resources include the availability of legal or accounting advice, medical and dental care, and a number of well-trained financial counselors who will work with those in need. Accountability is an essential part of any good benevolence program.

No successful benevolence program will happen until God's people in the local church decide to get involved and make it happen.

83

"Because of the proof given by this ministry they will glorify God for your obedience to your confession of the gospel of Christ, and for the liberality of your contribution to them and to all" (2 Corinthians 9:13).

Church Benevolence Programs

Many churches are beginning to realize that they must give financial assistance to persons in their church and community. Benevolence funds and committees are being revamped or established with a genuine burden to *"do good to all men, and especially to those who are of the household of faith"* (Galatians 6:10). Because of the fact that virtually every congregation has experienced the abuse, misuse, or unwise management of such special funds, many churches have grown indifferent and overly protective in this area. In reality, the answer in this vital area is better planning, wiser management, and more realistic goals.

Our Lord told us, *"By this all men will know that you are My disciples, if you have love for one another"* (John 13:35).

There are many ways to show love apart from finances. However, it is impossible to deny that a great percentage of the needs within a typical church will be financial. The church is then confronted with a basic choice: Will they be "doers" of the Word or merely "hearers"?

"If a brother or sister is without clothing and in need of daily food, and one of you says to them, `Go in peace, be warmed and be filled,' and yet you do not give them what is necessary for their body, what use is that?" (James 2:15-16).

On the other hand, how does a benevolence committee genuinely and biblically determine who really deserves help? That is a vitally important question. It is just as damaging to give money to one who shouldn't receive it as to not give it at all.

There are some thoughts on practical ways to implement an effective benevolence program:

Screen applicants. That can be accomplished by thorough interviewing and the filling out of a questionnaire that provokes honest responses from the applicant. It is also important to have applicants submit a thorough budget and explain any anomalies in that budget.

The committee should be careful to be discerning, and yet still compassionate, of the real needs of the one seeking help.

Scripture tells us that clothing—and that might also allude to a roof over the head—and daily food are the key criteria in determining to whom the help should be given first. Certainly, then, our emphasis ought to be on meeting needs in these areas. How and when to help beyond basic food, clothing, and shelter needs can only be determined on an individual evaluation. The committee must realize that seeking wisdom through diligent prayer is an absolutely vital part of these evaluations.

With only rare exceptions, money should not be given. It is far better to provide the material items instead: for example, pay the rent, electricity, and purchase food. If the church is led of God to help, then it must face the issue of providing the long-term needs of some. That will include the widows (and divorcees who qualify), orphans, ill, and elderly.

The question always arises, "How much can we afford to give as a church?" On the other hand, Scripture says, *"He who is gracious to a poor man lends to the Lord, and He will repay him for his good deed"* (Proverbs 19:17).

If the one receiving the help is truly at a point of need, then a church must believe that they are literally lending to

85

God. The money is simply a vehicle of God's love. God promises that as long as His people are faithful to give of the resources He has given them, those resources are limitless.

CREATIVE HELP

Many times the need for assistance may be temporary, particularly where young couples are concerned. For instance: consider a young couple that has recently committed their financial matters to God. In the past, they have not been as diligent in this area as they should have been, and they failed to either get medical insurance or save money to cover a pregnancy. The hospital refuses to admit them without a $1,000 deposit. They have no human source for this money. The church has established a "Hope Fund" for critical needs such as this. A committee evaluates the couple's budget and needs and makes a commitment to make the funds available. The check is drafted directly from Hope Fund to the hospital. The couple has committed to a monthly amount at no interest to pay the loan back to the fund. The benevolence committee will monitor the couple through a monthly review by a lay counselor. If, at that time, the monthly commitment needs adjusting, the committee will evaluate the new amount and encourage the family to be diligent in repayment.

The main objective of the Hope Fund is to have funds available for genuine needs. It is also a means of: (1) helping Christians keep a good testimony before the world; (2) encouraging Christians to be more diligent in personal budgeting; and (3) providing no-interest loans for genuine emergencies that would have otherwise ruined a family's budget and testimony.

Some would object to such a fund, claiming that we should either give money away or not make it available at all. We must remember the Scripture that tells us, *"He who oppresses the poor reproaches his Maker, but he who is gracious to the needy honors Him"* (Proverbs 14:31).

Part 3:

Insurance and Investing

Avoiding "Get-Rich-Quick"

It is amazing how susceptible Christians are to get-rich-quick schemes and how logical they seem at first. A friend of mine once shared that he had invested several thousand dollars in a "fool proof" plan to buy surplus goods and resell them. The promoter promised a 10 percent per month return. He also presented the names of several people who had been "investing."

After risking a small amount of money for a couple of months and promptly receiving the promised return, my friend borrowed a large sum and invested it. The logic behind the loan was that he could borrow at 10 percent and earn over 100 percent a year. I'm sure you have already guessed the conclusion. The promoter had been bringing in more money to pay the interest to previous investors, and finally the circle got too big, and it collapsed, along with my friend's money.

Unfortunately, that is not a unique case. Every year, thousands of Christian families risk and lose money they cannot afford to lose seeking that "big deal." Can it be avoided? Most certainly, but not on the basis of human wisdom. There has never been a get-rich-quick scheme that didn't sound terrific on the surface. The promoters are a great deal better at disguising the bad deals than most people are at detecting them. Also, what may seem like a business deal to one person is get-rich-quick to another.

How then can a Christian avoid such schemes? The simple truth is that he cannot at long as he is emotionally caught up in his own desires and fails to yield control to God's wisdom. However, there is one source of wisdom that is not dependent on our attitude—God's Word. Our decisions can be aligned with God's by first considering His written principles. *"Trust in the Lord with all your heart, and do not lean on your own understanding"* (Proverbs 3:5). I have listed a few of the basic principles dealing with how to avoid get-rich-quick schemes.

1. *Stick with what you know. "By wisdom a house is built, and by understanding it is established"* (Proverbs 24:3). A great part of wisdom is recognizing our limitations. Seldom will anyone be duped into a get-rich-quick scheme in his area of expertise. It would be very difficult to convince a chicken farmer that someone could get rich quick in the chicken business. Unfortunately, there have been many people who lost a great deal of money trying.

The vast majority of people who make money do so in the field in which they have the most training and experience. Those who lose it usually do so in an area they know little about.

2. *Don't risk borrowed money. "A prudent man sees evil and hides himself, the naive proceed and pay the penalty"* (Proverbs 27:12).

It's one thing to speculate with money you can afford to lose and quite another to lose money that literally belongs to another. The former is called speculation; the latter is surety. It doesn't necessarily mean that the investment should be paid in total, but it does mean that the down payment should not be borrowed.

However, the only time an investment should be financed (leveraged) is when there is adequate value to cover any liability or when payments can be made from a known source of funds and are not dependent on the sale of the investment. Otherwise, you are presuming on an uncertain event.

"Do not boast about tomorrow, for you do not know what a day may bring forth" (Proverbs 27:1).

3. *Buy investments with utility. "She considers a field and buys it; from her earnings she plants a vineyard . . .She makes linen garments and sells them, and supplies belts to the tradesmen"* (Proverbs 31:16, 24). Utility simply means buying something of use to someone else.

Most get-rich-quick schemes deal with intangibles, or at least remote tangibles, such as oil wells, chicken farms, movies, motivational programs, and so on.

4. *Don't make quick decisions. "The plans of the diligent lead surely to advantage, but everyone who is hasty comes surely to poverty"* (Proverbs 21:5). The very essence of a get-rich-quick scheme is emotionalism. The promoter urges the potential buyer to act quickly before the opportunity is missed. The exact technique will vary, depending on the need. It may include pressure to become a "success," to avoid income taxes, or to "make it" for retirement. Above all else, a get-rich-quick scheme depends on convincing the prospect to buy without thinking about it too long. Once the money has changed hands, the promoter knows it's too late to back out.

The final ploy in closing is to develop an attitude of covetousness by hinting that another prospect is waiting to snap up the deal. What is the best way to avoid this trap?

"Rest in the Lord and wait patiently for Him; do not fret because of him who prospers in his way, because of the man who carries out wicked schemes" (Psalm 37:7).

5. *Seek good counsel. "The way of a fool is right in his own eyes, but a wise man is he who listens to counsel"* (Proverbs 12:15).

It is amazing how quickly someone who is not emotionally involved with a get-rich-quick scheme can spot its flaws. Good, objective Christian counsel should be a prerequisite to any major financial decision. That counsel is most objective when it comes from someone who has no profit motive involved.

One of the best sources of counsel is a Christian spouse. It is astounding how many times I have observed that a wife comes to the right conclusion using the wrong facts. Most women are generally more conservative than men and can provide a balance.

"House and wealth are an inheritance from fathers, but a prudent wife is from the Lord" (Proverbs 19:14).

SUMMARY

A get-rich-quick scheme is usually one that offers an excessive gain for the apparent risk. It usually involves an area about which you know little or nothing, requires a quick decision, and was recommended by a friend.

Satan will often provide one good deal before presenting the real loser. He knows that a Christian who is defeated in one area, particularly finances, will not be an effective witness.

To avoid these financial traps, you must establish your standards by God's Word: seek God's plan for your life, stick with what you know, seek good counsel, and wait on God's peace for acting.

"It is the blessing of the Lord that makes rich, and He adds no sorrow to it" (Proverbs 10:22).

The Purpose of Investing

Once I was asked a very penetrating question by a close Christian friend: "Why should we help rich people get richer?" The obvious answer is that teaching Christians to invest wisely is as necessary as teaching them to budget. God has commissioned us to help Christians to be better stewards, and that includes using surplus resources properly. In a very practical way, it is obvious that those with a surplus are able to give more to God's work than are others. That doesn't mean that everyone who has a surplus *will* give more, but that he *can*. One function of any ministry of finances is to teach Christians how and why to multiply their resources for giving. To do this, those with a surplus must be able to invest wisely.

HISTORY OF INVESTING

The first investment can be found in Genesis 3:23. Adam was cast out of the garden and told to cultivate the soil for his food. To do so he had to risk planting seeds that could have been eaten; thus, he became an *investor*. Farmers understand the principle of investing. Each year they are faced with a choice of eating all the seeds, selling all the seeds, or retaining some to replant. It would be a very short-sighted farmer who would either eat or sell his entire harvest. He would still have some harvest the next season from the seed that fell during picking, but it would be pretty slim. A wise farmer not only holds back some seed for replanting, but he also sorts out the best seed to insure a greater harvest. By doing so, he exercises self-discipline to achieve greater prosperity.

Contrary to what many people believe, God is not against prosperity. The Scriptures give evidence that one of God's blessings to those who love and obey Him is prosperity (2 Chronicles 16:9; Psalm 37:4; Proverbs 8:21). God hates evil attitudes. These include greed, covetousness, and pride. Attitudes like these are not isolated to those who have a surplus. They are abundantly evident even among the very poor.

JUSTIFICATION FOR INVESTING

A rational reason for not investing a surplus is to give it away to further God's work and to help the needy. However, there is no evidence in the Bible that God's plan was to *always* give away any surplus. Just the opposite is true. Saving was a sign of wisdom, while a lack was the sign of slothfulness. *"There is precious treasure and oil in the dwelling of the wise, but a foolish man swallows it up"* (Proverbs 21:20). Obviously, there are exceptions, but they were, and are, individual directives, not biblical principles.

In Matthew 25:14-30, several references are given to investing various amounts. In our economy today, the largest amount mentioned, five talents, would be equal to approximately $1,784,000, and the smallest, one talent, would be $356,835. The very intent of this parable is to reflect on the attitudes and faithfulness of investors in the absence of their master. If investing is prohibited or even discouraged, why would Jesus use it as an example and reward the most diligent? The obvious answer is: investing is just another part of stewardship—not more important than giving but not less important either.

91

PREREQUISITES FOR INVESTING

The number-one prerequisite for investing is *attitude*. Why are you investing, and how will the surplus be used? If a Christian wants God to entrust greater riches to him, he must be found faithful in the smaller amount first (Luke 16:10-11). To protect against the infectious diseases of greed and pride, the best weapon is a specific plan for returning the excess to God's kingdom. I find that once a commitment has been made to a disciplined life-style, regardless of the available income, the danger of greed and self-indulgence is drastically reduced.

The term used throughout Paul's writings is *contentment*. *"But godliness actually is a means of great gain, when accompanied by contentment"* (1 Timothy 6:6). In a society oriented to "more" and the "best," it is difficult to reach the right balance. Even within Christianity, the examples of those who could handle a surplus are few. Therefore, a plan to dispose of the profits is as important as a plan to invest the surplus.

LEGITIMATE REASONS FOR INVESTING

There are several legitimate reasons for a Christian to invest:

First, to further God's work. Some Christians have received a gift of giving (Romans 12:8). To them, the multiplication of material worth is an extension of their basic ministry within the Body of Christ. Even to those who do not have a gift of giving, investments are a way to preserve and multiply a surplus that has been provided for a later time. In Acts 4:34, the believers sold their assets and surrendered the proceeds to meet the needs of other believers. God blessed some with surplus to be used at a later date.

Second, family responsibility. We are admonished to provide for those within our own households (1 Timothy 5:8). That provision was never limited to the life span of a father. It extended to providing for his family even after his death. Not everyone can do so, but if those who are able meet their own needs, the church can concentrate on the needs of the poor. *"If a man fathers a hundred children and lives many years, however many they be, but his soul is not satisfied with good things, and he does not even have a proper burial, then I say, 'Better the miscarriage than he'"* (Ecclesiastes 6:3).

If parents believe that God wants their children to go to college, is it more spiritual to expect the government and banks to educate them than to store for the eventual need? The parable of the ant in Proverbs 6:6 says to "observe her ways and be wise." One of her ways is to plan ahead by storing. In a highly inflationary economy, even storing requires investing.

ILLEGITIMATE REASONS FOR INVESTING

There are also several unbiblical reasons to invest. Unfortunately, these represent the greater number of investors, Christian and non-Christian, because Satan has so thoroughly dominated our attitudes about money.

Greed. Greed is the desire to continually have more and demand only the best. *"But those who want to get rich fall into temptation and a snare and many foolish and harmful desires which plunge men into ruin and destruction"* (1 Timothy 6:9).

Envy. Envy is the desire to achieve based on observation of other people's success. *"For I was envious of the arrogant, as I saw the prosperity of the wicked"* (Psalm 73:3).

Pride. Pride is the desire to be elevated because of material achievements.

"Instruct those who are rich in this present world not to be conceited or to fix their hope on the uncertainty of riches, but on God, who richly supplies us with all things to enjoy" (1 Timothy 6:17).

Ignorance. Ignorance is following the counsel of other misguided people because of a lack of discernment. *"Leave the presence of a fool, or you will not discern words of knowledge"* (Proverbs 14:7).

There are many wrong motives for investing. The result of any of these is anxiety, frustration, and eventually a deadening of spiritual values.

Thus, as our Lord says, *"No servant can serve two masters; for either he will hate the one, and love the other, or else he will hold to one, and despise the other. You cannot serve God and mammon"* (Luke 16:13).

INVESTING TO SERVE GOD BETTER

Once a Christian has accepted the purpose of investing (to serve God better), the crucial decision is how much to invest. Obviously, there is no absolute answer. It is an individual decision made by a Christian after much prayer. With earnest prayer the decision is difficult—without it, impossible. There are some initial choices to be made that will greatly simplify the decision about how much to invest:

1. Before investing, give to God's work until you know that all of the needs God has placed on your heart are satisfied. Don't be misled into thinking that there will then be no more needs in the world. There will always be needs, but God doesn't place *every* need on anyone's heart. Giving, like spiritual discernment, is a matter of growth and practice. I believe the key here is: when in doubt, give. It is better to be wrong and give too much than to ignore God's direction and give too little. The Spirit is never dampened by too sensitive a will, only by developing calluses.

"Therefore openly before the churches show them the proof of your love and of our reason for boasting about you" (2 Corinthians 8:24).

2. Settle on a level of family needs that is God's plan for you. Too much spending on a family can rob surplus funds as surely as bad investments. Each Christian family must decide on the level God has planned for them and stick to it in spite of available surpluses. Remember that balance is essential. Too much is waste; too little is self-punishment.

"And whatever we ask we receive from Him, because we keep His commandments and do the things that are pleasing in His sight" (1 John 3:22).

3. Have a plan for the use of your potential surplus. One interesting characteristic about humans is that we can rationalize nearly anything, including reinvesting God's portion or saving it for Him. Therefore, it is important to settle on a plan for distributing the profits from investments before they arrive. Decide what portion is to be reinvested. Clearly, the greatest danger is to continually reinvest the profits and rationalize it because of taxes, lack of discernable needs, or a need for surplus security.

Do your planning *before* the money becomes available. One good way to do that is to give away a large percentage of the investment *before* it appreciates.

"Because of the proof given by this ministry they will glorify God for your obedience to your confession of the gospel of Christ, and for the liberality of your contribution to them and to all" (2 Corinthians 9:13).

Selecting Good Counsel

A commonly asked question is, "How can I find good Christian counsel?" But perhaps even more fundamental would be the question, "How can I tell when I find good Christian counsel?"

It is very difficult to give objective counsel when the counselor is selling a particular product. There is nothing wrong with product sales, however. Virtually everyone is a product salesman of one sort or another. But good, objective counsel must be separated from the necessity to sell a product; otherwise, a lot of objectivity is lost.

For instance, it would be very difficult to obtain objective counsel about what car would best suit your family's needs from a salesman who earns his living selling Hondas. He is going to be biased by his sales training, experience, and mostly by his need to sell a Honda. A good salesman will match his product as closely to your need as possible but will seldom suggest that you look elsewhere.

The bias toward a particular product is only one limitation in finding good counsel. Another critical limitation is finding counselors with "like" minds and attitudes, namely Christians. What makes it even more difficult is that there are many counselors who profess to be Christians but who give worldly advice. There are also many Christians who profess to be counselors but who give very unwise advice.

With all this confusion, I can thoroughly understand the difficulty and frustration of locating good Christian counsel, especially in the areas involving money. However, I know beyond a doubt that such counsel is available to anyone willing to take the time and effort to seek it out.

WHY BOTHER WITH COUNSEL?

There are many guidelines in God's Word for seeking and selecting good counsel. The purpose of counsel is to aid us in making our decisions, not to actually make them for us. Too often we want someone to tell us what to do. When you allow someone else to tell you what to do, with rare exception, you're going to get bad advice. Many times I've had someone share that an advisor told him to buy a particular investment that ended up losing money, while the advisor made money through that purchase. Sometimes the advice is both right and wrong, as in the recent instance of a Christian couple who bought into a whiskey-aging partnership—the investment was great (about 25-30 percent growth per year) but not for Christians. Under a very strong conviction about being both stewards and witnesses, they ended up selling out at a sizable loss. The other investors will probably end up making a sizable profit over the next ten years. The investment advice was accurate; the counsel was entirely wrong.

PRINCIPLES FOR SELECTING COUNSELORS

Principle 1: Christian counsel. Select your counselors on the basis of a common value system. For the Christian, that means those who acknowledge Jesus Christ as their Savior and Lord.

"How blessed is the man who does not walk in the counsel of the wicked, nor stand

in the path of sinners, nor sit in the seat of scoffers" (Psalm 1:1). In no way does that imply that non-Christians can't give good advice. Some of them give better advice than many Christians. But the standards by which decisions are made in our society today are quite often incompatible with God's standards.

Principle 2: Wise counsel. "He who walks with wise men will be wise, but the companion of fools will suffer harm" (Proverbs 13:20). The mere fact that someone is a Christian does not qualify him as an expert in every area of life. Too often Christians invest absolute confidence in the advice of someone solely on the basis of his salvation. The evidence that Christians can and do give bad counsel is all too evident today. The process of salvation does not eliminate attitudes of ego, pride, and greed in most of us. They are active by virtue of our self-will.

Additionally, many "Christian" counselors suffer from acute lack of common sense and wisdom. Wisdom comes from God, and in James 1:5 we are told, *"But if any of you lacks wisdom, let him ask of God, who gives to all men generously."* Therefore, both counselor and counselee must be in regular communication with God.

Most Christians have found that the majority of decisions they face can be answered on the basis of God's written Word, and that the wisdom they lack is the wisdom to understand (and accept) what God has already told them. Therefore, a counselor must be knowledgeable in his area of expertise and regularly in God's Word.

Principle 3: Multiple counselors. *"Without consultation, plans are frustrated, but with many counselors they succeed"* (Proverbs 15:22). No one can be expert enough in all areas of finance for anyone to depend upon his counsel exclusively.

Any financial counselor who would steer clients away from other qualified sources of advice qualifies as foolish.

"He who walks with wise men will be wise, but the companion of fools will suffer harm" (Proverbs 13:20).

The areas of taxes, securities, stocks, bonds, and real estate are so complex today that only with a variety of good counselors can you really get good advice. What inhibits most financial counselors from suggesting other advisors is the fear of losing a client or of a client's finding out that he has had bad advice. Counselors who are good at what they do and who seek the very best for their clients have no fear of losing them.

Principle 4: Weigh all counsel. "The naive believes everything, but the prudent man considers his steps" (Proverbs 14:15).

The purpose of counsel is to offer suggestions, alternatives, and options—not to make your decision. Even the best counsel in the world lacks an essential ingredient necessary to making decisions —God's plan for your life. Paul was given accurate, godly counsel not to return to Jerusalem in Acts 21. Paul listened and weighed that counsel against what God had impressed upon him to do and refused to be swayed from God's path for him.

Sometimes people call to ask what I think about some financial advice they have received. Often without offering any counsel at all, I ask them how they feel about the suggestions, and they will respond, "I really don't have a peace about doing it." Their decision was already made if they were willing to listen to their conscience. The investment may be great, but it's not for them. What is financial bondage? The absence of financial freedom. Anything that robs us of God's peace is contrary to God's plan for us.

HOW TO WEIGH COUNSEL

I have found that there are many people who know a great deal more about their area of expertise than I do. Those people I use as resources. But I have found that a lot more people know practically nothing about the areas in which they give advice. Those people I try to avoid. The problem is that it's sometimes difficult initially to tell the difference between the two groups. Later, when the good advice works, or the bad advice fails, it's a lot easier to see what they did or didn't know.

Test their counsel. When I'm evaluating someone's counsel in an area with which I am unfamiliar, I will pick a subject about which we should both be knowledgeable and test him. If I find his answers to be fundamentally wrong in an area I do understand, then I avoid his counsel in areas I don't understand.

Compare to God's Word. In Proverbs 3:5, we are told to *"trust in the Lord with all your heart."* Therefore, any counsel that runs contrary to God's Word should be counted as worthless. Recently, a friend was advised by his attorney to divorce his wife during a pending car accident lawsuit so that if she lost, she could file bankruptcy without endangering his assets. They could remarry later, he said, and everything would be all right. My advice was to divorce himself from ungodly counsel.

Test counselor's value system. Proverbs 13:5 says that *"a righteous man hates falsehood."* A consistent observation is that a man who will deceive someone else on your behalf will eventually deceive you as well, given the right set of circumstances. Just because someone calls himself a Christian does not mean that he holds to God's value system. Test the value system to see where his heart is.

Track record. Proverbs 21:5 says, *"The plans of the diligent lead surely to advantage."* A good test of a counselor's expertise is his past performance. If every financial advisor were graded on the basis of promises versus performance, many would grade rather low. Any time you choose to invest time and money with someone who has less than five years verifiable track record, you should assume that you're his on-the-job training.

References. Few people ask for multiple references from a financial counselor, and even fewer verify those references. A friend once asked me to check out an investment salesman for him from his own list of references. The very first reference spent ten minutes telling me what a poor job the man had done for him and ended up saying that he didn't even answer the salesman's calls anymore. Two more calls verified that this fellow never expected anyone to actually call a listed reference. Most people who list references try to list only the best; so, I assumed these were his best clients. Remember what Proverbs 21:29 says: *"A wicked man shows a bold face."* Most so-called "advisers" count on a good front to satisfy most clients.

HOW TO LOCATE GOOD COUNSEL

The best method for locating good, Christian counsel is from other Christians who have been helped. Quite often, if you'll just ask others at your church, someone will recommend a good resource. You can also call several of the sound pastors in your area. They will almost always know of the quality people in their communities. Lastly, there are several Christian professional associations, such as the Christian Legal Society, the Christian Medical Association, and the Fellowship of Companies for Christ. Obviously, not everyone involved with these associations is either Christian or expert, but it's a good starting point. With-out a doubt, the expert Christian counsel we need is available if we seek it diligently.

Insurance—Is It Scriptural?

Two questions are often asked: "Is insurance scriptural?" and, "Does owning insurance reflect a lack of faith?" The answer is both yes and no. Insurance is not specifically defined in Scripture; however, the principle of future provision is. Owning insurance does not necessarily reflect a lack of faith in God, though it is increasingly being used for that purpose. However, just as damaging are the secondary effects that insurance is having on our society: those of greed, slothfulness, waste, and fear.

Some have developed an insurance ethic that often rationalizes cheating where insurance companies are concerned. Many committed Christians are willing to use insurance funds to do things they would never consider doing with their own money.

Recently, a Christian physician and I were discussing the issue when he related an all too common event. A Christian patient of his was in need of some tests to diagnose a problem. The doctor suggested that she receive the tests as a hospital outpatient because the costs would be substantially less. "Oh, no," she said, "my insurance only pays if I'm admitted to a hospital for at least two days, and I want the best." Certainly, this Christian lady would never consider willfully cheating somebody—but didn't she?

"And if you have not been faithful in the use of that which is another's, who will give you that which is your own?" (Luke 16:12).

A counselee some time ago shared with me one of what he called God's "answers" to prayer. His car had been severely damaged in an airport parking lot while he was away on a trip, and, unfortunately, the "banger" didn't leave a note for the "bangee." He didn't carry collision insurance that would cover the damage because of the cost; so, he drove the car as it was for several weeks. Then one day he was hit from the rear in a multiple-car collision. Although the actual damage from that collision was slight, in getting an estimate for damages, he "neglected" to mention the previous damage done at the airport. Consequently, his car was entirely repaired by the liability insurance of the car that struck him from the rear. "What an answer from the Lord!" he exclaimed.

Unfortunately, this "answer" conflicted with God's Word. *"The perverse in heart are an abomination to the Lord, but the blameless in their walk are His delight"* (Proverbs 11:20).

I simply asked him to review a few passages of Scripture that dealt with this area, pray about it, ask God's direction, and then do what he felt God would have him do. He ended up repaying the insurance company for his share.

CURRENT ATTITUDES

Why is it that even committed Christians are tempted to cheat and rationalize it? Several factors are involved: One is that insurance companies are seemingly wealthy and impersonal. Inwardly, many people feel that to be wealthy, they must be dishonest and therefore are "fair game." Also, since they don't actually know anyone at the insurance company, it's not like cheating a person. Another reason is that we have developed a protection attitude in our society so prevalent that most Christians don't consider whether the insurance they pay for is really necessary.

BIBLICAL PERSPECTIVE

A Christian must believe that *all* resources belong to God. Therefore, the resources that are in the control of an insurance company are still God's. As such, we will be held accountable for how they are spent on us just as certainly as if the funds came out of our savings account.

"The righteousness of the upright will deliver them, but the treacherous will be caught by their own greed" (Proverbs 11:6).

PROVISION

God's Word teaches provision, not protection. Insurance can be used to provide where a potential loss would be excessive. That is especially true when another's loss must be considered, as in automobile liability coverage.

"A prudent man sees evil and hides himself, the naive proceed and pay the penalty" (Proverbs 27:12).

That point was brought home clearly to me as I sought to insure our ministry buildings. A group of Christians had purchased our property and had given it to us to develop a counseling center. Even minimal insurance coverage turned out to be several thousand dollars a year. After seeking God's will, the answer became very clear. Certainly, if God was able to provide buildings initially, He could also replace them if necessary. So the erstwhile insurance money went to buy teaching materials.

"And call upon Me in the day of trouble; shall rescue you, and you will honor Me" (Psalm 50:15).

God does not want us to be foolish; He wants us to be responsible. Too often

insurance is used to shift our responsibilities to someone else. Between the government welfare programs and the growth of insurance plans for virtually everything, the Christian community has been duped into believing that they don't *need* each other. That is a lie from the deceiver to suit his purpose. But when God decides "enough is enough," we will again discover the reality of Psalm 73:25. *"Whom have I in heaven but Thee? And besides Thee, I desire nothing on earth."* Prior to Christ's return, we will again be molded into a working body, and no amount of insurance will be able to buffer us from needing each other. The community plan described in Acts 4:34 will be our "insurance" plan. That does not mean that the use of insurance is unscriptural, but that the misuse of it is.

NET EFFECT OF AN INSURANCE ETHIC

Unfortunately, one of the bad side effects of relying so heavily upon insurance to buffer every little problem is that we also buffer God's guidance. There is no evidence in Scripture that God promises or desires to buffer His people from every difficulty or inconvenience. In fact, conversely, evidence exists that these are specifically allowed to redirect us or allow us to "test" our faith (Romans 5:3; 2 Corinthians 8:2; Philippians 3:7; James 1:3). Thus, there is a transfer of trust from God to insurance if it is used in excess.

The apparently easy access to insurance company funds promotes an attitude of slothfulness both financially and spiritually. Financially, because there is less incentive to save and anticipate problems; spiritually, because there is less need to pray about future needs, of others as well as our own. Those who have access to employer-paid, low deductible insurance plans have a tendency to forget that not everyone in their community has the same opportunity. Legitimate needs within Christian families go wanting because others aren't aware that not everyone can afford the high cost of insurance.

The net effects from the misuse of insurance are to raise both the cost of insurance and the services that feed off of it. Much of the increased cost of credit is passed on to consumers (including those who pay cash); the increased cost of insurance abusers is passed on to the diligent. Obviously, that discourages conservatism and encourages even more abuses by others. The tendency is to say, "I want to get my fair share, too."

INDIVIDUAL RESPONSIBILITY

An overwhelmingly simple principle stands out in God's Word: individual responsibility. It really doesn't matter what others are doing. God holds each of us individually responsible for our actions.

"But let each one examine his own work, and then he will have reason for boasting in regard to himself alone, and not in regard to another" (Galatians 6:4).

Each Christian must examine every area of daily life frequently to determine if it is up to God's standards. The best quick test is whether or not there is a peace about the actions.

Health. Health insurance provides a good benefit by making good health care available to most families. Unfortunately, adequate health care is now *dependent* upon insurance coverage. It costs more to stay one day in a hospital in Idaho than at a fancy hotel in New York City. That doesn't mean that everyone should give up health insurance, but that, as Christians, we must use it as we would our own money. Never sign a bill without thoroughly reviewing it. Require doc-

umentation for every expenditure. Ask for a reasonable estimate before committing to any health care plan or hospital stay. If you are an employer, check into higher deductible plans that may cost less but provide better catastrophe care. Give incentives to employees who do not abuse the insurance plan.

Life. The purpose of any life insurance plan is to provide for those who cannot provide for themselves. Many Christians have too little, while others have too much. It always baffles me to counsel a Christian who has purchased an enormous amount of life insurance to protect an estate that is probably far too large anyway.

"When there is a man who has labored with wisdom, knowledge and skill, then he gives his legacy to one who has not labored with them. This too is vanity and a great evil" (Ecclesiastes 2:21).

On the other end of the spectrum are those who have the ability to provide for their families if they died unexpectedly but apparently don't think they need to. Both examples reflect disobedience to God's principles. *"If a man fathers a hundred children and lives many years, however many they be, but his soul is not satisfied with good things, and he does not even have a proper burial. then I say, `Better the miscarriage then he'"* (Ecclesiastes 6:3).

Other insurance. To decide what is the correct balance, a simple test can be used. Can you provide for an unexpected loss yourself? If so, then to pay out money for insurance is a waste of God's resources. Great emotional appeals can be made for protecting everything from the dishwasher to possible termites. At what point should we say enough? That point has been reached when a Christian looks around and finds that trusting God no longer seems necessary for future material needs (Philippians 4:19).

Part 4:

Borrowing and Lending

Surety—What Is It?

Surety must be one of the least taught and least understood principles in God's Word. It's hard to understand why when you consider the number of references to surety in the book of Proverbs. Any time there is that much teaching on a single subject and it's still being violated, then you must conclude that Satan is at work to deceive us. The fact that so many people can violate a basic principle about money and get away with it for a long time does not negate the principle. It merely means that the cycle has not run its full course yet. I trust that Christians will decide to change—not because they have to, but because God's Word says to. One certainty is, just wait, eventually the economy will confirm the wisdom of God's Word.

In a literal sense, surety means to deposit a pledge in either money, goods, or part payment for a greater obligation. Surety means taking on an obligation to pay later without a "certain" way to pay.

"A man lacking in sense pledges, and becomes surety in the presence of his neighbor" (Proverbs 17:18).

WHY IS SURETY WRONG?

Obviously, surety is not a biblical law —it is a principle. A principle is a biblical guide to keep you on God's path and out of the world's traps. You don't get punished for violating a principle unknowingly; you suffer the consequences. The consequences of violating the principle of surety is that you presume upon the future. In other words, when you sign surety for a debt, you pledge your future. If you have omniscient insights into the future, then there is really no danger. But,

since only God has omniscient insight, when you sign surety, you presume upon God's will.

"Come now, you who say, 'Today or tomorrow, we shall go to such and such a city, and spend a year there and engage in business and make a profit.' Yet you do not know what your life will be like tomorrow. You are just a vapor that appears for a little while and then vanishes away" (James 4:13-14.)

WHY SO MUCH VIOLATION?

If surety is such an obvious biblical principle, why is there so much violation today? I would venture to say that over 95 percent of the Christians in America have, or will have in the future, violated the principle of surety. Why? Because surety is a modern day mechanism to "get rich quick." It allows us to buy things we really can't afford to own and allows us to speculate on the future. The fact that so many have speculated and have got away with it—even prospered—has dulled us to the fact that a get-rich-quick attitude eventually catches up with us.

"The plans of the diligent lead surely to advantage, but everyone who is hasty comes surely to poverty" (Proverbs 21:5). Nowhere is this seen more often than in the purchase of homes and cars. These industries are built on surety. They require an ever-expanding source of credit, and, with rare exception, the borrower pledges to pay regardless of any outside circumstances.

Co-signing. *"He who is surety for a stranger will surely suffer for it, but he who hates going surety is safe"* (Proverbs 11:15). Because co-signing is the most widely known form of surety, one would be led to believe that no Christian would sign for the debts of another. That simply is not the case. Many Christians sign for the debts of another. Why? Sometimes it's actually to avoid their scriptural obligation to give. It's easier to sign and allow someone to borrow than to give to their needs. Most of the time, however, Christians co-sign either out of ignorance of what God's Word teaches or out of misguided conviction and guilt. They feel guilty about what they have materially and co-sign for a friend. What happens, then, is if the borrower cannot repay and the co-signer has to pay, a friendship is lost.

Usually, the borrower feels guilt, then, and will avoid the co-signer. Remember, the definition of a distant friend is a close friend who owes you money and can't repay.

Practically speaking, when you co-sign a note for someone else, you allow him to borrow beyond his ability to repay. Why do you suppose that a banker requires a co-signer? Usually because the person borrowing is a high risk and lacks the ability to repay under certain circumstances. Remember this: God's people are to be counted among the wise, and the Word says that a man lacking in sense pledges.

BUY NOW, PAY LATER

If surety is taking on an obligation to pay without a certain way to pay it, then virtually every home mortgage is surety. Some states have laws that prohibit mortgage lenders from collecting a deficiency on a home mortgage, but most do not. The only thing that has kept most lenders from suing a defaulting home buyer is that inflation was driving up prices and

there were few actual losses. However, many home buyers in states where prices have dropped during the last few years have been sued for defaults. It is quite possible that economic circumstances in the future could place many others in jeopardy. They will find that assets they thought were debt-free are actually pledged as surety against their home loan or another mortgage loan.

A few years back, I saw a vivid example of the problems brought about by surety through a Christian doctor's circumstances. He and his partner initially came to discuss an apartment complex they were considering buying. It seems that they could buy this complex, with an appraised value of over $4 million, for less than $2 million. It required that they put about $100,000 down and personally sign notes for the rest. My counsel from God's Word was, "Don't do it—no matter how good the deal looks." Well, they didn't like that advice, so they shopped around until they located some counsel they liked better and they "bought" the complex (against their wives' advice, too). Less than a year later, it was discovered that the buildings had been insulated with a hazardous substance, and the health department condemned the entire complex. In the meantime, the original lender, a foreign company, had sold their note to another lender, who threatened to sue to protect his interests. Ultimately, the complex was demolished and the property resold. Their final debt ended up at about $1 million, upon which they are now making payments.

There are no sure things economically, and God's Word anticipates that: *"Know well the condition of your flocks, and pay attention to your herds; for riches are not forever, nor does a crown endure to all generations"* (Proverbs 27:23-24).

APPRECIATING VS. DEPRECIATING

Often I have heard someone say, "I know you're not supposed to borrow for depreciating items such as cars and clothes, but it's OK to borrow for appreciating assets because they're always worth more than you owe." There are two basic flaws in that logic: First, if anyone can pick out assets that can only appreciate, let me know, and we'll get every Christian to buy some. Second, God's Word doesn't say that it's bad to sign surety for a depreciating item but acceptable for an appreciating item. It says that if you sign surety, eventually you'll suffer. *"He who is surety for a stranger will surely suffer for it"* (Proverbs 11:15a). Again, the simple truth is that no one can guarantee appreciation, and the time at which an asset might have to be sold may be the worst time, not the best. Avoid surety on appreciating or depreciating items.

EXISTING SURETY

The question is often asked when discussing surety, "What if I am already signed as surety?" You can only do what you can do. Fortunately, God doesn't expect more out of us than we are capable of doing. If you can get out of surety, you should. But if you cannot, then work at reducing the liability and paying off the debts early. If you can't avoid surety in your business right now, then start planning toward a time when you can. If you never decide to be debt free, then most probably you never will be.

Hundreds and perhaps thousands of Christians now operate major businesses totally debt free as a result of deciding to do so on the basis of God's Word. Most of them would have never believed it was possible. One automobile dealer who had to borrow well over $1 million in 1973 now operates totally on a cash basis. He now makes more money than he ever has before and is practically unaffected by fluctuating interest rates. The same could be said about home builders, restaurant owners, and Christians in virtually every area of the economy.

HOW TO AVOID SURETY

"Do not boast about tomorrow, for you do not know what a day may bring forth" (Proverbs 27:1).

Let me repeat—surety is a principle—not a law. It is an observation that pledging for debt leads to financial ruin. While not pledging does not guarantee financial success, it does eliminate any "contingent liability," meaning a future obligation to pay when you might not be able to.

Does that mean that a Christian should never borrow? No, God's Word does not prohibit borrowing—although it doesn't encourage it either. But scriptural borrowing would be limited to contracts where the means to pay is certain. That means that the lender agrees to accept pledged collateral in total payment of the outstanding debt at any time.

For instance, if you wanted to purchase a piece of land for $10,000 but could only put up $1,000, you would finance the remaining $9,000 with the land pledged as total security. Therefore, if ever you couldn't continue to pay the note, the land would be surrendered and the debt canceled. There would be no contingent liability because you always have a certain way to pay. Would it be ethical to give the collateral in lieu of payment? Certainly, if that's what your agreement stated. There will be many opportunities to buy where the property will not stand for the debt. You must be willing to walk away from them even if they are good deals. As Christians, if we are to seek God's best, that means avoiding surety.

Borrowing:
A Biblical Perspective

When you review the history of borrowing and lending, it is clear that we are living in a unique period of time in regard to credit. Prior to this century, a lender had almost absolute authority over a borrower. If a loan wasn't repaid exactly according to schedule, the borrower forfeited everything he owned to the lender. If the debt wasn't satisfied, the borrower was thrown into prison and became a bond-servant until every penny of the debt was repaid.

Today, almost the opposite extreme exists. The borrower has a legal method to avoid repayment of almost any indebtedness, regardless of how frivolously the money was spent. Eventually, the borrower will discover that the lender's authority has not been overruled, since it is established by God; it has merely been temporarily diverted. Ultimately, it will be the lenders who will come out on top.

I recently did a survey of several seminar groups to determine if they thought borrowing was scripturally forbidden. Over 70 percent responded that they believed the Bible prohibited borrowing. Perhaps it would be a lot easier if God's Word did prohibit a Christian from borrowing, but it does not. There is not a verse directing God's people *not* to borrow money (not even Romans 13:8). However, no Scripture *encourages* borrowing either. Borrowing is always discussed in the Bible as a negative rather than a positive principle. It would seem to be a consequence of disobeying God's statutes or rules of economics.

"He shall lend to you, but you shall not lend to him. . . So all these curses shall come on you and pursue you and overtake you until you are destroyed, because you would not obey the Lord your God"* (Deuteronomy 28:44-45).

GOD'S MINIMUM

The absolute minimum that God's Word establishes for any borrower is found in Psalm 37:21: *"The wicked borrows and does not pay back, but the righteous is gracious and gives."*

If we don't want to be counted among the wicked, we must repay any debt we owe. Knowing that should cause any Christian to avoid unnecessary borrowing for any reason. It really doesn't matter if the "circumstances" are beyond our control. If we make a debt, we're stuck with it.

"If therefore you are presenting your offering at the altar, and there remember that your brother has something against you, leave your offering there before the altar, and go your way; first be reconciled to your brother, and then come and present your offering" (Matthew 5:23-24).

GOD'S PROMISES

Unfortunately, we live mostly by sight rather than by faith. Those who are overwhelmed by debts will require faith that God knows their needs and will provide them. I have seen God provide for those who, by faith, trusted Him even to the point of losing every material possession they had. In many instances, God's provision came from a totally unexpected source and only after the commitment had been made.

I recall a Christian real estate developer who had lost every asset during an economic downturn. His three "Christian" partners all filed bankruptcy, and he was left with the total debt of slightly more than $600,000. After seeking counsel, he and his wife determined that they could not file voluntary bankruptcy, and in accordance with Matthew 5:40, they surrendered every possession they had except their clothes. They literally begged their creditors (mostly banks) not to force them into bankruptcy and promised to pay what they could above their basic living expenses. Over the next two years, they were able to pay about $20,000 on the debt, which didn't even cover 20 percent of the interest. However, they did have many opportunities to share their testimony and were able to counsel dozens of families who were having financial and spiritual difficulties. Their two children, who were in college when the crisis hit, dropped out for a year to help with the finances and then went back to school on working scholarships.

In the third year, the economy recovered rapidly, and the properties that secured the debts began to sell. Some sold at modest profits and reduced the indebtedness to about $400,000. The last and biggest property sold for more than $400,000 above the total outstanding loans, and the bank returned the surplus to them, even though they had no legal obligations to do so. In less than three years, God had provided a means to pay off all the debts and a great surplus besides. The man's ex-partners approached him about their "share" of the profits. His response was correct: "If you don't share in the losses, you don't share in the profits."

THE ONLY BIBLICAL WAY TO BORROW

Perhaps the most abused and least understood financial principle in God's Word is "surety." Surety is assuming an obligation to pay an indebtedness without a "sure" way to pay it. Surety means that we presume upon the future. If everything goes as we expect, we'll be able to pay the loans back. But if things go wrong, as they often do, we may be left in debt. A common example of surety is an automobile loan. When you borrow to buy a car, the car is pledged as collateral. But since the outstanding loan often exceeds the sale value of the car, the borrower must also personally endorse the note. If the payments cannot be met and the car is repossessed and sold, the borrower is liable for any deficiency. Since there is no *certain* way to pay the debt, surety results. Only if the collateral totally secures the loan can you avoid surety.

If Christians would observe this one caution associated with borrowing, the most they could lose is the security they had pledged against a loan.

"Do not be among those who give pledges, among those who become sureties for debts. If you have nothing with which to pay, why should he take your bed from under you?" (Proverbs 22:26-27).

After sharing that principle in a seminar, many times a Christian in the audience will respond, "Why, if I did that, I'd hardly ever be able to borrow money." To this I would have to respond, "Right!"

PRESENT DAY APPLICATION

Most of us were born into a debt-dominated society. Those under thirty cannot remember a time without home mortgages, automobile loans, and credit cards. However, just because these things are normal to our time, it does not make them normal to God's plan. It is important to remember that credit is not the problem; it's the *misuse* of credit. The misuse of credit can be traced back to some basic biblical root problems:

1. *Get-rich-quick.* Much debt exists because it seems faster and simpler to borrow than to save. Most of our economic cycles can be traced directly to the availability, or the lack of availability, of credit.

"The plans of the diligent lead surely to advantage, but everyone who is hasty comes surely to poverty" (Proverbs 21:5).

2. *Lack of trust.* Continual borrowing, regardless of the apparent worldly logic, is an evidence of a lack of faith in God. Many Christians either don't understand God's promises or don't believe them. God says that He knows our needs and will provide them in His time according to His plan. Borrowing is not a sin, but dependence on credit is an indication that a Christian has not yielded all rights to God.

"For all these things the Gentiles eagerly seek; for your heavenly Father knows that you need all these things. But seek first His kingdom and His righteousness; and all these things shall be added to you" (Matthew 6:32-33).

3. *Ignorance.* According to God's Word, ignorance is the absence of wisdom; wisdom comes from the mouth of God, and, therefore, God's Word is the cure for ignorance (Proverbs 1:32; 2:6; 3:4-6). Worldly wisdom says to multiply your goods and wealth by borrowing excessively. God's Word says that it is better to have a dry crust of bread and peace than a feast with strife (Proverbs 17:1). The vast majority of divorced couples say debts were the number one cause of strife in the family. Many families are having debt-funded "feasts," but great strife as

well. According to the Research Institute of America, the average American family pays one-fourth of their spendable income on debt.

"NECESSARY" BORROWING

In our society, it is nearly impossible for a young couple to buy a home without borrowing. However, with home loans has come a lifetime-debt mentality that causes couples to think in terms of what they must pay per month instead of what the total cost is. Unfortunately, most couples today don't ever plan toward a debt-free home. Worse, they don't even recognize the *need* for it. I have often heard someone say, "It's all right to borrow as long as the item appreciates." That's good common sense, but not a good biblical principle: First, God's Word doesn't state what borrowed money should be used for. Second, nothing appreciates forever, not even houses. Houses appreciate artificially because of the availability of cheap credit.

BUSINESS BORROWING

Most businesses are run on credit today. In fact, so widespread is the use of borrowed capital that many businessmen (including Christians) believe you cannot operate on a cash basis. That is not true—it is a dupe of Satan. Obviously, the debt-free can't sink as quickly. One long-range goal of every Christian businessman should be to become debt free. God never promises quick growth—He promises a solid foundation.

"He is like a man building a house, who dug deep and laid a foundation upon the rock; and when a flood rose, the torrent burst against that house and could not shake it, because it had been well built" (Luke 6:48).

Lending to Others

There's an old saying that the definition of a distant friend is a close friend who owes you money.

That's not always true, but it has enough truth in it to cause us to evaluate lending as a biblical principle. Let's first evaluate lending from a human viewpoint.

Why would anyone want to lend another person money? There are several logical reasons:

1. *To make a profit.* When you place money in a savings account, you have *loaned* the bank money. Obviously, you would like your money back, plus interest. The interest represents a profit on the loan you made.

2. *Because they have a need.* You may know someone who is short of funds for a business or a personal need, and you want to help but don't feel you can give the money.

3. *Because they asked you.* Many Christians lend money to someone because they were asked and are too timid to say no. That is typically true where close friends or family are involved.

THE HISTORY OF LENDING

There is no record of a society that operated for any period of time without borrowing and lending. Our society is a very rare instance where the laws favor the borrowers over the lenders. So lending is *not* a new principle. It is historically as old as man's written records and was common to Moses, Solomon, and Paul. Solomon's words in Proverbs 22:7 become much clearer in light of this: *"The rich rules over the poor, and the borrower becomes the lender's slave."*

BIBLICAL PRINCIPLE

It would be much simpler if God's Word merely said to be neither a borrower nor a lender. God doesn't say that anyone *has* to be a lender, but He also doesn't say you cannot be a lender. If you're a Christian in the lending business, this is a vital biblical issue. For if God's Word prohibited lending, the prohibition would, of necessity, carry over to working for a lender. Many Christians who work in banking have asked if they should be involved in a lending business. There may be reasons God would not want an individual to be involved in lending because of the morals or ethics of the day, but not because lending itself is unscriptural.

It is interesting that lending is one of the blessings promised by God for being obedient to His ways. Deuteronomy 28:12 says, *"The Lord will open for you His good storehouse, the heavens, to give rain to your land in its season and to bless all the work of your hand; and you shall lend to many nations, but you shall not borrow."*

Thus, God promises a surplus that can be loaned, at interest, to enhance His people's prosperity. There are many principles about collecting that must also be observed if we are in service to God, but clearly lending is not prohibited scripturally.

LENDING AT INTEREST

There is little Scripture dealing with the specifics of lending and charging interest, but what there is would seem to be very clear—don't charge interest to

110

your "brothers." *"You shall not charge interest to your countrymen: interest on money, food, or anything that may be loaned at interest"* (Deuteronomy 23:19).

A loan can be made to anyone, but loans to those within God's family are to be a demonstration that God can provide without charging interest to one another. I personally believe this admonition relates to basic needs (food, shelter, clothing) and not to investment loans, but that is my opinion.

In regard to lending to others, God's Word says, *"You may charge interest to a foreigner, but to your countrymen you shall not charge interest, so that the Lord your God may bless you in all that you undertake in the land which you are about to enter to possess"* (Deuteronomy 23:20).

Thus we *can* charge interest on loans to nonbelievers. That doesn't mean that we *have to* charge interest. God may well convict someone to extend a loan at no interest as a testimony and a door-opener to be able to share the message of Christ.

LENDING VS. GIVING

It should be clear by now that lending is not unbiblical—even lending at interest, under most circumstances. But there are conditions under which God would have us give rather than lend. That is particularly true where basic necessities are involved. However, the difficulty is deciding what constitutes a necessity. Is a house a necessity? What about a car or a college education? Needs vary by the society in which we live. A car may be a need for me but an extravagant luxury for an African. We may believe we're suffering by the lack of a comfortable home, and someone in Lebanon feels blessed by finding a rundown apartment that still has electricity.

The principle of lending without any consideration for whether or not the money can be repaid is shown in Luke 6:34: *"And if you lend to those from whom you expect to receive, what credit is that to you? Even sinners lend to sinners, in order to receive back the same amount."*

The obvious meaning is to give to those who have needs and would logically never have the ability to repay or reciprocate.

COLLECTING

God's principles of lending and collecting do not require a Christian to sit passively by if someone refuses to pay what is due. However, neither does it allow us to use the devices of the world to collect. There are boundaries within which we are to operate that are much narrower than those of the world. It is certain that if a Christian is involved in lending to any extent, especially in business, he will be tested in the area of collecting.

"Then summoning him, his lord said to him, `You wicked slave, I forgave you all that debt because you entreated me. Should you not also have had mercy on your fellow slave, even as I had mercy on you?'" (Matthew 18:32-33).

BOUNDARIES

Collecting from Christians. Christians are clearly admonished in Paul's letter to the Corinthians *never* to take another Christian before the secular court for *any* reason. That would certainly apply to the collection of debts. *"Does any one of you, when he has a case against his neighbor, dare to go to law before the unrighteous, and not before the saints?"* (1 Corinthians 6:1).

We are told that it is better to be

defrauded than to lose our witness by suing one another (1 Corinthians 6:7). According to Matthew 18:15-17, we are to confront the sin publically, even before the church if necessary. Recently, a ministry was formed to provide Christians with an organized method to settle disputes. The group is called The Christian Conciliation Service. Using objective, non-biased lay-volunteers, they will act as a Christian court to settle disputes between believers.

Collecting from non-Christians. Many Christians assume that since Paul said not to sue other Christians, then it must be OK to sue non-Christians to collect debts. Just because there is a direct reference not to sue a Christian, that does not mean we *should* sue non-Christians. There are no direct references to not suing your mother or father, either, but several other Scriptures would clearly indicate that we should not.

To understand the principle of suing non-Christians to collect personal debts, it is necessary to look at our broad purpose. Our purpose as Christians is to represent our Lord Jesus Christ. We are told in Romans 10:9 to "believe" in our hearts. That means to "live in accordance with." In other words, we are to let our lives demonstrate what our mouths say. In Luke 6:30-31 the Lord says, *"Give to everyone who asks of you, and whoever takes away what is yours, do not demand it back. And just as you want people to treat you, treat them in the same way."*

That does not absolutely state that a Christian should never sue to collect a debt. But it certainly does imply that God desires a much higher standard of behavior from believers than is expected of others. Everything we do must be measured against eternal values and not short-term profit or loss.

"Giving no cause for offense in anything,

in order that the ministry be not discredited" (2 Corinthians 6:3).

BUSINESS LOANS

Perhaps one of the most difficult areas associated with lending is that of business loans. Usually, that is where credit is extended for services or products. Obviously, the lender has incurred some out-of-pocket expenses for time, utilities, and products, and when the loan is not repaid as agreed upon, an additional hardship is experienced. It is easy to understand that the lender, Christian or not, would feel resentful. Therefore, a special caution must be added here to not strike out in vengeance, but to deal in love with those who don't pay. There are several alternatives to suing or to using a collection agency.

Contact the individual directly. Many people who feel they can't pay a bill will avoid the creditor out of embarrassment. Many times a well worded letter or phone call stating your willingness to work out a reasonable repayment plan will help to restore the relationship.

"A gentle answer turns away wrath, but a harsh word stirs up anger" (Proverbs 15:1).

Sometimes harsher means are necessary. I recall a Christian newspaper publisher who was having great difficulty collecting on accounts from Christians in his church. He had tried everything including a request to go before the church, but the pastor refused to let him do that. Finally, in frustration, he published a "special" church edition of his newspaper listing the names of the Christians who owed for previous advertising but would not pay. He pledged that the money would go to a missionary program to remove all hint of personal motives and distributed the papers within the church. His collection went up to almost 90 percent within a week. *Note:* Be sure you consult an attorney before attempting any similar action.

Collecting Debts

Collecting is actually the other side of borrowing, because for every borrower there must be a lender. In our generation, most Christians have been either a borrower or a lender or both. What are a Christian's alternatives in collecting loans he has made? Recently, a Christian asked me about God's principles of collecting debts and about lending money to others who ultimately will end up in debt. Should a Christian extend credit to another person, knowing the many admonitions in God's Word against excessive borrowing?

EXTENDING CREDITS

There are virtually no Scripture references prohibiting the extension of credit; indeed, the burden of prudence is placed on the borrower, except in the case of interest. For the lender, the Scriptures describe the methods of collection and whether or not interest should be charged.

"You may charge interest to a foreigner, but to your countryman you shall not charge interest, so that the Lord your God may bless you in all that you undertake in the land which you are about to enter to possess" (Deuteronomy 23:20). *"When you make your neighbor a loan of any sort, you shall not enter his house to take his pledge"* (Deuteronomy 24:10).

The implication throughout most of the Scripture dealing with lending is that a loan could be made to anyone, but interest could not be charged to brothers.

On closer scrutiny, I believe that admonition applies specifically to loans made for basic needs or personal income and not to investment-type loans.

Certainly, no one has to make investments, and loans made in this regard would not be to the widows, orphans, or needy described as needing assistance. However, just because a Christian is not prohibited from doing something does not necessarily mean that it is the best or could not be prohibited for an individual. Let me use myself as an example. Although lending is acceptable spiritually, I believe that God has directed me to give, not lend, to others. Accepting this as God's plan for my life would greatly influence any type of investments or businesses in which I might be involved. That is important for every believer to keep in mind. The principles are there for general direction, but they in no way detail God's unique plan for each of us.

Understanding the scriptural guidelines for debt collecting should certainly make a Christian more cautious about extending credit, specifically for a Christian engaged in supplying basic needs, such as housing, food, and medical or dental care. The charging of interest is prohibited, and under some circumstances collection would be prohibited as well. I have counseled many doctors, dentists, and attorneys not to extend credit to their patients. Individuals who can't save and pay very possibly won't pay later, either. It would be far better to know in advance that someone couldn't afford to pay and treat him as a ministry than to carry him as a delinquent account and cause unnecessary financial pressures in his family.

Those who cannot pay should be screened by a Christian financial counselor to assess their financial position and have the fees adjusted accordingly. Those who can pay should do so, or an exchange of some kind should be made. I know of a doctor who offers reduced-fee clients the opportunity to paint, clean, and repair in exchange for his services. Another has set up a child-care clinic as a ministry and asks non-fee clients to work as volunteers to help others who cannot afford proper child care. The guiding principle here is that free care should be the professional's option, not the patient's. And by allowing the needy to work rather than adding another debt to their load, he becomes a friend rather than an involuntary authority.

COLLECTING

Supposing a Christian is owed a legitimate debt, what are the limits on collection?

1. *Collecting from Christians.* One counselor told me that he classified anyone who didn't pay as non-Christian, thereby removing the restriction against lawsuits. Unfortunately, it's not that clear-cut. Many Christians, through ignorance or otherwise, find they have borrowed more than they can repay, just as non-Christians do. It would seem abundantly clear from Paul's exhortation in 1 Corinthians 6 that Christians aren't to sue each other in the world's courts, even at the risk of being wronged and defrauded (1 Corinthians 6:7). We are to demonstrate to the unsaved world that God's people love and honor each other regardless of the personal cost. God never promised that it would be simple or painless to be a follower.

"More than that, I count all things to be loss in view of the surpassing value of knowing Christ Jesus my Lord, for whom I have suffered the loss of all things, and count them but rubbish in order that I may gain Christ" (Philippians 3:8).

If a Christian creditor has been wronged by a nonpaying brother who will not submit to a plan of authority as outlined in Matthew 18:15-17, the first step is not collection of the debt, but rather discipline in the faith to correct the sin. Failure to pay a debt or to go before a Christian review group is not a sin—it is the outside reflection of an inner problem with authority. Once a Christian has exhausted scriptural remedies, if the debt remains unpaid, it should be forgiven and forgotten.

"But if you bite and devour one another, take care lest you be consumed by one another" (Galatians 5:15).

2. *Collecting from nonbelievers.* It would be simple to take the position that, since Paul limited his discussion on not suing to believers in 1 Corinthians 6, it must be all right to sue nonbelievers. Such an assumption would be too broad. Paul stated that suing a brother would bring shame to the Body, but he did not imply that suing nonbelievers would be acceptable.

"Giving no cause for offense in anything, in order that the ministry be not discredited" (2 Corinthians 6:3).

3. *Using collection agencies.* Is the use of a collection agency the same as suing? Not necessarily. However, for a Christian, the collection service becomes an extension of his own witness. It is important to consider what kind of witness a typical collection agency presents. Since in the collection process a partnership is formed, it would seem clear that only other believers should be used to pursue an obligation owed to a Christian. The certainty is that whatever image the collection service presents will be reflected back to the creditor. Just selling the collection accounts does not relieve that obligation on the part of a Christian creditor. I believe clearly that a Christian must first

115

determine the need of those in debt before resorting to any formal collection process.

"But whoever has the world's goods, and beholds his brother in need and closes his heart against him, how does the love of God abide in him?" (1 John 3:17).

4. *Collecting from a corporation.* A corporation, whether an insurance company, supplier, or contractor, is an entity, as opposed to an individual. It is literally a legal entity existing only under the law. When formed, the individuals associated with a corporation purposely relinquish their rights to the public law. In fact, for many corporations, there is no recourse or communication to them except through the channels of the law. When an insurance company signs a contract to pay for damages incurred to their client, they clearly state that in the event of an impasse on damage claims, they will use the court as the arbitrator. As far as I can determine, the Scripture is silent on this particular issue, leaving the decision to go before the law or not to the individual. Each Christian must test his motives and be willing to abandon any action if God so directs.

"Let your character be free from the love of money, being content with what you have; for He Himself has said, `I will never desert you, nor will I ever forsake you'" (Hebrews 13:5).

BEST POSITION

With the emphasis on "rights" in our country, it is common and accepted to force payment from anyone who owes, even if it requires the harassment of suing. A Christian must always keep in mind his primary purpose for being here: to lead others to the Lord. Continually God's Word stresses mercy and forgive-

ness in every aspect of our lives. Because of God's mercy to us, He forgave our debt. In the same manner, God requires us to forgive the debts of others, some of which will be financial.

"And be kind to one another, tenderhearted, forgiving each other, just as God in Christ also has forgiven you" (Ephesians 4:32).

Since that is the position given in Scripture, it should be the norm for God's people. Once a Christian realizes that, he should plan to make the extension of credit uncommon rather than a common event.

Knowing that God may well call upon us to forgive a debt, particularly one of necessity, means that a lender should know the spiritual character of the borrower thoroughly. Then the burden for repayment is shifted to the borrower, and collection becomes a matter of a gentle reminder. What a witness it would be to the unsaved if collecting debts between Christians would be as simple as a handshake.

However, until more Christians adhere to the principles of repayment, it is up to the lender to be very prudent and not extend credit to those who cannot reasonably repay it. It would be far better to turn down someone who could not pay than to have to spread the costs of a bad debt over those who do pay. Let the choice be yours, not theirs.

"A prudent man sees evil and hides himself, the naive proceed and pay the penalty" (Proverbs 27:12.) The burden of repayment clearly rests upon the borrower.

God may well bring someone who cannot or will not pay debts to you for help and counsel. If you operate on a cash-only basis, those people can be identified and dealt with as a ministry. Otherwise, they will be just one more bad debt. For a business that has bad accounts receivable, each debt must be evaluated on a cash-by-cash basis. The scriptural principle of collection must be considered before extending credit to any business or individual.

Part 5:

Business

Bankruptcy—Is It Scriptural?

Bankruptcy is a subject that is very personal to the several hundred thousand people who use it each year. About half of the personal bankruptcies are taken by young couples who have charged and borrowed far beyond their abilities to pay. They see bankruptcy as their only release from the financial bondage that threatens their marriages and sometimes their health.

In a recent counseling session, a couple revealed that they owed $6,000 in credit card bills, $11,000 for a previous consolidation loan, and $15,000 for a family loan to buy a home. "Obviously," the husband said, "another consolidation loan won't help. The only thing that will help us is a fresh start." A friend in their church had offered to lend them the money to file for bankruptcy. They came for counsel because of a wise pastor who knew that bankruptcy would be just another "quick fix." A review of their financial history convinced me, and them, that history would repeat itself if they didn't change their past habits.

It's amazing that the average family filing for bankruptcy only owes about $4,000. The problem is that it's usually composed of many small bills, and most of them are delinquent. They may have the capacity to pay their creditors, but that would require at least two years of financial sacrifice. We are a generation of "quick-fix" addicts, and the idea of absolutes has been taught for a long time, even inside Christianity.

BANKRUPTCY IS A SPIRITUAL INDICATOR

God's Word teaches that the way we handle our money is the clearest reflection of our spiritual value system. Excessive debts, even bankruptcies, are not our problems—they are the external indicators of internal spiritual problems. Literally, they are a person's attitudes being reflected in actions. That is not to indict those who are in debt or who file for bankruptcy, but only to reflect what Christ said:

"He who is faithful in a very little thing is faithful also in much; and he who is unrighteous in a very little thing is unrighteous also in much. If therefore you have not been faithful in the use of unrighteous mammon, who will entrust the true riches to you?" (Luke 16:10-11).

I recently received a call from a pastor who was considering filing for bankruptcy because of a very heavy debt burden. He was fearful of his creditors obtaining judgments or even garnishments against him. "It's not fair that they can attach my salary," he said. "I won't be able to feed my family." I asked if they had tricked him into borrowing their money. They had not. Then I asked him to put himself in the place of the lender. If that lender were in his congregation, would he respond to a salvation message delivered by a pastor who had bankrupted to avoid paying a debt? Second, I asked him to consider what Christ would do if He were in his position. After all, isn`t that what we're instructed to do as Christ's followers? We are to do nothing that would be solely for our own benefit.

"Do not merely look out for your own personal interest, but also for the interest of others" (Philippians 2:4). Also, we are to be imitators of Christ. *"Therefore be imitators of God, as beloved children"* (Ephesians 5:1).

This pastor stood up to his burden, asked for the forgiveness of his creditors, and cut up all of his credit cards. He confessed his error before his church and found several kindred spirits in the congregation. There was some wagging of tongues, to be sure, but in great part there was healing and understanding.

REPAYMENT IS A VOW

I believe a principle that has been greatly overlooked in our generation is that of making a vow. A vow is literally a promise. When someone borrows money, he makes a promise to repay according to the agreed-upon conditions of the loan. Once an agreement is reached, repayment is not an option. It's an absolute as far as God is concerned. The rights all fall to the lender, and the borrower literally becomes the lender's servant.

"The rich rules over the poor, and the borrower becomes the lender's slave" (Proverbs 22:7).

As representatives of Jesus Christ before the world, Christians are admonished to think ahead and consider the consequences of their actions. That's why Scripture teaches so many principles dealing with borrowing and lending, and especially the misuse of credit. But once a Christian borrows, he's made a *vow* to repay.

"When you make a vow to God, do not be late in paying it, for He takes no delight in fools. Pay what you vow! It is better that you should not vow than that you should vow and not pay" (Ecclesiastes 5:4-5).

IS BANKRUPTCY ALLOWABLE?

A counselee once asked, "Would God direct someone to go bankrupt?" My answer was, "I don't see how, since that would refute His own Word." God's Word says a wicked man borrows but does not repay (Psalm 37:21). God desires that we be righteous, not wicked.

"But would God forgive me if I go bankrupt?" he asked. God says He will forgive *any* sin, past, present, and future, if we confess that it is wrong. Bankruptcy is a legal remedy, *not* a scriptural remedy. It's understandable that under the pressures of excessive debts a Christian would yield to a quick-fix, but it doesn't make bankruptcy any more scriptural.

THE YEAR OF REMISSION AND/OR JUBILEE

One counselee told me that bankruptcy was a biblical principle based upon the year of remission discussed in Deuteronomy 15:1-2. According to God's Word, there was to be a release of debtors every seventh year. However, this was a direction between God's children and was always an option of the lender, not the borrower.

The year of Jubilee, as discussed in Leviticus 25:10, was literally the seventh year of remission. Again, the same principle was involved. It was the responsibility and option of the lender, not the borrower, to release debts.

WHAT IF YOU HAVE NO ALTERNATIVE?

I was working with a young couple who had accumulated nearly $40,000 in business debts before they closed their doors. They were being hounded by creditors on every side. They had sold their home, one car, and virtually every worldly asset to reduce the debt from about $60,000. They didn't want to go bankrupt and tried to negotiate any kind of repayment with their creditors but to no avail. Creditor after creditor filed judgments against them. The bottom line was that virtually every creditor told them to file bankruptcy and get it over with—all at one time. They told the husband they wouldn't work with them because he had no assets and that they would rather write off the debts through bankruptcy.

My counsel was that he was not responsible for what the creditors did or didn't do. He was responsible before God for his actions. I recommended that he respond literally according to Proverbs 6:2-3. He should humble himself before his creditors and ask them to work with him. They, unfortunately, refused and forced him into involuntary bankruptcy. Once they filed bankruptcy against him, he was legally, but not scripturally, released from the debts. He has diligently worked ever since to pay off the debts, one at a time, and will continue to do so with God's help.

WHAT ABOUT INVOLUNTARY BANKRUPTCY?

An involuntary bankruptcy can be initiated by several creditors who wish to attach all available assets and force an individual or corporation to liquidate. A good biblical case can be made for the position that since the creditors initiated the action, they have settled any and all claims. But in our society, this action is often necessary to pre-empt a debtor from liquidating all assets and spending the money. For a Christian, the obligation to repay according to the original terms still exists.

"Do not withhold good from those to whom it is due, when it is in your power to do it" (Proverbs 3:27).

CHAPTER 13 BANKRUPTCY

According to the federal bankruptcy code, an individual can elect to come under a court administrated repayment plan, commonly called a Chapter 13. The court determines how much of the indebtedness an individual can pay and then directs the creditors to operate within that plan. I can find no biblical reason prohibiting a Christian from using such remedy, provided that once the court-appointed percentage was repaid, the remaining portion was also repaid. That would also be true of a Chapter 11 reorganization for corporations.

The key element in any decision involving a legitimate loan made to a Christian by another person is that our actions honor the Lord. In a society that is obsessed by desires for quick riches and then quick outs to the havoc that they reap, God has no "easy-in, easy-out" principles. We serve a holy and righteous God who desires that all men come to the saving knowledge of Jesus Christ. If any willful action on our part impedes that process in the life of another, it displeases Him. Just try to share your faith with a creditor involved in a bankruptcy, and the true loss will be evident.

"A good name is to be more desired than great riches, favor is better than silver and gold" (Proverbs 22:1).

What Is Christian Business?

Obviously, there is no such thing as a "Christian business." A business is a legal entity, such as a corporation, partnership, or proprietorship and, as such, has no spirit or soul. It may, however, reflect the values of the principal owners or managers. It is the reflection of these values that determines whether or not a business is labeled Christian or non-Christian.

A business is a tool to be used by God in demonstrating the truth of the gospel. In James 1:22 we are told to be "doers" of the Word. A business is the perfect environment for doing Christ's truth.

APPLYING GOD'S RULES

One of the best ways to determine whether a business is being used to serve God is to look at the policies governing the day-to-day actions. If a Christian is truly committed to Jesus Christ and to serving His purposes, then the business will be run according to His principles and precepts. Obviously, that means that a Christian must first understand God's rules. Anyone attempting to follow God's plan for business will discover a startling difference between what the world says is normal and what God says is normal. Therefore, the committed Christian must accept that he is merely a manager of God's business. If God's Word says to do something a particular way, the committed Christian *will* do it. If the Word says not to do something, then he *will not* do it. Without a doubt, such decisions can potentially cost something economically. But the right decisions will also yield something even greater —God's wisdom and peace.

An additional reward that God promises those who follow Him is prosperity. After all, what kind of witness would we be if we failed every time we followed God's rules? Indeed, the opposite is true. God wrote the rules of business economics, and through the ages, those who followed God's path have prospered while bringing countless lost souls into God's eternal family.

"For its profit is better than the profit of silver, and its gain than fine gold. She is more precious then jewels; and nothing you desire compares with her" (Proverbs 3:14-15).

WHAT IS THE PURPOSE OF BUSINESS?

If a Christian business is to be used to serve God, it has but one overriding purpose—to glorify Him. Acknowledging that will make decisions much simpler. Each decision, hiring, firing, paying, promoting, and so on, must be made in harmony with God's written Word. Obviously, God's Spirit leads us day-by-day, but always within the boundaries of what He has chosen to commit to the written Word.

BALANCE IN BUSINESS

The purpose of a Christian's business is to glorify God. The day-by-day functions are the things we do to accomplish that purpose. No one function is more or less important, and each must be done with excellence. For instance, if the business aspects are neglected for the sake of evangelism, quite often the business will fail. If the ministry functions are neglected to generate profits, the business loses

124

its witness in the world.

That can certainly be observed in our society today. Often the term "Christian" in conjunction with a business brings to mind an image of a Bible-toting evangelist who doesn't pay his bills and tells the creditors he's just "trusting the Lord" for their money. On the other hand, there are many Christian-run businesses that are extremely profitable and are operated honestly and ethically, but few people even know the owner is a Christian. In his business life, he's a secret service Christian. Obviously, these extremes do not constitute every Christian-run business but too few present a balanced image of good business based on biblical principles.

THE FUNCTIONS OF A BUSINESS

There are five basic business function that together constitute the activities of a Christian *business*.

Function 1: Evangelism. There is no tool more effective for evangelism than a business dedicated to the Lord. Not only can employees be won by a dedicated owner or manager, but, similarly, so can suppliers, creditors, and customers. The key here is the *walk*, not the talk.

Function 2: Discipleship. Evangelism is sharing Christ's message of salvation with the lost. Discipleship is training Christians to grow stronger in their faith. In a business, that effort should be directed by the owner or manager to those immediately under his authority. It is they who will then be able to disciple the others under their authority.

"And the things which you have heard from me in the presence of many witnesses, these entrust to faithful men, who will be able to teach others also" (2 Timothy 2:2).

"That's well and good," you say, "but what if my managers aren't saved?"

If they aren't saved, then you simply back up to function 1. An excellent program for evangelism is the Christian Businessmen's Committee (CBMC) life-style evangelism. It is ideally suited for developing a witness with managers.

Function 3: To fund God's work. A business is the best tool for funding God's work ever created. A properly run business can generate excess capital to meet needs, share the gospel, and still continue its operations day-by-day. There are many creative ways to use such funds to further God's work. Obviously, giving to your church and to ministries is good and necessary to do God's work, but there are many ministries available within the business itself. For instance, several Christian businessmen have hired full-time counselors who work with employees who have personal problems. Often, when one business is too small to afford a counselor, several businesses have combined to use a common counselor. Also, many businessmen have funds available for needy employees. Other provide cassette tape lending libraries and books as internal ministries to employees.

Function 4: Provide for needs. A business must provide for the needs of the employees, creditors, customers, and owners. That is done by paying salaries, paying for supplies and equipment in a timely fashion, and providing a quality product at a fair price. In our modern business environment, the principle seems to be to meet the owner's needs, wants, and desires first, then pay the employees what is necessary to keep them off his back. Many creditors are paid late, or not at all, and the customers are viewed as a necessary evil.

If a Christian business owner accepts meeting needs as a normal part of God's plan, his business will play an effective role in evangelism and discipleship.

When employees know that those in authority put the needs of others ahead of their own, they will respond.

Function 5: To generate profits. Any business must be able to make a profit if it is to continue operations. Sometimes Christians seem to believe that God will bless them supernaturally, while they ignore every pretense of good management. If you believe that, you haven't studied God's Word very thoroughly. God's Word directs us to think and plan.

"The mind of man plans his way, but the Lord directs his steps" (Proverbs 16:9).

I have counseled enough Christians in business to know that many claim to operate by faith, when, instead, they are being slothful. God's Word does not teach us to sit on our hands, waiting for Him to reveal His perfect will. We are to be active. In other words, we are not to be observers of God's plan, but participants in it.

"The soul of the sluggard craves and gets nothing, but the soul of the diligent is made fat" (Proverbs 13:4).

KEYS TO GENERATE A PROFIT

The keys to generating a profit according to the principles in God's Word are not complicated. Many businessmen have followed them during their lifetimes and have been leaders in their industry. Some, like J. C. Penney, R. G. LeTourneau, Stanley Tamm, and Walt Meloon, became known, not only for their astute business acumen, but also for their Christian witness.

Acknowledge and obey God's eternal wisdom in operating your business. In other words, seek God's counsel first.

"Trust in the Lord with all your heart, and do not lean on your own understanding. In all your ways acknowledge Him, and He will make your paths straight" (Proverbs 3:5-6).

Too often, we seek God's wisdom but then violate the most basic principles taught in His Word. Remember what Christ taught in Matthew 21:31. Those who do what their Father says will inherit the kingdom of God.

Seek godly counsel in major decisions. Psalm 1:1 tells us, *"How blessed is the man who does not walk in the counsel of the wicked,"* and Proverbs 15:22 says, *"Without consultation, plans are frustrated, but with many counselors they succeed."* Outside of God, a man's primary counselor is his wife. Proverbs 31:11 says, *"The heart of her husband trusts in her, and he will have no lack of gain."* That is a resource that few men utilize.

Often, drifting is the result of a lack of accountability. Too many Christian business owners are not really accountable to anyone. An accountability group of three or more godly men who know God's Word will provide the counsel God directs us to seek.

The Purpose of a Business

I t is enlightening to reflect on what the Bible has to say about business. Many Christians say they have a Christian business, but what does that mean?

Obviously, the actual business entity is neither Christian nor non-Christian. A Christian business, therefore, is one that is controlled by a Christian. The more control this Christian has, the more the business can reflect his or her spiritual values.

It is interesting to see how many Christians would like for God to make them a success so that they can be a witness for the Lord and how few really are witnesses once God does. Clearly, a Christian in business can be used by the Lord, but only if the correct priorities have been pre-established. One key to being useful to the Lord is making decisions on the basis of God's Word and not on circumstances, feelings, or what is acceptable to society.

THE PURPOSE OF A CHRISTIAN'S BUSINESS

The purpose of any Christian, in business or otherwise, is to glorify God, not just to make a profit. *"Whatever you do, do your work heartily, as for the Lord rather than for men"* (Colossians 3:23).

As in any other area of service, it is important to establish a priority system. We can quickly become so involved with the urgent things of this world that we neglect the important things. Early in a business career, the urgent thing is to make payroll. Later it becomes urgent to make a greater profit or build a bigger company.

Therefore, it is important always to strive for balance in business. That is true in a spiritual sense just as in a material sense. For example, sales are important to any business, but if a manufacturing company applies 100 percent of its labor force to sales, the imbalance will be readily apparent. One of the priorities of a business should be to lead others to the Lord. But if all other functions are ignored in pursuit of evangelism, the work will be short lived. Therefore, the priorities really mean "What are my goals, and can my goals be balanced to achieve the overall objective of serving God while meeting material needs?"

Goal 1: Salvation. Compared to eternity, the profile of a business is rather trivial and a lifetime of work rather insignificant. If used wisely, though, a business can change the lives of countless lost people. When the primary thrust of a businessman's outreach is to insure that others within his sphere of influence hear the promises of Jesus Christ, a whole new perspective takes place. There is an old cliché that seems applicable here: "If it doesn't work in your life, don't export it." Nothing speaks louder than a phony, and nothing will turn others off more than a businessman who lives carnally and talks spiritually. However, if we wait until we're perfect, we'll never share Christ's claims. God expects application, not perfection.

There is no group more accessible to a businessman than his employees. It never ceases to amaze me that a businessman will spend thousands of dollars to travel around the world to speak to lost people about Christ, when there are many unsaved in his own business who have never heard the truth clearly from him. Often it is the fear of rejection that makes us first seek out those we don't know.

Once the message has been taken to the employees in an inoffensive manner, then it should be presented to others, such as suppliers, peers, and customers. Sharing Christ with others through the business environment should not be done under compulsion, nor should witnessing be used as a club. God prepares the hearts of men through the Holy Spirit and then provides the opportunity to share in a meaningful way.

A forced sharing is what we do for God; fruitful sharing is what God does through us. It is important to keep in mind that in the daily routine of operating a business "as unto the Lord," God will provide these opportunities to share. It is not necessary to sacrifice good business practices, and consequently the business, in order to serve the Lord. Satan would have us believe that serving the Lord requires abandoning good common sense. Indeed, serving the Lord provides good common sense.

"Then you will discern the fear of the Lord, and discover the knowledge of God. For the Lord gives wisdom; from His mouth come knowledge and understanding" (Proverbs 2:5-6).

Goal 2: Use of funds. The first use of funds is to honor the Lord. Proverbs 3:9 says, *"Honor the Lord from your wealth, and from the first of all your produce."*

We can look at the Scriptures on sharing from any perspective, and they still say the same thing: God wants the first part of our increase. That is not a requirement; it is a promise. It is God's promise that by our honoring Him materially before the world, He will in turn honor us. Literally, we acknowledge His lordship. If Christ is Lord, then He is owner as well; our money is His to preserve or disburse as He sees fit. We only manage it for Him until He returns. Therefore, the firstfruits from any business should be surrendered in the name of the Lord. Where, how, and how much? That is a subject for a later principle.

The second use of funds from a business is to meet the needs of its employees.

In Deuteronomy 17:15-20 God establishes the standards for his leaders. One is to live moderately. Those who do not observe this simple rule often lose sensitivity for others who have less, and many become callous and corrupt. Any Christian businessman intent on serving the Lord must keep in mind Christ's example to this world.

"But Jesus called them to Himself, and said, `You know that the rulers of the Gentiles lord it over them, and their great men exercise authority over them. It is not so among you, but whoever wishes to become great among you shall be your servant, and whoever wishes to be first among you shall be your slave'" (Matthew 20:25¬27).

To men, authority and position mean power and wealth. To God, they mean responsibility. A Christian businessman who seeks to serve the Lord will also belong to those faithful employees who helped to build the business.

The third use of funds is to pay suppliers and creditors on time. There is no poorer witness than a businessman who is consistently delinquent on accounts. It is the responsibility of every Christian businessman to budget wisely and live on surplus funds, not accounts payable. Many businesses operate on the principle of "I'll pay when and if it's convenient." They ride their creditors to the limit, believing that it is easier to owe someone else than to cut back during tough times.

"Do not withhold good from those to whom it is due, when it is in your power to do it. Do not say to your neighbor, `Go, and

come back, and tomorrow I will give it,' when you have it with you" (Proverbs 3:27-28).

Goal 3: Discipleship. Once the goals for witnessing and the use of money have been determined, the next goal is to disciple those who have been won to the Lord. Obviously, for spiritual growth new Christians must be directed into a sound, Bible teaching church. But to help them become witnesses in the business environment requires some specialized training. The same principles that have become a part of your life should be ingrained within them.

"A the things which you have heard from me in the presence of many witnesses, these entrust to faithful men, who will be able to teach others also" (2 Timothy 2:2).

It is difficult to share Christ in a meaningful way in any relationship. That difficulty is amplified even more for the salesman in someone else's office. That does not mean we should abandon witnessing, only that our sensitivity to the leading of the Holy Spirit is vital. Many time young, exuberant, and ill-trained Christians leave a trail of disaster behind them. Instead of picking the ripe fruit they mow down everything in their path. Obviously, the other danger is that a new believer will be timid to the point of becoming a "secret service" Christian.

A sound discipleship program is a good beginning. The teaching can be accomplished through written materials, audio, or video, but an essential element to the program's success will be the extent of personal follow-up and accountability. Every new disciple should ideally spend several months in a study plan where he meets regularly with one other person to discuss victories and defeats.

Does all of this sound difficult and time consuming? No doubt about it; God's way does not equate success with large numbers. The first step is to start with one or two who are truly seeking God's best. Once they are trained, they can help train others. In our society of instant potatoes and Minute Rice, God still prepares Christians the old-fashioned way—over time.

THE PRINCIPLE OF SUCCESS

I would trust that by this point your image of a successful Christian businessman, owner or otherwise, has changed somewhat. While it's true that one essential element of a Christian business is a profit, it is not the most important element. There are many unsaved and uncaring men and women who have developed profitable businesses without the slightest regard for God. No, to qualify for God's round table requires much higher standards than just net profits. Consider these questions:

1. When people think of you, do they focus on your business success first or your visible image as a disciple for Jesus Christ?

2. Do your employees and close business contacts know and respect your unwavering stand for the Lord and His principles?

3. Does your family receive a fair share of your time and view the business as ministry as well?

4. Are the bills paid on time and debts kept within the ability of your business to pay?

5. Does the Lord's work receive the best (firstfruits) from the business?

6. Does the business produce a good product or service at a fair price from the customer's perspective?

7. Does the business generate a reasonable profit to continue operating?

"For to a person who is good in His sight He has given wisdom and knowledge and joy,

while to the sinner He has given the task of gathering and collecting so that He may give to one who is good in God's sight. This too is vanity and striving after wind" (Ecclesiastes 2:26).

Unequally Yoked

As always, a study of a particular principle from God's Word must begin with two pertinent questions: What does God's Word say about the subject and why?

In 2 Corinthians 6:14 Paul writes, *"Do not be bound together with unbelievers; for what partnership have righteousness and lawlessness, or what fellowship has light with darkness?"* Clearly, the "what" is specific in that believers are admonished not to be yoked to nonbelievers. But then other questions arise. What is a yoke, and how far does the principle extend? Does it cover only marriages or extend also to business relationships?

These questions can only be answered by knowing the answer to our second primary question: Why? I trust that you will discover, as I did, that the reason such an instruction is given to Christians is clear. We are to operate with a value system so different from the nonbelieving world that on a day-by-day basis we will be in conflict with the norm. Our purpose in life is to glorify God in every decision and every action. A non-Christian could not and would not accept decisions made from that perspective. However, before I get ahead of myself and discuss the "why," let's look at the "what" from God's Word.

WHAT IS A YOKE?

Two distinct types of yokes are presented in the Scriptures. One is a collar used on slaves to show their total subjugation. The second, which is of concern here, is a harness used to link two working animals together. In 2 Corinthians 6:14, when Paul says, *"Do not be yoked together with unbelievers"* (NIV*), the yoke referred to is a farm implement.

The yoke was a common everyday device used to couple oxen together for plowing or hauling. The oxen were matched as closely as possible so the burden would be distributed equally. The two animals had to be trained to work together, even walking stride for stride so that the heavy wooden bar would not rub the skin off of their backs as they worked.

Once connected by the yoke, the oxen were no longer two who could choose to go their own way; rather, they became one working unit. It was extremely critical that the yoked animals be closely matched in size, strength, and temperament. If one animal was larger, the weight of the yoke rested upon the smaller and fatigued it rapidly. If one was much stronger, he pulled the bulk of the attached load and would also fatigue more quickly. And even with two physically matched animals, if one would not yield to the task (and kicked against the traces), then the obedient animal suffered some whiplashes as the owner disciplined the wayward one. The yoke bound them together for the purpose of accomplishing a task, and without mutual compromise it could not be done.

Hence, the analogy of a yoke to a marriage is an accurate one. A marriage should be two people pulling in common bond toward compatible goals and sharing the load equally.

* *New International Version.*

131

WHY AVOID A YOKE

People with opposite goals and values will not be compatible. When they are linked together either in marriage or business, their differing values will ultimately create conflicts. Christians are admonished not to be yoked together with unbelievers because the very purpose of our lives will be sidetracked.

When decisions must be made that involve spiritual principles, the unbeliever cannot be expected to be motivated by God's Spirit. Even elementary decisions, such as giving to the Lord, become sources of friction in an unequally yoked relationship.

A FINANCIAL YOKE

It is necessary to take the broad principle of a yoke and narrow down its applicability to the area of finances. But first we must look at what does not constitute a yoked relationship.

Employee/employer. When two or more people are related in a work situation by employee-employer agreement, they are not yoked. There is an authority relationship, but they are not bound together by either verbal or written agreement (Titus 3:1; Ephesians 6:5; Colossians 3:22; etc.). They are not expected to carry the same load, and either party is free to terminate the relationship according to the predetermined agreement.

Stock ownership. Normally, stock ownership would not create a yoke. The stockholder is not bound to the company, except to the limit of his financial risk. Actually, there is an authority relationship, but the authority rests in the hands of the stockholder. There is no attempt to create a binding, equal relationship.

However, each relationship must be reviewed individually. If the intent is to create an equal, binding relationship between two or more people, then a yoke exists.

Other than a marriage, there is no better defined yoke between two or more people than a partnership. The intent of a partnership is to create a binding business relationship where all parties are equal in responsibility, authority, and liability. Indeed, the law deals with partnerships in this manner. If one partner commits to a business decision, all partners are bound by it.

All of the partners' assets, both business and personal, are jointly and individually pledged. Partnerships are difficult under the best of circumstances but can become completely untenable if all the partners do not have compatible financial and spiritual goals. Indeed, a Christian may find himself in a situation where God chooses to discipline one partner through finances, and thus all other partners are equally affected.

It is not necessary to attempt to define every type of contractual relationship dealing with business. The intent is the important determination. If the intent is to create an equal and binding relationship, then a yoke is created.

INTENT

There is no absolute method of predetermining what creates a yoke and what does not. Marriages and partnerships fit the description of yokes nearly perfectly, so in those cases we are admonished not to be bound to unbelievers.

The admonition for Christians not to be yoked to unbelievers should not imply that nonbelievers are less honest people. The principle is given because the believer and nonbeliever are not working toward the same ultimate goals. Literally, the believer must be willing to pay any price to serve God, while the unbeliever will not be willing to do so. Thus, their attitudes are incompatible, and ultimately, they will clash.

"And whatever you do in word or deed, do all in the name of the Lord Jesus, giving thanks through Him to God the Father" (Colossians 3:17).

When a believer and a nonbeliever can maintain a partnership without conflict over the spiritual goals of the company, it is normally because the believer has compromised God's principles (Romans 12:2).

NOT ALL THINGS ARE PROFITABLE

Just because we can have partnerships with other believers does not mean that we should. Paul said, *"All things are lawful for me, but not all thing are profitable"* (2 Corinthians 6:12*a*). Stretching that principle a little, we can say, "Any two Christians can be partners, but not all should be."

There are different levels of maturity, commitment, and human compatibility. Choosing a business partner should be done with the same caution with which you would choose a spouse.

EXISTING PARTNERSHIPS

If you are already in an unequally yoked business situation, observe the principles taught by Paul in 1 Corinthians 7. If you have the opportunity to be released from the partnership, you should arrange to be. But if you don't have the opportunity, make your partner's salvation your number-one item of prayer. A general observation I would add is that through the consistently godly life-style of a Christian partner, an unsaved partner will often decide either to join God's family or to sever the partnership.

Keeping a Vow

While I was teaching at a conference for professional athletes, an interesting question was asked about a pending players' walkout in the National Football League. The question was, "As Christians, what should our response be toward the strike?"

In order to get the problem in perspective, it is necessary to understand a little background information. Each player signs a contract with an NFL team for his services. Once drafted by a team, he has no option to negotiate with another team—he is stuck with either striking an agreement with the team that drafts him or sitting out a year if they won't trade him. Once signed with a team, he must play for them. The team, however, can drop him at any time up to the regular season with little or no compensation. Basically, he is bound to the team, but the team is not bound to him. Salaries are negotiated individually, and older, higher-paid athletes are often replaced by younger, lower-paid athletes.

That particular year, the players' association (an involuntary association set up to negotiate with the team owners on general compensation items, such as retirement benefits and uniform salaries) had asked for a percentage of total profits to be shared with players. To support that demand they had asked the players to participate in a walkout if necessary. Thus, the question was asked: "What do we, as Christians, do?"

MAKING A VOW

It is clear in God's Word that a vow of any kind is not to be taken lightly.

Once someone has given his word, it becomes a binding contract to be fulfilled. Thus, before agreeing to any terms, it is assumed that an individual has carefully considered the consequences.

For the current generation, that concept is rarely taught and seldom applied. A vow is deemed something made under one set of circumstances that may be broken under another. Thus, a vow to pay a creditor is ignored when the usefulness of the product wears out. Indeed, all creditors can be avoided by a perfectly legal arrangement called bankruptcy, if necessary. When a couple gets married, they exchange vows or promises to each other. They promise to love each other and forsake all others no matter what. That will hold true, even if the other partner becomes a drunk, a thief, disabled, ugly, or old. Today, though, the common attitude is, "If it doesn't work out, I can always get out," and usually that's what happens. The original conditions that made the promises seem legitimate change, and one partner begins to think he got a bum deal. Usually it happens because, being older and wiser, he believes he could have negotiated a betted "deal."

LEGAL LOOPHOLES

The more prevalent this attitude becomes, the trickier the contracts or vows become. Everyone tries to leave loopholes so that if he changes his mind, he can always get out. Then the vows become clouded with attorneys and legal jargon, and a simple contract becomes the meeting ground for adversaries.

GOD'S PROMISES

The reason most Christians are not able to claim God's promises is because they are not willing to meet His prerequisites. First John 3:21-22 explains that God will answer our prayers when we do the things that are pleasing in His sight and keep His commandments. Few scriptural principles are clearer than that of keeping our vows—literally keeping our word both to God and to others.

"It is better that you should not vow than that you should vow and not pay" (Ecclesiastes 5:5).

A SURVEY OF VOWS

First, it's important to note that God never promised us fairness in this life. Many times we will be bound to a higher standard than those with whom we deal. Quite often as a result, we will come out second best in a two-man contest. In Psalm 73, Asaph confessed that he envied the arrogant until, as noted in verses 17-18, he *"came into the sanctuary of God; then I perceived their end. Surely Thou dost set them in slippery places; Thou dost cast them down to destruction."*

A promise that should govern our daily lives is found in Psalm 101:7. *"He who practices deceit shall not dwell within my house; he who speaks falsehood shall not maintain his position before me."*

HONESTY

A Christian's usefulness to God is directly proportional to his honesty. When we give our word and then go back on it, we have made our "yes" "no" and our "no" "yes." *"He who walks in his uprightness fears the Lord, but he who is crooked in his ways despises Him"* (Proverbs 14:2).

Honesty goes beyond not telling an outright lie; it must include being reliable to fulfill promises made. God's Word calls that "loyalty." Loyalty on a Christian's part is not ultimately to another person. Indeed, few people are really deserving of our uncompromising loyalty. Our loyalty is to God and His Word. In being loyal, we become instruments for God to show others His loyalty. It would really be a tough life for us if God changed His mind whenever the "deal" wasn't right. Our only hope rests in the fact that God is loyal to His promises, regardless of how bad His end of the deal is.

"Many a man proclaims his own loyalty, but who can find a trustworthy man? A righteous man who walks in his integrity —How blessed are his sons after him" (Proverbs 20:6-7).

PRIDE

The opposite of humility is pride. Pride is perhaps the major sin in Christendom today. Pride—the desire to be first—leads to greed—a craving for more. When someone backs down on a vow that has been made in good faith, it is usually either because of pride or because of greed. The real problem lies in the fact that when someone dishonors an agreement just to gain a little better deal, he is the real loser, because more money won't help replace what's been lost: integrity.

"Everyone who is proud in heart is an abomination to the Lord; assuredly, he will not be unpunished" (Proverbs 16:5).

TRUST

Many times Christians read through the Bible without grasping the fact that the truths presented are life's handbook. God's Word says that everyone will be accountable for his words and actions on the Day of Judgment. Jesus Christ said that our real motives are shown by our decisions about money. Many compromising Christians are going to be saddened to learn that their treasures were just wood, hay, and stubble. When it really counted, they couldn't be trusted in a small thing, so God never used them in larger things.

"No one can serve two masters; for either he will hate the one and love the other, or he will hold to one and despise the other. You cannot serve God and mammon" (Matthew 6:24).

RIGHTS/RESPONSIBILITIES

We are so conscious of our rights today that I believe our rights will ultimately cost us our freedom. In the area of contracts, many people believe it's their right to strike a better deal later if the circumstances change. What about our responsibilities? The word means to be accountable for our actions. Christ said His followers must be willing to surrender their rights and become His stand-ins. It is inconceivable to think that our Lord would have made an agreement with someone and then change His mind and try to negotiate a better deal. As a carpenter, I rather imagine Jesus delivered His products at the agreed-upon price, regardless of what His costs were or what the market was doing.

In Matthew 20, Jesus gives us just such an example of being satisfied with a bargain once struck. Various workers were hired during the day at an agreed-upon sum, which happened to be exactly the same amount. At the end of the day, those who had worked all day for the same wages as those who had worked only one hour were grumbling at the landowner because they felt they had been cheated. The landowner's response was, *"Friend, I am doing you no wrong; did you not agree with me for a denarius?"* (v. 13).

The issue wasn't whether or not the wage was sufficient—it was just that someone else got a better deal, and that wasn't "right."

WHAT WE DESERVE

The one certain rule of contract law is that once a contract is made, one party can't arbitrarily decide to modify or cancel it. As Christians, we can be truly thankful that God's contract with us is binding and firm. Otherwise, He might give us what we deserve. However, God says that if we wish to be forgiven, we must forgive others. If we wish to exercise God's promise to call upon Him in our day of trial, we must pay our vows.

"Offer to God a sacrifice of thanksgiving, and pay your vows to the Most High; and call upon Me in the day of trouble; I shall rescue you, and you will honor Me" (Psalm 50:14-15).

AUTHORITY

Once a Christian has agreed to submit to an authority as in the case of a professional athlete by contract, he is admonished to give honor to that authority, even if the authority doesn't deserve it. Clearly, the apostle Paul did not condone or approve of slavery, but in Ephesians 6:5, he admonishes Christian slaves to be obedient to their masters, and not to give eyeservice, but to do their work sincerely, as unto Christ. When a Christian honors his authority, God promises his rewards will come from the Lord.

"Knowing that whatever good thing each one does, this he will receive back from the Lord, whether slave or free" (Ephesians 6:8).

In conclusion, James puts it into proper perspective: *"But prove yourselves doers of the word, and not merely hearers who delude themselves"* (James 1:22) and, *"Therefore, to one who knows the right thing to do, and does not do it, to him it is sin"* (James 4:17).

Each believer will have to decide before the Lord what vows he has made and in each case be willing to fulfill them —regardless!

Financial Honesty

Recently a businessman asked me, "Do you think it's possible to be totally honest in our business society?" Since that particular individual was a very committed Christian, I had no doubt that his question was an honest one.

He went on to explain that he didn't purposely cheat anyone, but even when negotiating a sale, the common practice was for the seller to begin at a price higher than desired, knowing that the buyer always started with a price lower than he knew was acceptable. As I considered his question, I realized what he had asked must be a conscious thought on the heart of many sincere Christians: "Can you truly be honest and, if so, at what cost?"

MONEY IS AN INDICATOR

The Lord says in Luke 10:10a, "He who is faithful in a very little thing is faithful also in much." The small thing to which the Lord is referring is money. Naturally, this also includes the pursuit of money.

God has placed us in a physical world and expects us to live in it. Why is that? God could miraculously provide for us on a day-by-day basis if He chose to do so. Why then has He determined to leave us in a materialistic society, subject to the same problems and temptations as those who totally reject His ways? After all, the one who truly seeks to follow God's will will surely suffer at the hands of those who live only to please themselves.

The answer becomes clear in the light of God's Word. In Philippians 2:15, Paul tells us to hold ourselves above this wicked generation so that we can prove ourselves blameless. Thus we become "lights" in a world of darkness. We are placed in this society by God so that He can reveal Himself through us. For this to happen, we must avoid the devices of the accuser and hold to standards of the Lord.

Satan works through guile and selfishness and labels them "shrewdness" and "ingenuity." God calls guile "deceit" and selfishness "greed." "He who winks his eyes does so to devise perverse things" (Proverbs 16:30a). "For where jealousy and selfish ambition exist, there is disorder and every evil thing" (James 3:16).

WHY THE DISHONEST PROSPER

There is little doubt that in the short run a deceitful person will seem to prosper. But it doesn't take long for others to recognize his dishonesty, so he must continually seek out new prospects. Sometimes the deceitful person may gain materially as a result of his craftiness. We must remember that Satan does have limited authority over this earth and can indeed provide riches. The problem with his supply is that it is always accompanied by fear, anxiety, anger, greed, and resentment.

Every Christian must accept God's Word as the standard for doing business. Only the Lord's provision brings with it peace and contentment (Proverbs 10:22; Proverbs 3:4-6). It is also within God's power to grant material blessings to those who truly follow His directions. "Riches and honor are with me, enduring wealth and righteousness" (Proverbs 8:18). But many times God elects to store those riches for distribution in eternity, in which case the rewards are multiplied a thousandfold (Matthew 6:20).

The biggest loss associated with following the worldly path is the loss of God's full blessings. Many Christians fail to experience God's blessing because they conform to the image of the world (Romans 12:2). God declares that if we do not respond correctly in such a trivial thing as money, we will not be entrusted with any greater possessions.

"If therefore you have not been faithful in the use of unrighteous mammon, who will entrust the true riches to you?" (Luke 16:11).

MATERIAL WITNESS

It becomes clear that God has placed us in this materialistic world not only to witness to the unsaved, but also for the purpose of examining our relationship to Him. There can be no clearer reflection of the true value system of a Christian than the way he handles his money and the way others are treated where a profit or loss is concerned.

Can a Christian be honest in our society? He *must* be to experience the fullness of God's power and love. There will be times when it will seem that others take advantage of that honesty. The Lord knew that would happen. *"If anyone wishes to come after Me, let him deny himself, and take up his cross daily, and follow Me"* (Luke 9:23). There is often a price to be paid for following in the path of Christ, but there is also a great reward as a result of doing so.

The Lord told us that a house built upon sand would fall when the storms come, while one built upon the rock would survive. We are in the midst of a materialistic storm today, and every Christian must decide whether to build upon the solid rock of God's Word or the shifting sands of society. The decision to do business by the world's normal standards—guile and deception—is a decision to deny Christ.

"No servant can serve two masters; for either he will hate the one, and love the other, or else he will hold to one, and despise the other. You cannot serve God and mammon" (Luke 16:13).

OBEDIENCE TO GOD

The principle passed down to us throughout the Scripture is: we don't serve God because of what He can do for us; we serve Him because He is God. Job understood this principle when he told his friends, *"Though He slay me, I will hope in him"* (Job 13:15).

Nebuchadnezzar, about to cast Shadrach, Meshach, and Abednego into the furnace because they did not worship the idol he chose, mocked God by saying, *"What god is there who can deliver you out of my hands?"*

They responded, *"If it be so, our God whom we serve is able to deliver us from the furnace of blazing fire; and He will deliver us out of your hand, O king. But even if He does not, let it be known to you, O king, that we are not going to serve your gods or worship the golden image that you have set up"* (Daniel 3:15b, 17-18).

Each Christian must come to the position where God's approval is more important than the world's riches. Then, and only then, will the full measure of God's peace and power be experienced.

"But prove yourselves doers of the word, and not merely hearers who delude themselves" (James 1:22).

Retirement—Is It Scriptural?

The flow of our modern society has changed the way we live. One of the most far-reaching changes is our attitude about retirement. Retirement, to most, means that period of time in our latter years when we can stop work and start enjoying life.

FUTURE ATTITUDES

We like the idea of retirement. After all, we worked hard to get where we are, and we "deserve" to enjoy it. Unfortunately, though many are geared to look forward to retirement, most do not have the means to do so. Therefore, at ages sixty-five to seventy, they are forced to retire and become wards of the state. We see them on the rolls of welfare and Social Security. They require the help of their own children, who are unable or unwilling to help because they are strapped financially by indulgent life-styles.

BENEFITS OF RETIREMENT

Obviously, not all retirement is wrong any more than all borrowing is wrong. It is a matter of degree. The problem is that we seem to do everything to excess today. In some professions, such as athletics, age is a critical factor, and retirement is inevitable. In other professions everyday stress eventually burns a person out. But there are other instances in which retirement is encouraged to attract workers, such as in government-related jobs. Retirement provides at least some benefits to society: (1) it makes room for younger, more aggressive people to be able to progress; (2) the shift to a lesser income at retirement necessitates a mod-erate life-style. Those who don't moderate their life-styles end up back at work; and (3) the goal of retirement creates savings that can be used to help build and create jobs for others.

LIABILITIES OF RETIREMENT

The biggest liability associated with retirement today is the mass notion that everyone should be made to retire. The truth is that the majority of those over sixty-five cannot afford to retire, and we cannot afford for them to retire. But since the idea of retirement has been sold to Americans over the last forty years, we now accept it as normal. It is not normal, either biblically or historically. There are some who can retire and a few who should retire, but most people (particularly Christians) should not consider traditional retirement.

Retirement for Christians should mean freeing time to devote to serving others more fully without the necessity of getting paid for it. If Christian retirees have this motivation in mind while looking forward to "retirement," then the Lord really will find us doing Hs work when He returns.

A second liability is the diversion of funds needed for God's work into retirement plans. Many of those funds will never be used because they far exceed the reasonable amount the retiree will need. Others won't be used because they will be lost or dissipated by inflation long before retirement. The only funds that should ever be allocated for retirement are those left after giving what God has directed and meeting family needs.

BIBLICAL GUIDELINES

Since the Bible is our guide for day-by-day living, it is always necessary to verify what we're doing against that guide. Retirement, as we know it, is found only in one place in God's Word. Numbers 8:25 refers to the retirement of the Levites from the tent of meeting. The Levites were directed not to own land or accumulate riches but to receive their living from the tithes and offerings of God's people. As a reward for their service and obedience, they were retired at age fifty.

Other than that single event the people were not directed to retire. That does not mean they could not retire, but that it was not normal. The normal system of retirement that we see throughout God's Word is a sabbatical. The first sabbatical given was a day of rest each week called the Sabbath. Additionally, the Jew was required to let his land lay idle every seventh year.

Wouldn't it be great to take retirement through sabbaticals? That would mean we would work six years and take the seventh off. That year could be utilized for continued education, missions work, new technology training, or simply to enjoy our families while we are still young.

"Six years you shall sow your field, and six years you shall prune your vineyard and gather in its crop, but during the seventh year the land shall have a sabbath rest, a sabbath to the Lord; you shall not sow your field nor prune your vineyard" (Leviticus 25:3-4).

BALANCE BETWEEN TOO LITTLE AND TOO MUCH

As stated many times before, one of the key principles in God's Word is balance. We seem to be a society of extremes. We borrow, spend, and work excessively during our early years— and then we want to quit altogether. For the vast majority of people, retirement is literally an impossible dream. They spend everything they make on a current basis and will actually save very little toward retirement. Even worse, a majority of sixty-five-year-olds will still owe on their homes for ten years or more. They are still in debt at retirement age and find it impossible to reduce their income needs substantially. For them, retirement will mean near poverty and dependency on the government. It is difficult to imagine that they are following God's direction.

For that group, their imbalance reflects a total lack of planning for the future. Granted, we shouldn't just stop working, but Christians should be wise enough to realize that, as we get older, our ability to maintain our income declines. Savings laid aside and invested wisely at an early age can be used to supplement income needed at an older age.

On the other side are those Christians who have planned too well for retirement. They have enough stored for at least three lifetimes already, and they continue to store even more. They have diverted funds that could be used to feed starving people and to change lives for eternity into a retirement account simply because it is a good "tax shelter."

"And he said, 'This is what I will do; I will tear down my barns and build larger ones, and there I will store all my grain and my goods. And I will say to my soul, "Soul, you have many goods laid up for many years to come; take your ease, eat, drink and be merry." ' But God said to him, 'You fool! This very night your soul is required of you; and now who will own what you have prepared?'" (Luke 12:18-20).

HOW MUCH IS ENOUGH?

Every Christian needs to realistically face some planning questions.

1. *Why should I retire?* You may be forced to retire because of your chosen vocation (such as an airline pilot). It may be company policy to retire at sixty-two or sixty-five. But it may also be that the decision is totally under your control, and you shouldn't retire.

"For by me your days will be multiplied, and years of life will be added to you" (Proverbs 9-11).

2. *What will I do?* You should have a clear-cut picture of your life post-work. How will you spend your time, and how will you keep involved with God's work? Without a doubt, in our society we isolate the elderly from the young. In doing so we subvert God's plan for sharing learned wisdom. Make your plans to include involvement with younger families who need the benefit of your acquired wisdom.

"A gray head is a crown of glory; it is found in the way of righteousness" (Proverbs 16-31).

3. *What if my retirement plan fails?* It really grieves me to see so many of God's people depending on an economic system that is so clearly operating outside of God's rules. It no longer seems to be a question of what we will do *if* the economy fails, but *when*. Most Christians are tied up in intangible assets, which could be gone in a financial crisis. Perhaps the best retirement plan of all is a service skill that others need.

"A prudent man sees evil and hides himself, the naive proceed and pay the penalty" (Proverbs 27:12).

4. *What if I can't retire?* Many Christians simply need to give up the American concept of retirement and acclimate themselves to earning a living for the rest of their lives. That is probably true for the majority of Christians. Therefore, if you fit into this category, you need to plan your career by stages. The first stage would be to work until a given age (fifty to fifty-five) with the goal of being totally debt-free, including on your home. Once your children are grown, you need to seek retraining in a skill area that requires less physical strength—programming, accounting, art, or woodworking. These skills will successfully carry you throughout your lifetime.

Obviously, any plan such as this requires both husband and wife. If the husband is the primary wage earner, then enough life insurance must be maintained to adequately provide for the wife.

"By wisdom a house is built, and by understanding it is established; and by knowledge the rooms are filled with all precious and pleasant riches" (Proverbs 24:3-4).

HOW TO USE YOUR RETIREMENT PLAN

Many retirement plans are so restrictive that you have little or no control over the use of the funds. That would include IRAs, company retirement, and Social Security. However, many plans allow a reasonable amount of self-direction. That is particularly true of "vested" retirement plans, such as Keogh and private pension plans. As much as possible, these funds should be invested in economic growth areas, such as land, houses, and businesses.

Business Ethics

Perhaps nothing reflects the decline of our society more than the state of current business ethics. It is not at all uncommon to read about major companies paying bribes to government officials or providing large kickbacks to company purchasing agents.

On a smaller scale, many sales companies offer incentives to buyers from other businesses in the form of coupons for merchandise, vacations, cash, or Christmas gifts. These are available on a voluntary basis in spite of the fact that nearly every company has established rules against their purchasing agents accepting such items.

"A wicked man receives a bribe from the bosom to pervert the ways of justice" (Proverbs 17:23).

THE COST OF COMPROMISE

There is a price to be paid for every compromise, especially to God's Word. That price is the loss of peace from God. Compromise at any level results in further compromise until finally the conscience is seared, and right and wrong are no longer distinguishable. *"And just as they did not see fit to acknowledge God any longer, God gave them over to a depraved mind, to do those things which are not proper"* (Romans 1:28). An employee who will pad his expense account and rationalize it will eventually pad his income and rationalize that as well.

"Bread obtained by falsehood is sweet to a man, but afterward his mouth will be filled with gravel" (Proverbs 20:17).

Fortunately, nobody is worthy before God. Our greatest advantage is the fact that God doesn't have much talent to work with down here. He will restore anyone who will acknowledge his sin and return to His way. If God commanded us to forgive each other seven times a day (Luke 17:4), how much more will He forgive us?

"If we confess our sins, He is faithful and righteous to forgive us our sins and to cleanse us from all unrighteousness" (1 John 1:9).

BECOMING A LIGHT

In our society, most people are looking for guidance and unwavering commitment to principles. Unfortunately, when these can't be found, many people fall dupe to the humanist's argument that "values are established by society." The end result of this lie can be seen in the abuses of our day—drugs used to escape reality, sexual immorality, a high rate of divorce—and ultimately in the collapse of society itself. Why do people turn to enslavement through a form of government like Communism? It is because it offers an uncompromising set of principles that seem to represent stability.

In reality, only Christ assures both stability and love. It is the responsibility of every believer to adhere uncompromisingly to the set of values presented in God's Word. These values encompass the business as well as the personal life. A Christian must decide either to follow Christ or to follow Satan; there is no middle road. A business will be dedicated to the furtherance of either God's kingdom or Satan's. If the primary purpose of a Christian in business is to be a success and make money, then God's way is *not* for him. Christ promised that following His way would cost something.

"And He was saying to them all, 'If anyone wishes to come after Me, let him deny himself, and take up his cross daily, and follow Me'" (Luke 9:23).

Certainly taking a stand for Christ won't always be admired, because it will cause a great deal of discomfort to those who know of Him but don't serve Him. Christ Himself said He came not to bring peace but division (Matthew 10:34). That is not a division based on pride, position, or anger, but on principle. The liars and the thieves will cheat those who obey godly principles, and it is quite possible that the ways of the wicked will cause them to prosper. A Christian must remember that all that is seen is not all that there is.

"The wicked earns deceptive wages, but he who sows righteousness gets a true reward" (Proverbs 11:18).

BUSINESS GOALS

The number-one goal of a Christian businessman must be to share Christ with others. The business is merely a tool to reach people who may never be reached otherwise. The method will vary according to the business and number of employees. One businessman may choose to call the employees in and give them his testimony. Another may use outside speakers in a weekly devotional.

The next step should be a plan for regular fellowship through a company devotional time that employees are invited, but not pressured, to attend. The important principle is to take a stand and present Christ's message to the lost and the wandering (Colossians 1:28). Once a plan has been implemented for sharing with employees, the next step is to share the message with suppliers and customers. Obviously a direct approach is not always possible, so other methods, such as written materials, may be utilized.

In addition to the spiritual goals established, a company should have some straightforward business goals. If the owner's goals are merely to make a lot of money, build a lot of buildings, and leave it all to their children, how are they different from those of non-Christians?

1. *Pay a fair wage.* Many Christian employers are guilty of paying some employees less than a livable wage. To hire someone at such a low wage is in direct violation of the principle of fairness. *"You shall not oppress a hired servant who is poor and needy, whether he is one of your countrymen or one of your aliens who is in your land in your towns"* (Deuteronomy 24:14).

To pay less than is reasonably needed to live places the employee in a position of not being able to provide for his family. If a job will not support a livable wage for a man with a family, then do not hire those who have families, for doing so will result in short-term, disgruntled employees.

2. *Build a good product.* "A good name *is to be more desired than great riches, favor is better than silver and gold"*(Proverbs 22:1). A company is known by the quality of its products or service. What a great witness it would be if every time a customer encountered a Christian-run company what was remembered was the quality.

3. *Make a fair profit.* It is an interesting observation that the primary thing that holds prices in line even for Chris-

tian-run companies is competition. Given a situation where little or no competition exists, most Christian businessmen will escalate prices until buyer demand drops off. Such pricing sounds like good business, but it is scriptural? *"Better is a little with righteousness than great income with injustice"* (Proverbs 16:8). Should a Christian in business, whether offering a factory product or a doctor's services, charge what the traffic will bear? Wouldn't it be a testimony to the Lord and His people if Christians established prices and fees on the basis of what is fair both for them and their customers?

4. *Be a godly leader.* *"Where there is no guidance, the people fall, but in abundance of counselors there is victory"* (Proverbs 11:14). Above all else, a Christian employer should be a godly leader. That means a life free from sin and corruption. Too often Christians are guilty of hypocrisy by taking a stand outside the business environment but not living it inside the company.

PURPOSE OF BUSINESS

Does that mean, then, that Christians are supposed to be losers and never be successful? Obviously not, but priorities must be established outside of what the world calls success. Christ warned us that a man could gain the entire world and forfeit his soul in the pursuit of it. The purpose of a Christian in business is the same as any other Christian—to glorify God and lead others to Christ.

A business is nothing more than a tool to accomplish God's work. Making money and acquiring success are by-products of putting God first (Matthew 6:33). Both employees and employers need to take a stand based on God's Word and become lights to their unsaved

counterparts. Will such a stand cost business? Almost beyond a doubt, it will initially. For some employees it may well cost them their jobs, if those jobs include bribes and other types of deceit. However, God's Word promises that He owns everything and that He delights in helping those who completely sell out to Him.

"For the eyes of the Lord move to and fro throughout the earth that He may strongly support those whose heart is completely His" (2 Chronicles 16:9).

COST OF COMMITMENT

It is not necessary to speak of Christ with everyone you meet in order to serve the Lord. Obviously there are situations in which sharing is not possible or productive. However, being a"silent witness" is a rationalization for being no witness at all. If Christ is first in someone's life, he will share Him with others. Good wisdom will determine the method; the Holy Spirit will provide the opportunity. For employees who are restricted by employer rules, it may mean using dinners or other opportunities outside of business hours. For employers it means using every available opportunity to glorify Christ in words and in actions, both to employees and to customers.

I recall a story that a Christian businessman told me about one of his key employees. That employee had secretly been praying for God to touch him and heal him of a desire for other women. The employee suffered a divorce and an emotional breakdown that led him from one counselor to another and ultimately to an attempt at suicide. One day, after nearly three years of depression, he came in elated to announce that he had found Christ as his Savior and had turned his life over to Him. The president congrat-

145

ulated him and shared that he also was a Christian and had been praying for him. To this, he exclaimed, "Why didn't you tell me where you got your strength and peace? I just thought it was because you owned the company."

Paying a Fair Wage

I once asked a group of Christian employers, "How much should a Christian employer pay employees?" The answer ranged from minimum wage, as a legal requirement, to a large bonus for special employees. But not a single answer was confirmed on the basis of our source of truth—God's Word. Those Christian employers weren't just the run-of-the-mill Christians, either. They were mostly dedicated men and women seeking to do God's will as well as they knew it.

The difficulty is that in our generation, and in many previous generations, we have been conformed to the image of our world. In fact, in most instances we are indistinguishable in our daily activities. Our words may be different, but our faith is not always reflected through our works. I find that many Christian employers take an identical approach toward employee wages as do most non-Christian employers.

BUSINESS CYCLES

Anyone who has read much business history recognizes that management attitudes go in cycles. When business is depressed and jobs are few, the managers and owners call the shots, and labor really can't do much about it. During those times wages are often cut, benefits are cut, and most new employees are recruited at reduced wages. Then the cycle reverses, business gets very good, trained labor is in short supply, and wages are forced up by organized labor unions.

Prior to the twentieth century, the cycles affected only a relatively few industries. Today, with our mass media, they develop quickly and in virtually every area of business. What we have developed is a traditional adversary relationship between owners and workers, where each tries to exploit the other whenever possible.

THE PRINCIPLES OF FAIR PAY

I believe the overwhelming principle about paying employees according to God's Word is fairness, but *not* fairness according to the world's standards. God is not concerned about what others think is fair, but what He thinks is fair. If you were to review all the passages dealing with paying employees and boil them down to a simple principle, I believe you would be left with two options regarding pay. You must either pay someone what he needs to live on or only hire those who can live on what you're able to pay. Once someone is in the employment of a Christian, we are obligated to meet his basic needs to the limit of our ability to do so.

"You shall not oppress a hired servant who is poor and needy, whether he is one of your countrymen or one of your aliens who is in your land in your towns" (Deuteronomy 24:14).

Quite obviously, then, each employee's need level must be determined. Arriving at an actual dollar amount is difficult, but I have found some fundamental steps helpful. First, survey your employees to determine if they feel that they are making enough to live on. Then, have an experienced, qualified financial counselor work with them to develop a minimum family budget. Review that budget yourself, and simply put yourself

147

in the employee's position to see if you could live on it.

WHAT CAN YOU PAY?

Obviously, some businesses do so poorly that paying adequate salaries is not always possible. But if that situation continues over an extended period of time, there has to be a doubt about the wisdom of continuing the operation. If God can direct by supplying, He can also direct by withholding. Perhaps the most obvious examples of this are some Christian organizations, most notable in recent years, Christian schools. Many of them pay so poorly (and seldom) that almost no one but the administration can live above the poverty level. If God has truly directed this effort, then adequate salaries should be the norm.

More often than not, the failure of most businesses to pay adequate salaries at the lowest levels is really one of choice rather than necessity. If you look at the assets of the company, the salaries of management, and particularly the indulgences of the owners, most often there is more than enough for the lowest paid employees to be paid fairly. Secular business philosophy teaches that "to the victor belongs the spoils." That translates into a trait the Bible calls selfishness.

"He who shuts his ear to the cry of the poor will also cry himself and not be answered" (Proverbs 21:13).

It is important for a Christian employer to review every attitude in the light of God's Word to determine if it meets God's minimum. It would be very difficult to stand before a group of employees and testify that you are a Christian and want to operate your business by Christian principles while many of them know that they can't meet even the basic needs of their families. Of course, you are not responsible if their financial problems are caused by their own indulgences.

WHOSE NEEDS COME FIRST?

A commonly practiced but seldom expressed principle of management today is to do what you have to do to keep the employees pacified. In other words, respond according to the pressure they can exert. Thus, most wage negotiations become battles between adversaries. That has never been part of God's direction for meeting needs and building businesses. And that is exactly why we are now studying Japanese management to figure out why they are more productive. Their success isn't really very difficult to understand—they simply built a management system around a biblical principle known as caring.

"Do nothing from selfishness or empty conceit, but with humility of mind let each of you regard one another as more important than himself; do not merely look out for your own personal interests, but also for the interests of others" (Philippians 2:3-4).

Since the Japanese don't have business management schools to teach that principle, it must be applied at the root level, face to face. They don't allow a "we against them" attitude in management. Instead, each employee shares in the financial success of the company.

If Christianity simply practiced what God's Word teaches on this subject, the world would be studying our management techniques, because we would have contented employees sharing in the most profitable businesses in the world. Instead, we are virtually nonidentifiable from the world.

SCRIPTURAL WARNING

God's Word offers some sober counsel to believers who fit into the worldly mold of indulging while others in their care suffer. Deuteronomy 17 describes the kind of leader God desires for His people. The same characteristics would apply to a leader today.

"Moreover, he shall not multiply horses for himself. . . . Neither shall he multiply wives for himself, lest his heart turn away; nor shall he greatly increase silver and gold for himself" (Deuteronomy 17:16-17).

James amplifies this and describes those who would act selfishly in the blunt language of a prophet. *"Come now, you rich, weep and howl for your miseries which are coming upon you"* (James 5:1). *"Behold, the pay of the laborers who mowed your fields, and which has been withheld by you, cries out against you; and the outcry of those who did the harvesting has reached the ears of the Lord of Sabaoth. You have lived luxuriously on the earth and led a life of wanton pleasure; you have fattened your hearts in a day of slaughter"* (James 5:4-5).

BALANCE

God's Word does not suggest that a Christian employer has to pay the highest wages around and certainly not to the detriment of his business. What is required is that at least minimum needs are met and that we are not cheating our workers of their fair wages. No employer will lose by following God's principles for paying people. What you lose in current cash you make up for in long term stability. However, too much of a good principle can often backfire. If you pay everyone the maximum amount possible and don't lay aside any surplus funds, then economic cycles will play havoc with the business.

Every phase of a Christian's business must mesh together, and a part of that is anticipating difficulties. We live in a physical world and are subject to natural forces as well. It does not mean God can't or won't intercede on our behalf—He can and often does. But when you set out in a leaky boat, you may get wet. *"There is precious treasure and oil in the dwelling of the wise, but a foolish man swallows it up"* (Proverbs 21:20). Remember that the better the business does, the better everyone does.

SOWING AND REAPING

"Do not be deceived, God is not mocked; for whatever a man sows, this he will also reap" (Galatians 6:7).

The principle of sowing and reaping is usually directly applicable to dealing with other people, and since employees are other people, it applies to them as well. When an employer is able to exercise total control because of prevailing economic circumstances, there is an opportunity to demonstrate with actions what words can never do. Literally, you are sowing attitudes into the lives of others. They will often take root, grow, and return to you. So, if you sow love and caring, you reap the same. If you sow indifference and contempt, you'll reap that also.

LET US BE DOERS

Quite often, Christian business leaders fall short in the "doing" end of God's Word. I have observed that one reason many Christian business owners travel to give their personal testimony is that they have a rather cool reception at home. Obviously, you can't please everyone.

149

Whatever you pay, there will be those who don't think it's enough or who will resent the fact that someone else makes more. But the principle is very clear—you don't have to please them. Just please God, and you'll do fine.

To Sue or Not to Sue

The question of lawsuits comes up frequently in our business seminars, particularly during a recession time when a lot of people don't pay their bills. A study of this principle turns out to be a study on rights and motives.

Does a Christian have a right to sue another person? Obviously, lawsuits are a common matter today. The reasons range from emotional distress caused by a neighbor's barking dog to legitimate losses caused by faulty products or personal injuries suffered in an accident. Many lawsuits are simply blatant fraud for the purpose of personal profit. Certainly for Christians, those kinds of lawsuits must be regarded the same as stealing.

But what about the right to justifiable legal remedy? How should a believer respond when cheated by another individual or corporation? Does it make a difference whether or not the offender is a Christian? What if a Christian is sued? Is countersuit a justifiable defense? Obviously, these are questions that can only be answered in the light of God's Word.

WHAT IS A LAWSUIT?

The purpose of a lawsuit is to provide someone who has suffered a loss at the hands of another party a legal means to recover the property or other damages from the offender. In practicality, it is one person's accusing another of an offense and requesting that a judge or jury make a decision about guilt or innocence and compensation.

Suing is certainly not a new concept. It is apparent from Paul's writing in 1 Corinthians 6 that lawsuits were common place in the first century. Unfortunately, suing today has become a first, rather than a last, recourse. As Christians, we must be able to discern what our rights are scripturally.

PERSONAL LOSS

Many lawsuits are initiated because of personal loss suffered due to the negligence or deceit of another. A common example is defective merchandise. Most department stores have a return policy that helps avoid such conflicts, but what about those that do not? Do you have the right, as a Christian, to pursue such matters into the secular courts?

Since a corporation is a legal entity established to protect the owners, I can find no scriptural basis for not bringing suit against one for legitimate losses. A corporation is a court-established entity that has no humanity and thus may be compelled by law to accept its legal responsibilities. In the case of an insurance company, that is particularly evident. The purpose of an insurance company is to provide financial remedy for losses. Recourse for inequitable settlement rests in the law. In reality, the company has contractually bound itself to compensating a liability of a client.

That certainly does not imply that God cannot or will not change the actions of corporate officers—only that a corporation has no personal rights in scriptural terms. That is not to say that a Christian should sue a corporation. God may well convict someone to give up the right to sue for several reasons, not the least of which is to have a witness in the lives of the principals involved. Also, God wants us to learn the principle of giving up our rights, and this may be an exercise in yielding a right. The guideline in regard to a suit against a corporation has to be twofold: motive and personal conviction. We must be certain about both; and if we have any doubt, we should stop.

PERSONAL LAWSUITS

What are our rights and options when we have a legitimate case against another individual for a loss? First, let's address the best defined situation—one Christian against another. The principle covering this situation is found in 1 Corinthians 6. We are directed to take our case before true believers when a brother is involved.

"Does any one of you, when he has a case against his neighbor, dare to go to law before the saints?" (1 Corinthians 6:1).

The recourse provided when two Christians are involved is outlined in Matthew 18. The principle is simple: We are to take any offense directly to another believer. First, we are to see him alone, then with a witness, if necessary, and ultimately, we are to take him before the church. The purpose in every instance is for restoration in the faith, not collection. That procedure, if taken seriously, would certainly serve as a testimony to the unsaved. All too often, however, the witness is a negative one—first, because Christians ignore the admonition not to sue one another; and second, because the unsaved see our motives as self-centered. It is clearly a matter of giving up rights; something we would rather not do.

"Actually, then, it is already a defeat for you, that you have lawsuits with one another. Why not rather be wronged? Why not rather be defrauded?" (1 Corinthians 6:7).

I would like to be able to tell you that by giving up this right to sue, God will intervene to recover the material assets lost, but no such promise is made in God's Word. God may choose to do so—but He may also choose not to.

"And someone in the crowd said to Him, 'Teacher, tell my brother to divide the family inheritance with me.' But He said to him, 'Man, who appointed Me a judge or arbiter over you?'" (Luke 12:13-14).

SUING NONBELIEVERS

Since the direct implication of 1 Corinthians 6 is of one believer's suing another, what about suing nonbelievers? There are no direct references to suing a nonbeliever, but there are some very revealing indirect references.

It is important to bear in mind that God's Word deals much more with our attitudes than with our actions. Many people have the right actions but the wrong attitudes. The Pharisees had many of the right actions but the wrong attitudes. When a Christian has the attitude towards others that God requires, most actions will change toward them.

"Bearing with one another, and forgiving each other, whoever has a complaint against anyone; just as the Lord forgave you, so also should you" (Colossians 3:13).

Above all, God's Word teaches us to surrender our rights, even to the unbeliever. That means literally to put others first, even when they are wrong.

"Whoever hits you on the cheek, offer him the other also; and whoever takes away your coat, do not withhold your shirt from him either. Give to everyone who asks of you, and whoever takes away what is yours, do not demand it back" (Luke 6:29-30).

That attitude can be very costly when you live in a society of opportunists. The result may be personal loss. A Christian friend recently told me of an instance where someone cancelled a contract with him and flatly told him, "I know you won't sue me because you're a Christian." Once you've taken a stand for the Lord, it may well cost you materially. Not every believer is willing or ready to live by God's highest standard. But when the decision is solely ours and the loss is solely ours, the question becomes, "Do we really believe it all belongs to God?" Most human counsel will run contrary to God's perfect will. The fairness of the situation is of primary importance to the Lord.

ALLOWABLE DEFENSE?

A Christian asked about his scriptural right to defend himself when accused by someone else. His particular case involved a dispute over a real estate fee that the accuser said was due him. Everyone involved in the sale (broker, buyer, attorney) unanimously agreed that the claim was false. In fact, it was found that this individual had used the same ruse several times before. Many times the fee was paid just to avoid the inconvenience of a court battle. The question he asked was, "Can I and should I defend myself against an unjust claim?"

I believe the answer can be found in Paul's defense against unjust claims throughout the book of Acts (16:37; 22:25; 25:11). Paul did not attack his accusers, nor did he attempt to extract any compensation from them. But he did vigorously defend himself against their claims, several times even reciting Roman law applicable to his case. As long as our motives are right and we are not seeking retribution, we can, and often should, defend the rightness of our actions. In this particular case, the claim was dropped the day the case was to go to court. It was clear that the accuser knew he would lose.

RECOURSE FOR A CRIME

Although a believer is instructed not to sue another for personal loss, the same is not true for criminal action. By law a criminal act is committed against the whole of society. A Christian who has knowledge of a crime is obligated to report that crime and allow the law to respond. The only exception would be when the law is in conflict with God's Word. As Peter stated in Acts 5:29, *"We must obey God rather than men."* It may also be necessary to testify in court as a witness.

That does not relieve our responsibility to forgive the offender. Rather, it is our responsibility to obey the authority established by God. *"Let every person be in subjection to the governing authorities. For there is no authority except from God, and those which exist are established by God"* (Romans 13:1).

Work as unto the Lord

"**W**hatever you do, do your work heartily, as for the Lord rather than for men; knowing that from the Lord you will receive the reward of inheritance. It is the Lord Christ whom you serve" (Colossians 3:23-24).

In addition to supplying our physical needs, work plays a very important role in our spiritual lives. It provides the opportunity to put into practice spiritual principles that would otherwise be mere academics. A Christian can study every passage in the Bible dealing with serving others and read every biography of those who were noted servants, such as George Mueller, and still not really understand the principle of surrendering rights.

On the job, however, the opportunity to yield our rights presents itself every day. The way we do our work provides the best exterior reflection of our commitment to serve the Lord in a real, physical way. It doesn't matter whether that work is in the home, on an assembly line, or in a corporate office. Our true Christian beliefs will be reflected more clearly there than in any other environment outside the immediate family relationships.

The chain of relationships from family to work is so intertwined that the apostle Paul listed them as a series in Colossians 3—first, husband-wife relationships (vv. 18-19);second, parent-children relationships (vv. 20-21); and third, authority-work relationships (vv. 22-23). Paul knew that unless a Christian had all of those managed properly, his life could not manifest joy, peace, or contentment. A great deal of teaching is available now on the first two areas—marriage and children. However, little has been written on an equally large area of difficulty—work.

CURRENT ATTITUDES

For too many Christians, work is a necessary evil, while for others it is an area of "worship." Obviously, both are extremes and represent a spiritual imbalance. Many Christians view their jobs with drudgery. Literally, jobs are just a means to earn money so that they can enjoy themselves. They are dissatisfied with their vocation, disgruntled on the job, and resentful of others' success. A by-product of all this mental anxiety is quite often fatigue on the job and restlessness at home. To compensate, they fill their lives with endless outside activities. For nonbelievers, these are usually hunting, fishing, boating, skiing, and so on. For the Christian, they may be church activities and civic functions. None of these activities is bad in itself; in fact, they are quite good unless the activities are a substitute for the lack of fulfillment at work.

Somehow Christians have been duped into believing that work is a secular activity and therefore one shouldn't expect to feel spiritual about a job. That attitude destroys our greatest area of outreach and witness. Few Christians who view their work as a chore have much of a witness on or off the job.

Proverbs 22:29 says, "*Do you see a man skilled in his work? He will stand before kings; he will not stand before obscure men.*"

RESENTMENT

It is amazing how clearly spiritual problems are reflected on the job. I once taught at a company meeting, and afterward one of the employees cornered me to let me know how oppressed he was. It

154

seemed that everyone else received bigger raises and better promotions, but he always did the most work. He went on and on until I told him I had to go. On the way out, the owner told me he believed the man could be a key employee, but he always had his feelings hurt about decisions even remotely affecting him, and he was resentful of anyone else's recognition. It was obvious that he had a spiritual problem that was being reflected in a physical way.

Such problems are not unique to industry alone. The leader of a large Christian organization once related that he had less trouble with employees when he was in business than he did in the ministry. He said, "I once naively thought that I could deal with Christian staff differently. On the contrary, in great part they see the other staff members as competitors, and if I do something extra for one, many of the others resent it." It would seem that we failed to teach Christians that the job is an extension of their walk with the Lord, not isolated from it.

BIBLICAL ADMONITION

It is fortunate for all of us that God's Word is both simple and complete. No subject affecting our lives is left to our own imagination. Those who are resentful about the success of others, whose feelings are hurt because of the lack of recognition, or who use a job as their alter egos all suffer from the same spiritual malady—they are in service to men instead of God. Unfortunately, men will always fail; fortunately, God never will. If a Christian approaches a job with the attitude that some person must recognize him as the best, there will almost always be disappointment, because the first time the boss forgets to show appreciation, resentment creeps in.

PRAISE OF MEN

To get the praise of men is not difficult in business. Just do what they want, when they want it, and how they want it. The trick is guessing what, when, and how. One bad guess, and the praise is gone. It might require dropping a bomb on your coworkers from time to time, because if you're to get the praise of men, you certainly can't allow someone else to get it.

"And He said to them, 'You are those who justify yourselves in the sight of men, but God knows your hearts; for that which is highly esteemed among men is detestable in the sight of God'" (Luke 16:15).

It is interesting to note that those workers whom bosses praise most highly are usually the ones who require the least praise. It takes a lot of energy to remember to praise someone for everything he does right. What a joy it is when a boss finds a quiet, efficient, self-starter who continually looks after the interest of other employees. Those qualities are so rare that the boss is torn between promoting that person and keeping him at the present job because it is so easy to get the work done.

I have found a common characteristic in Christians who don't rely on praise from men: they take literally the principle of work in Colossians 2:23-24. *"Whatever you do, do your work heartily, as for the Lord rather than for men; knowing that from the Lord you will receive the reward of the inheritance. It is the Lord Christ whom you serve."*

The key is that they look to the Lord for their rewards and in doing so find that His standards of conduct are so much higher than men's that they surpass any boss's expectations. It is not that they don't want continual praise from men, but that they don't need it.

155

HOW TO BREAK THE TRAP

1. *Be honest.* The first step is to confess to God that any attitude of resentment, ego, pride, or desire for praise is unacceptable and needs to be corrected. First John 1:9 says, *"If we confess our sins, He is faithful and righteous to forgive us our sins and to cleanse us from all unrighteousness."*

2. *Admit openly.* The next step is to seek the forgiveness of those who may have been offended or hurt. Acknowledge this as a personal weakness and ask their help in detecting and correcting it in the future. Galatians 6:2-3 says, *"Bear one another's burdens, and thus fulfill the law of Christ. For if anyone thinks he is something when he is nothing, he deceives himself."*

A word of caution is necessary here. Do not expect everyone to appreciate or understand your actions. Remember that you serve Christ, not men. It is for your relationship to Him that you need to correct the problem . That is equally true of a housewife whose husband and children seemingly never "appreciate" her. Correct your attitudes and actions, and leave the results to God.

3. *Take correct action.* Satan's number-one weapon is defeat, but God's number-one promise is victory. When you find that the original problems have returned, never allow yourself to dwell on them. Confess them again, publicly if necessary. Many times a little ego deflation is necessary to make a commitment firm. That will also require that you forgive any offense that someone else commits against you.

Colossians 3:13 says, *"Bearing with one another, and forgiving each other, whoever has a complaint against any one; just as the Lord forgave you, so also should you."*

4. *Spiritual renewal.* Since the problems are spiritual, the solution must be spiritual also. The only source of spiritual renewal is the Holy Spirit. Examine your daily spiritual life honestly. Do you spend time regularly in prayer and the study of God's Word? Without regular spiritual food, even the most determined Christian will develop spiritual anemia. Group prayer, conferences, and church are not substitutes for a personal relationship with God. If Christ needed to withdraw and be alone with God, we must also.

Romans 12:2 says, *"And do not be conformed to this world, but be transformed by the renewing of your mind, that you may prove what the will of God is, that which is good and acceptable and perfect."*

Multi-Level Sales Programs

The subject of multi-level sales is an emotional subject to many. There have been good and bad effects on the lives of people who engage in this fastest growing area of consumer sales.

WHAT IS A MULTI-LEVEL SALES PROGRAM?

In reality, every product is sold by a multi-level system. The manufacturer marks it up and sells it to a retailer who marks it up again and sells it to a customer. This is a delivery system that has proved very effective over the centuries.

The multi-level plan we will discuss is different in two ways: First, the products are usually sold through part-time sales people who sell primarily to personal acquaintances and friends; and second, there are several levels of distributors, each making a percentage on the sales of those under his authority. In most programs, distributors are encouraged to recruit others to sell for them, thus expanding their sales volume and income.

Many multi-level companies have grown from no sales to billions in less than a year. Usually the end price is higher than a similar product in a retail store because of the markups at the various levels of distribution. Consequently, the incentive to buy must be greater. That incentive is created in two ways: First, most sales are made by direct contact through referral—friends and family first. Second, the buyers of the product are recruited to sell it and thus make extra money themselves.

ASSETS AND LIABILITIES

In counseling Christians involved with many of these multi-level sales programs, I have found both assets and liabilities within them. Before looking at the scriptural principles relating to them, it would be helpful to look at some assets and liabilities.

Part-time employment. Most of these plans provide the opportunity for part-time income without working at an office. Thus, most are oriented toward wives and mothers who can work out of their homes. That lowers their overhead costs and, in general, allows them to choose their own hours.

Small investment. A second asset is that most programs require very little capital investment to get started—usually under $50.

The liabilities are generally related to priorities rather than products. Quite often, what started out to be a part-time job ends up as an all-consuming passion to sell more products or recruit more prospects. After a while, everybody is viewed as a prospect, and every social activity as a sales platform. When a particular program is approaching its zenith in an area, Christians are stepping all over each other to recruit new salespeople and move to the next level in the company. A lot of otherwise well-meaning Christians have severely damaged their credibility and witness by becoming known as "Mr. and Mrs. Multi-level" in their community.

WHY GET INVOLVED?

There are many reasons why a Christian would be attracted to a multi-level program. Some are good and acceptable, while others are purely destructive. Perhaps the most destructive motive is the most common—get-rich-quick. Many multi-level plans (called pyramids) stage high-pitched emotional meetings that insinuate if you're content where you are financially, you're lazy and have failed God. Interestingly enough, almost all such promotions are aimed at the Christian community and receive an acceptance there.Why? Because many Christians are trusting and gullible with regard to anything having a spiritual ring to it.

Another reason many Christians get involved with these hyped-up programs is purely fad. Christ described us quite accurately as sheep, and a lot of people follow wherever somebody is leading. *"The naive believes everything, but the prudent man considers his steps"* (Proverbs 14:15).

Still others get involved with multi-level sales because of a need for money. My caution to these people is always to be patient in building a product sales organization. Be sure the product is not just a passing fad, and be sure it's meeting a genuine need for the ultimate user. *"Prepare your work outside, and make it ready for yourself in the field; afterwards, then, build your house"* (Proverbs 24:27).

Last, many Christians get involved in multi-level programs out of a genuine desire to help other people. Several Christians I know check out various companies and products to screen out the deceptive ones. They stock products from the best and then help others who need more income by putting them into business. The real test of their motives can be found in the fact that they themselves refuse to profit from their investment in other people. *"The righteous is concerned for the*

rights of the poor, the wicked does not understand such concern" (Proverbs 29:7).

THE TRUE TEST OF ATTITUDE

Before getting involved with any kind of public-oriented program, it's necessary for a Christian to test his motive. Then it's necessary to retest that motive periodically to be sure that simple greed has not taken control. Otherwise, everyone becomes a prospect. If most Christians would approach evangelism with the same zeal with which they approach product sales, we would saturate our communities with God's Word.

Anytime Christians look upon others as a source of revenue rather than service, they are caught in Satan's most common trap—greed. *"Do nothing from selfishness or empty conceit, but with humility of mind let each of you regard one another as more important than himself"* (Philippians 2:3). Many young Christians who were hungry for fellowship have been hurt immeasurably by other Christians who deceptively asked them over for an evening, only to attempt to recruit them to sell their product line.

Even more devastating are those who use the church environment to prospect. They have violated a God-given trust. A couple I was counseling related that they visited a church in their community and were asked twice that day by members of the church if they used a particular company's products. They responded that they didn't, and shortly thereafter received three visits from members of the church to sign them up. Be assured that they sought out another fellowship immediately.

"A brother offended is harder to be won than a strong city" (Proverbs 18:19a).

Anything that we do, as Christians, must be approached with an attitude of service to others. That requires more than lip service, where a Christian rationalizes constant prospecting by saying that it's ultimately for *their* good.

God wants us to be unusually astute in the things of God and innocent in the guiles of the world. The only way to consistently test our motives is always to consider others first. Every new recruit that a Christian acquires should be thoroughly apprised of the benefits and liabilities of direct product sales. Also a Christian must adopt a nonaggressive sales attitude when there might be even the slightest motivation to prospect from a fellow believer. Since God really is the Creator of the universe, He knows what our needs and their needs are. If He can hang the stars in the sky, He can surely build an effective sales organization without any guile on our part.

"For we are not like many, peddling the word of God, but as from sincerity, but as from God, we speak in Christ in the sight of God" (2 Corinthians 2:17).

KNOW GOD'S PLAN FOR YOU

Selling products door-to-door or friend-to-friend is not for most people. It requires two basic ingredients in order to be successful: first, service to God; and second, service to others. That's the same plan to be successful in any field. If someone is into multi-level sales just for money, ego, pride, or greed, then there will never be enough. *"He who loves money will not be satisfied with money, nor he who loves abundance with its income. This too is vanity"* (Ecclesiastes 5:10).

A Christian must know God's individual plan for his life. Most Christians don't know what God's plan for them is and consequently get led into many schemes that disrupt their lives.

BE HONEST

In summary, I would say that the concept of multi-level direct sales is not wrong, but quite often its practices are. Anytime a Christian must trick another person into listening to a sales pitch while promising fellowship, it is wrong. Anytime a Christian is more interested in selling a product than in ministering to someone else's needs, that person is in service to money and not to God.

Each believer must test his own attitudes before the Lord. One Christian can be involved in a multi-sales program serving God and convincing others about Jesus Christ, while another is acting greedily and selfishly, storing up wrath for the day when even our attitudes will be revealed.

"Set your mind on the things above, not on the things that are on earth. . . . Do not lie to one another, since you laid aside the old self with its evil practices" (Colossians 3:2, 9).

How to Identify Business Bondage

Financial bondage applies to more than just indebtedness. Certainly those who owe more than they can pay are in bondage. But those who have a large surplus and live in fear or pride are also in bondage. Literally, financial bondage is anything material that interferes with our relationship with God. Thus, the individual who has a surplus of $100,000 a year to invest, but spends all of his waking time worrying about how to multiply it and protect it, is in as much bondage scripturally as someone else who can't pay his credit card bills.

The key to whether or not someone lives in bondage is one's attitude. We are servants of the living God, and when material things bind us, we cannot fulfill our function.

"So that you may walk in a manner worthy of the Lord, to please Him in all respects, bearing fruit in every good work and increasing in the knowledge of God" (Colossians 1:10).

All of this is to point out that just as financial bondage does not apply merely to debt, neither does business bondage apply only to failure. A Christian whose business involvement pre-empts God's greater plan for his life is in bondage. And it really doesn't matter that the efforts are materially successful or that large sums are given to God's work. God has never been impressed by our worldly successes. What He wants is our obedience to His will for our lives.

"No one can serve two masters; for either he will hate the one and love the other, or he will hold to one and despise the other. You cannot serve God and mammon" (Matthew 6:24).

SYMPTOM 1: OVERCOMMITMENT TO WORK OR SUCCESS

"It is vain for you to rise up early, to retire late, to eat the bread of painful labors; for He gives to His beloved even in his sleep" (Psalm 127:2).

Overcommitment is a term that cannot be defined in hours and minutes. One person can work ten hours and still maintain the correct priorities, whereas another may work ten hours on the job physically and another ten mentally even while at home. Overcommitment to business is usually a sign of fear, specifically the fear of failure. Most times a Christian will rationalize an overcommitment because "it's for my family."However, when put to a vote, most wives and children would decide otherwise.

Perhaps the most graphic consequence of that particular symptom is the swing toward liberalism in our young people. An overcommitted parent can supply things to his children but not direction and certainly not balance.

SYMPTOM 2: AN AIR OF SUPERIORITY

"Instruct those who are rich in this present world not to be conceited or to fix their hope on the uncertainty of riches, but on God, who richly supplies us with all things to enjoy" (1 Timothy 6:17).

Any of at least a hundred scriptural references could be used to demonstrate God's view of our human tendency to elevate people because of their worldly success. It is even worse when a Christian begins to adopt an air of superiority because of his stewardship over some of

God's resources. There is no greater deterrent to a consistent walk with the Lord than false pride and self-elevation. Unfortunately, there is a very common tendency for those in management or ownership to assume these characteristics or symptoms.

Usually, an air of superiority begins with the internal attitude that says, "I started this business; I can do what I want to with it," or it can take a more directed course toward people, especially those who are hourly employees. A Christian executive who establishes a social barrier between himself and assembly workers or truck drivers will find that a spiritual barrier exists as well. But that means the Christian executive is in bondage—the bondage of phony superiority. Anyone who believes that God's message of salvation was primarily carried to or through the world by the educated and well-mannered needs to reread God's Book on evangelism.

"For who regards you as superior? And what do you have that you did not receive? But if you did receive it, why do you boast as if you had not received it?" (1 Corinthians 4:7).

Those in positions of authority must exercise great caution to maintain the proper balance. Authority actually means responsibility according to God's Word. The single example of perfect leadership was Christ. He consistently told His followers that He came to serve, not to be served. By showing kindness and concern, He did not weaken His authority. He knew, as we should, that His authority and position were in God's kingdom. The leaders and followers of His day tried to convince Him to hold Himself above the poor. This He refused to do, and He condemned the practice.

"But the greatest among you shall be your servant. And whoever exalts himself shall be humbled; and whoever humbles himself shall be exalted" (Matthew 23:11-12).

The question is often asked, "How can I maintain discipline if I get too close to my employees?" The answer is that if they know that you're applying God's principles fairly and consistently, then they will also know that administering justice along with compassion is a part of that plan. Justice without compassion is callousness, and compassion without justice is weakness. It should also be noted that you're not trying to make pets out of those under your authority. Nobody likes a condescending boss. What you should be striving to do is to treat all men equally.

The symptom of superiority is difficult to overcome. Those Christians I know who struggle to overcome it have discovered something in common. As soon as they begin to treat everyone they meet equally and fairly, some obnoxious employee immediately begins to see how much he can get away with. God's Word says not to look down at others, but it doesn't say that work rules can't be enforced. Some of those who resent authority must either be taught to respect that authority or be released.

SYMPTOM VS. PROBLEM

The symptom may be an air of superiority, but the real problem is either ego or pride. *"Pride goes before destruction, and a haughty spirit before stumbling"* (Proverbs 16:18). The way to deal with pride is to consciously put others first. Certainly it's difficult and without a doubt runs contrary to popular business management principles. But God wrote the book on business management, and if we really believe that everything belongs to Him, then we believe it is His plan we are to follow. Remember that the purpose of a Christian's business is to glorify God.

SYMPTOM 3: SELFISHNESS-INDULGENCE

"Come now, you rich, weep and howl for your miseries which are coming upon you. Your riches have rotted and your garments have become moth-eaten" (James 5:1-2).

A commercial for a luxury car once showed a late night scene in an office parking lot and a haggard looking executive walking up to his expensive car saying, "Sure I've had to sacrifice a lot, but I've earned the right to the best." What that commercial didn't show is that in real life often that executive is working on a second marriage, has rotten kids, and is desperately trying to indulge himself to prove that it has all been worth it. A thousand years from now it won't have made much of a positive impact on eternity, I imagine.

Far too often those who control a business adopt a "me first" attitude. They poorly pay many employees, establish their own retirement plans without thought to their employees' needs, and reap most of the available surplus for themselves. More often than not the owner will sell out a successful business, realizing a great profit and leaving the employees with little or nothing to show for the years of their lives they invested. Certainly they received their wages, but a Christian has to ask, "Does my responsibility end at payday?"

SYMPTOM VS. PROBLEM

The symptom may manifest itself through selfishness and indulgence, but the real problem is greed. We all have an inborn attitude of greed—always desiring more. Until it is brought under God's authority, we will not be good stewards. Consequently, we settle for trinkets now when God really desires to pour out His blessings upon us.

"You ask and do not receive, because you ask with wrong motives, so that you may spend it on your pleasures" (James 4:3).

SYMPTOM 4: CONFUSION-DISORGANIZATION

"The sluggard does not plow after the autumn, so he begs during the harvest and has nothing" (Proverbs 20:4). Almost in total contrast to the overcommitted workaholic are those Christian businessmen who apply themselves at the minimal level. They're content to operate with sloppy records and poor work quality, and they exist in a mediocre society without a real Christian testimony.

Christians are instructed to be excellent in everything they do. *"Whatever you do, do your work heartily, as for the Lord rather than for men"* (Colossians 3:23). That is a part of our testimony before the unsaved.

God's way is not a cop-out; it is the best. It is astounding how mediocre society has become. We build defects into our equipment and appliances because of shoddy workmanship and wonder why we aren't competitive. As Christians, we should accept excellence as our minimum standard. The quality of our personal efforts should be so high that the unsaved around us are drawn to the Lord through our witness. Instead, few Christians really have such a testimony.

Without a doubt, excellence is an attitude that God commands of us. It would be very difficult to convince others that Christianity is the only way if the Christians they see are sloppy and in a state of confusion. Usually, these conditions result in frustration and anger for the Christian and for those around him.

SYMPTOM VS. PROBLEM

The symptom is disorganization, but the underlying problem is slothfulness, which is generally a by-product of a lack of commitment. In other words, it's an "I don't care" attitude. That is so uncharacteristic of a Christian that one would have to question God's leadership in the life of a slothful or lazy person. Anyone can have lapses of excellence caused by pressures, health, or overwork. But continual laziness is a sure sign of spiritual problems (1 Peter 4:11).

Too Busy to Serve

Nothing interferes more with our ability to serve God than our need to earn a living. An observer from 100 years ago would be awestruck by the improvement in our living standard and by the amount of leisure time our technology has provided. Few North Americans regularly work more than a fifty-hour week; most work forty-four hours or less. In addition, we now live an average of eighteen years longer than we did 100 years ago and have at least one-third more disposable income per family. When all of these factors are weighed together with the fact that in America alone there are perhaps 20 million Christians, it would seem clear that we ought to be getting out the message of Jesus Christ much better than we are.

The simple truth is that most Americans are too busy to serve God. We have grown complacent and comfortable in God's blessing and have forgotten the first commandment. In the meantime, immorality and cults have grown to alarming proportions because their advocates are more zealous in their support. Since God asks for obedience rather than demanding it, many Christians simply ignore the very reason for their existence: to glorify God. Without exception, God has a unique and meaningful plan for every believer, and it does not depend on age, income, or ability.

It is also clear that God calls each of us to fill his gap. Just as Esther did, every believer must decide either to be used by God or to be bypassed and another chosen instead. What a loss that we will allow temporary comforts and laziness to rob us of true riches both now and for all eternity!

"Since all these things are to be destroyed in this way, what sort of people ought you to be in holy conduct and godliness" (2 Peter 3:11).

TIME OUT, PLEASE

Most Christians would never "refuse" to do God's will; it's just that the timing is not right. When God calls us, He wants obedience first and worldly wisdom last. We have allowed the *urgent* things of this society in which we live to over-shadow the *important* things. That fact is neither new nor unique to our generation. In fact, Christ experienced it in His walk on earth and predicted it for us. He left a parable of God's calling men to follow Him. They were invited to a dinner, but most were far too busy to attend right then. They wanted to be part of what was happening but had a great many responsibilities.

"And you will be blessed, since they do not have the means to repay you; for you will be repaid at the resurrection of the righteous" (Luke 14:14).

CONSIDER THE COST

Service to Jesus Christ is demanding. It may actually mean that we will have to work as hard for God's kingdom as we do for earthly riches. Few salesmen consider it a great imposition on their time to tell about their product line. Being a success at anything requires dedication, training, and perseverance. It would be a very hungry company that trained its salesmen to expect perfect success on every call. Just one turndown and they would give up, considering themselves a failure. Instead, the key to successful salesmanship starts long before they ever see the first product. In fact, it starts at the job interview. A good sales manager knows that not everybody can be a good salesman, and many don't even want to be. Christ knew that not everybody will serve God, and most won't even want to.

Some would like to have a foot in both worlds. They are willing to be called Christians provided they can pick the times and places to serve. *"But Jesus said to him, 'No one, after putting his hand to the plow and looking back, is fit for the kingdom of God'"* (Luke 9:62).

These people are actually worse off in this life than they were before. they are content to know about God but are fruitless fakers who must generate false blessings. They are poorly nourished spiritually and quickly waste away until there is real doubt in their minds about their salvation.

"And other seed fell on rocky soil, and as soon as it grew up, it withered away, because it had no moisture" (Luke 8:6). They truly fall prey to every wind of doctrine because they are too busy to grow firm roots.

THORNS OF LIFE

"And the seed which fell among the thorns, these are the ones who have heard, and as they go on their way they are choked with worries and riches and pleasures of this life, and bring no fruit to maturity" (Luke 8:14).

In the parable of the sower, Christ defines the thorns as worries, riches, and pleasures of this world. At first glance, one could assume that committed service to God then would necessarily yield peace, but peace with poverty and blandness. Judging from the way Christians avoid total service to God, this would seem so.

However, Jesus Christ said that total service to God would yield peace and blessings within His will: *"For all these things the nations of the world eagerly seek; but your Father knows that you need these things. But seek for His kingdom, and these things shall be added to you"* (Luke 12:30-31).

Each of us has experienced the thorns of this world. Everything around us is moving at a frantic pace. A family can hardly get one car paid off before another is needed. Only twenty-five years ago our goal was a high school education to get a good job—now it's a college degree. Family life is degrading because it now takes both spouses working to hang on to the "good life."

GOOD WORKS

To a lesser degree, but just as misguided, are Christians who apply themselves to fruitless effort in the name of the Lord. They busy themselves to the point of exhaustion going to conferences and countless church activities and serving on many committees. However, they are rarely, if ever, quiet enough for the Lord to direct them. They are irritable and often envious of others. They are working at God's work but not *in* it. Even those who walked with the Lord suffer from this busy malady from time to time.

Once when Christ was visiting Martha's home, she complained to the Lord that she was stuck doing all the things while Mary was just sitting and listening to Jesus. Jesus told Martha, *"You are worried and bothered about so many things; but only a few things are necessary, really only one, for Mary has chosen the good part, which shall not be taken away from her"* (Luke 10:41b-42).

Many Christians have taken on a life

of meaningless works to avoid the reality of serving God according to His will. The fruits of true service cannot be denied (Galatians 5:22-23), whereas the effects of human work cannot be hidden. I once heard someone ask how to determine if one's service was truly being blessed by the Lord. One response was, "Ask his pastor." Another was, "Ask his friends." But the best and by far the most enlightening was, "Ask his family."

SOWING AND REAPING

Most Christians are familiar with the principle of sowing and reaping as it applies to giving—though few really believe it. That same principle applies to sharing time in the Lord's work. Just as God can multiply the fruits of our labor, He can also multiply the use of our time. Any good administrator knows that ten minutes spent in productive effort is more valuable than two hours spent in confusion and frustration. Therefore, one of the first things a busy, frustrated, overworked Christian needs to do is dedicate the best part of the day, week, month, and year to the Lord. To do so will mean reordering priorities at work and at home and establishing some sound goals (Luke 6:38).

GOAL SETTING

Personal. No other goals are going to be meaningful until the first and most important one is settled—one's relationship with God. In Psalm 51:10-13, David tells us of some prerequisites to teaching others God's way: assurance of salvation, a steadfast spirit, the Holy Spirit's control, and a clean heart. If any of these is missing, then utter frustration will result. If a Christian's first priority in life is God, then an understanding of God's way is mandatory. That means personal Bible

study. It also means a personal prayer life dedicated to the needs of others as well as personal needs.

Family. Most families drift for lack of a rudder—the father's leadership. If a family's most important need is a godly father, then this need is far more important than all the material possessions a parent can provide.

Work. There is nothing wrong with being successful even when measured by worldly standards—unless one ends a failure by godly standards. The rate of divorce and bankruptcy among Christians is an undeniable indicator that Christians have been duped into accepting the world's yardstick as the first priority. Each Christian must ask, "Am I certain my priorities are in line with God's?" If not, then a change is in order—no matter what the cost in dollars and cents.

It is remarkable that usually those at the highest end of the material scale are the biggest violators of priorities (executives, doctors, attorneys, and so on). But equally guilty are many in full-time Christian service, with pastors leading the group.

"It is vain for you to rise up early, to retire late, to eat the bread of painful labors; for He gives to His beloved even in his sleep" (Psalm 127:2).

SUMMARY

We all, to a greater or lesser degree, suffer from being too busy to serve God. Some are so busy doing things for God that they fail to do the things of God. Some have already been called by God to go into full-time Christian service, but they weighed the call against the cost and decided they could serve God best where they were. Others clutter their lives with so much materialism that they never have time to listen to God. The urgent things crowd out the important things, and Christian service to others is shelved until "a better time."

We can all give thanks to those committed saints, from the apostles on down, who did not feel that fame and success in the eyes of men were as important as God's blessings. Without fear of contradiction, I can say that one day each of us will grade 100 percent of our success or failure on the basis of Christ's evaluation and none other. I trust that each of us will hear Him say, "Well done, My good and faithful servant."

Part 6:

Family

Husband-Wife Communications

Of all the relationships described in God's Word, none depicts the partnership better than marriage. However, this partnership is not like a business or social partnership in which two people are merely working together toward a common goal. The relationship could be better described as a "yoke" (Greek, *zugos*) where two are tied to the same harness, pulling to accomplish a common task.

A marriage is more than that. At the end of a day, a yoke can be removed, as it was with oxen, and they need not be joined together again until the next work day. A marriage is much more like the partnership of the left and right hands of the same person. They are perfectly matched but totally opposite. God's Word says that two people become one.

"For this cause a man shall leave his father and his mother, and shall cleave to his wife; and they shall become one flesh" (Genesis 2:24).

Understanding this can greatly enhance a marriage, because it virtually eliminates any idea that one person is subservient to another. They are merely different for the purpose of accomplishing various functions. One hand working alone will not accomplish half as much as two. Many tasks are impossible without two hands working together. It is truly enlightening to see how opposite couples really are. It would seem that opposites do attract. One will get up early, while the other stays in bed. One has a good sense of direction; the other gets lost. One is punctual; the other is always late. One usually talks; the other listens. There is an old cliché that is very true. "If husband and wife are identical, one of them is unnecessary."

NORMAL SITUATIONS

Unfortunately, in any relationship, a balance is hard to reach. Usually one personality will overwhelm the other, and a marriage will take on a one-sided tilt. More often than not, where finances are concerned, the husband makes all of the decisions, although in some families the wife takes on this responsibility.

The lack of training in such a fundamental and critical area of marriage is bad enough, but combined with little or no communication it can be disastrous. If a couple knows how to communicate, the natural balance will often keep them out of financial trouble. Most women have a decided fear of being in debt and will normally exercise restraint. If they find themselves in financial trouble, they will quickly seek help and do what is necessary to correct the situation. In general, that is not so with men. The majority of serious debts are the result of the husband's spending, and either his indifference, pride, or eternal optimism keeps him from seeking help initially.

It must be remembered that few families desire or plan financial problems. Most occur because of poor training, poor communications, and a childhood of conditioned desires. Too often, parents don't teach their children that their life-style was earned by many years of effort and usually started with several years of sacrifice. Equipped with a value system learned in a generally affluent home and a handful of credit cards, most young couples set out to duplicate or improve upon their parents' success. The result in the majority of marriages today is disaster.

TURNING IT AROUND

The first step in turnaround is to recognize that different is not inferior. God put different gifts and abilities in the marriage, and it takes two people working as one to succeed in the home. Since men are often guilty of excluding their wives from financial decisions, a concerted effort must be made to use her gifts and abilities as a counselor. Wives should remember that a counselor does not scream, cry, or throw temper tantrums. Honesty between partners is an absolute necessity. Almost anyone can handle a situation if he knows about it and is a part of the planning. It's the deceptions that later show up as crises that create distrust.

Get help. If the problems and the communication gap are very intense, most couples will need outside help to get on the right track. Seeking counsel for marriage or financial problems should be as normal as seeking medical counsel. God has established various gifts and abilities throughout His kingdom, and unless couples are free to use them, someone's ministry goes wanting. *"Without consultation, plans are frustrated, but with many counselors they succeed"* (Proverbs 15:22).

Many couples have been through the very same crises that others are now facing and have found God's solutions. Those couples must be willing to share their experiences so that others in the midst of problems will know to whom to turn for help. There will never be enough professional counselors to do the job. It is the function of the body of Christians to minister to others within the body as the need arises.

Set specific goals. In order to establish the right relationship about finances in the home, husband and wife together must establish specific goals. The first must obviously be to solve financial problems if there are any.

Any couple that has not done so previously should plan a weekend alone together where every aspect of the family's finances can be discussed and some specific goals agreed upon. Remember that any financial planning involves two people's seeking mutually compatible goals under the umbrella of God's plan for their lives. No one will ever understand God's plan better than those who are to live it. Two people operating as one with unity of mind will find God's plan.

"I love those who love me; and those who diligently seek me will find me" (Proverbs 8:17).

Quite often a reasonable compromise will be necessary when establishing goals. One may be more committed to giving than the other; a home may be more important to one, while a bass boat seems like a basic necessity to the other. The first and most important aspect is to discern God's overall plan and then adjust as necessary to make it work. One method is for both spouses to find the answers they can agree upon first, write them down, and pray about them before moving on to more controversial areas. When an impasse is reached over any area, such as food, clothing, or education, each should list five positions from his best to worst. Then each should discard their first and last and find one of the other three they can agree upon.

FINANCIAL RESPONSIBILITIES

Problems. If problems exist, the husband must assume the burden of direct control. He is to act as a buffer for his wife. That doesn't mean that the wife is not involved, but that he is the visible interface. One of the great causes of fear in most women, and ultimately strife in the marriage, is creditor pressure. The wife's responsibility becomes one of assisting and implementing the necessary financial controls, not frantically worrying about them. Quite often, the husband is concerned that his wife cannot make the adjustments to reduce spending. Usually, I have found the opposite to be true. If a husband will provide the direction and submit to the same controls, his wife will adjust as necessary. Communication and planning are the keys to success. It's a matter of determining where you are financially, having a plan that is fair to both, and talking about it calmly.

"With all humility and gentleness, with patience, showing forbearance to one another in love" (Ephesians 4:2).

Bookkeeping. Assuming that there are no major financial problems, the task of recordkeeping should fall to the one best equipped to do it. Due to many factors, not the least of which are time and patience, the wife is often a better bookkeeper. If that is so and both agree, then she should maintain the records once a workable budget has been agreed upon. They should review the budget and discuss any problems on a regular basis.

Children's discipline. It is difficult, if not impossible, to establish financial discipline in children unless both parents agree upon the goals and enforce the rules consistently. Parents cannot wait until a situation arises to see if they agree. They must meet it with a unified front.

The decisions should be based on the long-term goals of what is best for the children, not what necessarily pleases them. If a rule is established that the children must earn at least one-half of all entertainment money, and Mom slips them money without Dad's knowing about it, then they learn a double lesson: slothfulness pays, and authority can be manipulated. Eventually, an employer will correct that notion for them rather rudely.

"The hand of the diligent will rule, but the slack hand will be put to forced labor" (Proverbs 12:24).

DEVELOPING LONG-RANGE GOALS

Nowhere is it more important to cement the husband-wife financial partnership than in the area of establishing long-range goals. Long-range goals are objective and measurable and give a couple the opportunity to communicate in a critical area. An excellent way to find out the long-range objectives of your spouse is simply to ask. Most women are excluded from long-range financial planning by their husbands, which is ridiculous because most women are excellent money managers.

Many men would be very shocked to discover that their wives actually manage their money better than they do. It is far better to include the wife, make her a primary consultant, and educate her on what she must ultimately know about finances. A side effect is that she will probably help keep her husband out of a great many unwise get-rich-quick schemes.

Remember—neither spouse is always right or always wrong. Balance is the key, and God provides it through both. *"The mind of man plans his way, but the Lord directs his steps"* (Proverbs 16:9).

Should Wives Work?

Few subjects in Christianity are more controversial than that of working wives. Many Christians feel that it is wrong for married women to be employed full-time outside the home because of the effect it has on their families, especially the children. However, it would seem the alternatives are few for most low-to-middle income families today. What are the alternatives for Christian families?

SOCIAL OPINION

It is commonly accepted in our generation that the cost of maintaining and operating a home requires that both spouses work in most families. On the surface, that is true. It doesn't take much arithmetic to determine that the costs of new homes, cars, food, and clothing are beyond the income ability of the average family. Currently, the payments on the average new home would require nearly 70 percent of the average husband's pay. The logical conclusion, then, is that two incomes are needed. The fault with that logic is that it doesn't consider whether or not the average family needs the average home.

PRESSURES

More and more married women are beginning to accept the pressures of a job as normal. That is unfortunate because wives provide a good family balance for their husbands, who have a tendency to work too much and too long. If wives begin to adjust similarly, then ultimately the family will suffer.

Most men seek employment in their primary skill area, such as administration, mechanics, bookkeeping, and so on. However, that skill is rarely applied at home because the fatigue of the daily tasks necessitates a change to unwind. Since many women are the primary teachers, trainers, organizers, and planners in the home, these attributes may be lost to their families if they are fatigued by a daily work routine.

CURRENT SOCIAL SITUATION

The violation of basic biblical principles will result in basic biblical consequences. There are many direct and indirect consequences of women being pushed into the role of wage earners; not the least of these would appear to be the increasing divorce rate. Financial problems are listed as the number one source of marital problems in divorces. If two incomes would relieve this condition, then we should see fewer divorces. Just the opposite is true.

CONFUSED LOYALTIES

When wives shift their need for approval to their work, the problems are increased. There is often a mixed loyalty between the demands at work and at home. On one hand, a wife may sense a lack of closeness to her family as a result of the time spent away from home and the normal mental fatigue of work stress. On the other hand, she may recognize the need to dedicate even more time to the job in order to succeed.

MISPLACED PRIORITIES

Just as many Christian men abandon the important priorities—God and family—because they believe they must be a success "for their families," so many women now rationalize the same way. For example, in a counseling session the mother of two young children justified what she considered to be a perfectly logical position: "Certainly, I'm not able to be with my children as much as I would like, and I know that my husband really doesn't want me to work, but how could we ever buy a car or take a vacation if I didn't work?" In the future, many sixty-year-old women will look back as many sixty-year-old men now do and say, "I wish I had taken the time to be with my family when I had the chance."

POSITIVE BALANCE

Because there are so many negative side effects of working wives, does that mean that it is scripturally wrong for wives to work? Not necessarily. Satan can use anything out of balance, and he usually does. The fact that many women choose to work outside the home is *not* the problem. The fact that so many women think they *have* to work to maintain the family's finances is the real problem. Wives do not have to work. The proof of that can be seen in the tens of thousands of wives who do not work but still get along very well.

For those women who are involuntary heads of households, we, as Christians, must stand guilty before God for failing our responsibility to provide them an option.

BIBLICAL PRIORITIES

1. *Desire.* Nowhere in God's Word is there an admonition for wives not to work outside the home. But the lack of a prohibition does not automatically confer acceptability. There are no admonitions against holding one's head in a bucket of water, but there are logical consequences that should be avoided. The first priority of a working wife is a desire to work on her part. When a wife is compelled to work by design or circumstance, resentment will often develop.

"A joyful heart makes a cheerful face, but when the heart is sad, the spirit is broken" (Proverbs 15:13).

2. *Husband's approval.* Many working wives are able to gain a tacit approval by pressuring their husbands. Although many husbands do not actually agree with their wives' working, they relent under an emotional assault called nagging. *"It is better to live in a desert land, than with a contentious and vexing woman"* (Proverbs 21:19). This is not the approval that a wife seeks or requires, because it will eventually undermine the marriage relationship.

3. *Disciplined children.* The role of the mother as the teacher of her children is incontestable. The father usually provides the policy decisions, but it is the wife who establishes discipline and direction day by day. The success or failure of children as individuals will, in great part, depend on her success or failure as their guide.

"She looks well to the ways of her household, and does not eat the bread of idleness. Her children rise up and bless her; her husband also, and he praises her" (Proverbs 31:27-28a).

In our society today, we have arbitrarily determined that a child is prepared for outside contact and discipline at six years of age. That may or may not be true, and all parents must make their own decisions about how long parental supervision is necessary. The certainty is that with the current attitude of laxness in society, *more* direct input from the mother is needed, not less. The greater the trend grows toward women's fulfilling their emotional needs outside the home, the more rebellious and undisciplined their children become.

4. *Confused authority.* The next consideration is less measurable but just as vital: can a Christian wife, who is also an employee, handle the responsibilities of having two direct authorities? God's Word establishes the husband as the head of the household (1 Corinthians 11:3; Ephesians 5:23). For the working wife, the loyalties between job and family may get confused, and she may be duped into a feeling of independence that is actually rebellion. *"The wise woman builds her house, but the foolish tears it down with her own hands"* (Proverbs 14:1). If a wife senses this happening, she would be well advised to for go some financial flexibility to preserve her family relationship. In other words: quit.

FINANCIAL DANGERS

Need to work. There is rarely an actual need for a wife to work outside the home. It may seem so because of the standard of living the family has chosen or because of past habits, but more money made just means more money to spend. Some very specific goals should be established for the wife's income, or additional debt will result. At least once a year every working couple should re-evaluate their goals and objectives, particularly the purpose of the wife's income. A young couple would be well advised not to merge the wife's income into their budget. To do so invites future disaster in the event of children, illness, or the husband's job change. They should learn to live on the husband's income and use the wife's for one-time purchases, such as a car, furniture, down payment on a home—on a cash basis only.

Comfort and convenience. Even if the wife's income is used for extra comforts, such as new cars, vacations, and private school, there must be a continual self-analysis to determine if these things have become necessities.

"Let your character be free from the love of money, being content with what you have; for He Himself has said, 'I will never desert you, nor will I ever forsake you'" (Hebrews 13:5).

Husband's needs. Many women are duped by society into believing that they must establish a "separate but equal" relationship, and to do so they must be working. The effect has been to undermine the husband's position as the leader and protector of his family. Naturally, no woman wants to be a slave, nor does God's Word support any such attitude. God's Word describes the wife's role as that of equal spiritually and dependent materially (1 Peter 3:1-7). A husband's needs can best be met by a wife who trusts him totally and will yield her human rights to him (Proverbs 31:10-12). The husband, likewise, is commanded to love her, care for her needs, treat her as his own body, and accept the responsibility for the family (Ephesians 5:25; 1 Timothy 5:8; Ephesians 5:28). To best meet the needs of her husband, a wife must become his helpmate—supporter and companion. If working does not interfere with that role, then great. But if it does, then the marriage priority comes first.

Financial Authority in the Home

The lack of godly leadership in the home can be devasting to a family. Women are experiencing pressures as never before because they are carrying burdens God never intended they have. Why? Because many men are abandoning their leadership responsibilities. Regardless of what psychologists say, God has not made a woman to function well under stress, particularly financial stress. The result of husbands' subjecting their mates to such stress can be seen in every community counseling center.

I am frequently confronted with women who have assumed the responsibility of negotiating with creditors, keeping the bills paid, disciplining the children, and maintaining a home. More often than not, it is because their husbands will not accept the responsibility.

That is not to say all men are irresponsible. Fortunately, most are very responsible. However, with the current social trend towards "equality," more and more men are encouraged to ignore their God-ordained responsibilities in order to find peer approval.

Many woman who assume the leadership role in the home find they have destroyed their health, their peace, and their marriage. *"The wise woman builds her house, but the foolish tears it down with her own hands"* (Proverbs 14:1).

In a counseling session a young wife commented, "I have to control all the money in our home. My husband doesn't know how to handle it, so I took over."

There was little doubt that she dominated the family, including the finances, and even less doubt that she had reduced her husband's authority in the family to approximately that of a child. She justified her action on the basis that it was "necessary." However, the net result of her takeover was emotional and physical stress and nearly a total breakdown in marriage communications.

Almost the exact opposite situation had occurred earlier with another couple. The husband felt so strongly about his role as the authority in the home that he refused to allow his wife to participate in financial decisions. Since he continually made decisions without consulting her, she naturally felt he neither trusted nor respected her. Over their married years, she had withdrawn into a shell of quiet resentment.

BALANCE

Both situations reflect that God's plan for authority in the home is not an either/or situation. It is a joint effort with differing responsibilities.

In any relationship as intimate as marriage, there must be a sharing of responsibilities and abilities. God often uses opposites in a marriage to balance the extremes. If husband and wife are identical in nature, undoubtedly the decisions will be unbalanced. Thus, a spender is balanced by a saver. A sensitive, discerning wife is a great asset to any husband, providing that he's willing to listen to her. *"A prudent wife is from the Lord"* (Proverbs 19:14b).

The management of the household,

hence the burden, rests on the husband. *"He must be one who manages his own household well, keeping his children under control with all dignity (but if a man does not know how to manage his own household, how will he take care of the church of God?)"* (1 Timothy 3:4-5).

The wife's responsibility is to support her husband by following his direction—as opposed to nagging and pushing. Sometimes she must be willing to suffer with him and to let him fail if necessary: *"In the same way, you wives, be submissive to your own husbands so that even if any of them are disobedient to the word, they may be won without a word by the behavior of their wives"* (1 Peter 3:1).

SHARED RESPONSIBILITIES

For a wife to be submissive does not mean to be silent. She must take an active role in financial planning. The best way to do that is for a couple to dedicate one full day a year to doing some planning together. The place to start is deciding how their income will be allocated.

1. *Yearly budget.* Together husband and wife should establish a budget for everything to be spent during the year. Every item on the budget should be discussed thoroughly and prayerfully. The primary consideration should be to develop a fair, but reasonable, plan for family spending. I would recommend *The Financial Planning Workbook* as an excellent guide.

2. *Windfall plan.* In addition to the budget, which controls normal income, a family should agree beforehand on the disposition of additional income (gifts, overtime, and so on). The plan should be fair and equal for all concerned. The spending of extra income often frustrates the wife because her wants are ignored. Remember that a marriage is a true part-

nership, and partners share in all things, both profits and losses.

Without a doubt, one of the greatest potential sources of conflict is a "his money, her money" attitude. This is true with earned income and windfall income, such as inheritance. The minute a husband or wife attempts to segregate finances, the message is clearly communicated: "I don't trust you." For a husband or wife to reserve assets from a previous marriage or inheritance is to allow Satan to drive a wedge between two who are supposed to be one.

3. *Long-range plan.* Few women are involved in long-range financial planning. However, it is a statistical fact that more women will live to fulfill long-range goals than men. It's also a fact that many women don't want the bother of discussing things like business goals, wills and trusts, or investments. As a result, these plans lack the balance that God built into the marriage partnership. Planning is not an option, because if you wait long enough, they will become short-range plans with no alternatives available.

"For which one of you, when he wants to build a tower, does not first sit down and calculate the cost, to see if he has enough to complete it?" (Luke 14:28).

WHAT IT MEANS TO SHARE

Assuming there are no unresolved financial problems and a budget has been established that is fair and reasonable, there remains the decision of who keeps the books. There is no doubt that many wives are better at keeping financial records than their husbands. They usually have more time, patience, and motivation. There is no scriptural reason that the wife should not be the family bookkeeper, assuming that to do so is not an effort to take over. In fact, it's important for the wife to understand how to manage finances. Many widows are forced to make important financial decisions with little or no experience, and the results are often disastrous.

There should be a regular time set aside each month for husband, wife, and children to review the current status of the budget and make any necessary adjustments. During these sessions, problems should be discussed and resolved jointly. Obviously, in families where the finances are tight and there are existing debts, the tendency is to argue over finances. Couples must assess this realistically and calmly and determine if they need counseling help. Sometimes in Christianity counseling is viewed as the last step and, therefore, has an emotional stigma. That is absolutely false. God's Word says that counsel is a sign of wisdom (Proverbs 12:15; 13:20; 14:15; 15:22).

WOMEN AS HEADS OF HOUSEHOLDS

There are instances in which a woman is forced to become the head of a household as a result of divorce, her husband's death, or other reasons. In these instances, she has no choice but to assume an authoritative position.

A woman in this position should realize that, within the Body of Christ, God has provided the leadership she needs. The local fellowship she attends should be used as a source for counsel in establishing financial plans. Two things are important in this respect: Christian widows must be willing to let their needs for financial counsel be known, and the local church must equip itself to do this counseling under the control and direction of the church leadership. That will effectively eliminate any "fleecing of the flock."

The Wife's Role in Business

I would venture to say that in most businesses today the wife's role is nearly zero. It may well be that in the early stages of developing a business she was involved, but as the business grew and prospered, that involvement was lessened or eliminated. Through the intervening years, most wives become involved with raising the children and maintaining the home, while the husband builds a business. In itself that is not wrong, provided that the wife stays actively involved in the decision making and direction of the business. Unfortunately few do, and later in life when she would like to be more active again, it's nearly impossible.

CORRECTING AN IMBALANCE

When women are not included in the decision-making process, a real imbalance can occur in a business. If, as Christians, we believe that God provides helpmates with strengths that offset our weaknesses, then not to include them ultimately causes great imbalances. Of course, many men refuse to take counsel from their wives. That is usually a product of training and observation in their homes as youths; but it is also a by-product of something called *pride*. Most men, particularly those who control others, want to be independent, to be able to make the snap decisions that usually result in disaster. That is not to say that, merely by including his wife in routine business decisions, all errors are eliminated. But without hesitation I can say that most of the problems I have observed in Christian-owned businesses would have been lessened or avoided if the men had been willing to seek the counsel of their wives before making major decisions, particularly those involving large amounts of borrowing.

Why didn't they? Because they knew they would not be able to rationally convince their wives that such risks were appropriate. So, instead, they sought the counsel of men of like mind who assured them that they knew at least one other "gambler" who had done the same thing and had got away with it. *"House and wealth are an inheritance from fathers, but a prudent wife is from the Lord"* (Proverbs 19:14).

It may sound like I'm coming down too hard on men in business, but I believe it cannot be stated too strongly: when a man and wife are joined in marriage, they are no longer two—they're one. *"For this cause a man shall leave his father and his mother, and shall cleave to his wife; and they shall become one flesh"* (Genesis 2:24). Therefore, each brings a necessary part of God's wisdom to every decision.

EXCLUSION OF THE WIFE

What commonly happens in our generation is that, as the business either prospers or fails, the wife is the last to be consulted. In our past agrarian society both husband and wife were acutely aware of how they were doing financially. Usually, the man plowed and planted while his wife managed the home; but come harvest time everybody got involved. Consequently, she knew about as much as did her husband on a year-by-year basis. Today, many men build successful businesses only to find that they have little in common with their wives of many years and eventually divorce when the children are grown. All too often the catalyst is a younger woman in the office who seems to be all the things that the wife is not. Few Christian men would ever actively solicit such a volatile situation, but one-sided decisions often allow such situations to develop.

The other extreme is that news of a failing business is kept from the wife until the collapse is imminent. Obviously, most women realize when a business is in trouble but are usually not aware of the extent of the crisis. The result is often conflict and deep hurt when she realizes that even the office staff knows more about the difficulties than she does.

HELPMATE

By observation it would appear that most couples practice only extremes in business involvement: total or none-at-all. That means that the wife is either immersed in the day-to-day operation of the business or is totally isolated from any meaningful input. It is not necessary to go to either extreme. A wife can become a vital factor in decision making without functioning as a part of the daily office routine, but only if she is knowledgeable and informed. In reality, the wives who are actively involved in the office constitute only about 10 percent or less of the total; the other 90 percent represent the norm today. They are to be helpmates.

In Proverbs 31, an excellent wife is described. Above all others, her husband respects her counsel because she "fears the Lord," and fear of the Lord is a sign of great wisdom. A wife should be her husband's primary counselor. She provides balance to his decisions that can be provided by no one else. A husband who never, or seldom, accepts this counsel has

not honored his wife, and, according to 1 Peter 3:7, his prayers will be hindered.

That does not mean that a wife's counsel is always right and must be followed to the exclusion of all else. But it does mean that it should be considered and weighed as the highest priority.

In a recent counseling session a businessman asked if I felt it was all right for him to borrow against their home to expand the business. My response was to ask him if he had asked his wife how she felt about it. No further discussion on that particular issue was necessary. Inside, he knew it was a bad idea, and he also knew that his wife would say so. In discussing it, his wife did say she thought it was a bad idea, but she also said she would support whatever decision he made. He was shocked. He discovered at that point that he had a counselor who was willing to give advice, leave the results to God, and share the outcome. He decided not to borrow the money.

To the wives I would give this counsel: don't allow yourselves to be ignorant of your spouse's business. Don't demand though—ask. As a counselor, you must be willing to give advice, offer alternatives, and leave the results to God. If your advice is sound, you won't have to continually remind your husband about it; he'll know.

"The wise woman builds her house, but the foolish tears it down with her own hands" (Proverbs 14:1).

ACCOUNTABILITY

I believe one of the least taught principles in Christianity is accountability. That means being responsible for our actions. Many businessmen are not held accountable for their time, money, or attitudes today because they report to no one.

Throughout God's Word are directions that we hold each other accountable. *"And if your brother sins, go and reprove him in private; if he listens to you, you have won your brother"* (Matthew 18:15).

The more knowledgeable someone is of our routine the more accountable we become. That's why a great many businessmen do not want anyone to know too much about what they do, lest they become accountable according to God's standard. A Christian who is truly seeking to serve God will find that, next to the Lord, his wife provides the maximum accountability. After living in the same home with their husbands, most wives do not miss even a small thing. For instance, don't just ask your wife to sign the joint tax return each year; explain how that tax shelter is really questionable if the I. R. S. checks. See if she has a peace from the Lord about it, too.

If husbands can get to a point where they are willing to share every major decision with their wives, they will have made themselves accountable. Since we are all accountable before the Lord, this will save a lot of grief later.

Wives must be able to accept their responsibilities to give counsel and not decisions. If your feelings are easily hurt, you'll probably be excluded from most decisions by your husband just to avoid the grief. I have often found myself delaying asking my wife's advice when I know I've gone further than I should have into a decision, for fear I'll hurt her feelings. The more I find I can trust her reactions to be under God's control, the more liberty I feel to share a decision. Sometimes I sense that she is avoiding telling me how she feels because she knows it's not what I want to hear. I then remind her of Philippians 2—we must be of the "same mind" for God to bless us. If she shares what she believes is God's wisdom and I don't listen, than I am accountable. But if she agrees with a decision, believing it to be wrong, then she's accountable.

HOW TO GET STARTED

First and foremost, don't get discouraged. You may be one of those fortunate couples who discuss everything, but if you fall in the other 90 percent category, it will require a re-education. Make a commitment to make Christ the center of your marriage. If you do, then making decisions together is a fundamental part of your marriage and business. Even if the wife doesn't want to be involved, she must be in order to reach God's balance. Remember this as an incentive: wives outlive their husbands more than 80 percent of the time. Ultimately, she will be the decision-maker.

Set aside a regular time to discuss current events in the business and any pending redirections or problems. If you find you can't discuss things rationally right now, then write them out. I have found with many couples, when emotions flare and old hurts are dredged up, that having the wife write out her counsel helps considerably. If a major decision is pending, schedule time together to discuss it. Don't get sidetracked by feelings and neglect God's promise that "where two or three have gathered together in My name, there I am in their midst" (Matthew 18:20).

To the husband I would say that the commitment to begin involving your wife is up to you. If you don't want to make that commitment, then be honest with God about not desiring His best in your life. To the wife I would say that to the degree you are able to put aside old hurts and let God be the enforcer of your "rights," this plan will work. Be a counselor and a comforter, not a fault-finder.

"Nevertheless let each individual among you also love his own wife even as himself; and let the wife see to it that she respect her husband" (Ephesians 5:33).

Disciplining Children

One of the most neglected areas in most families has to be teaching children financial discipline. Even in families where Bible study and prayer is an established way of life, finances are rarely, if ever, discussed. Is it any wonder then that so many young couples suffer because of financial mismanagement? Where are our children to learn good financial principles if not from us?

"Train up a child in the way he should go, even when he is old he will not depart from it" (Proverbs 22:6).

The financial pressure placed upon young adults is impossible to resist unless they have been armed with an unshakeable source of strength—God's Word. In most schools today, a consumer economics class consists primarily of teaching them how to make out credit applications. The logic is simple—since "everybody" is going to need credit, we should concentrate on the best methods to obtain it. Whatever happened to the old principle of "if you can't afford it, don't buy it"? Whose responsibility is it to teach children the rules of self-discipline? Obviously, it is the parents'.

SELF-DISCIPLINE

The place to start is with the parents. It will do no good to teach financial discipline to children until the principles are active in the parents' lives. Kids have an instinct for detecting insincerity, and the old adage "Don't do what I do, do what I say" doesn't work.

A husband and wife who don't communicate about financial goals will not be able to convince their children that they have anything worthwhile to say, either.

It is important that adults develop self-discipline and use it. If parents continually buy luxuries on impulse, the children will come to expect the same privileges.

Parents who have not learned the discipline of balancing a checkbook should not be surprised to find that their children are sloppy in other areas of their lives.

Parents must set examples for their children. Unfortunately, it seems that kids are much quicker at mimicking bad habits than good ones. Why? Because being slothful and undisciplined requires less effort. Children, like most others, will usually seek the path of least resistance. Therefore, the authority must establish a positive, balanced example.

CHILD DISCIPLINE

"The rod and reproof give wisdom, but a child who gets his own way brings shame to his mother" (Proverbs 29:15).

If too much discipline is harmful, too little is disastrous. The evidence of too little financial discipline with children can be seen in the number of sixteen-year-olds driving new, high-powered cars and the millions of dollars wasted on rock concerts and trash movies. Every time I see a teenager whip out a credit card to buy gas, I wonder if he can really be expected to understand the principle of "owe no man."

MINIMUM STANDARDS

The principle behind establishing minimum standards is honoring parents. Tasks should be assigned with age and ability in mind. A child who makes a mess and leaves it for another to clean up or who drops clothes where they are removed does not show honor to his mother. Left to grow and mature, that dishonor will come out later in verbal abuse and disregard for the parents' feelings.

"A foolish son is a grief to his father, and bitterness to her who bore him" (Proverbs 17:25).

The best rewards for these jobs are verbal praise and privileges. For younger children a visual chart with smiling faces or stars works well.

The punishment for noncompliance should be determined by the age of the child and the frequency of violation. Recently I shared that principle with the parents of a totally undisciplined teenager. The mother said, "It won't work because our son really doesn't have an interest in anything." That turned out not to be true. He had a great interest in his car and his girl friend. However, his parents used him to pick up and deliver their other children, and his girl friend was their best babysitter. They were not willing to sacrifice themselves to discipline him.

DISCIPLINE—FAIRNESS—REWARDS

If you make rules, enforce them. That is sometimes difficult for parents, but discipline must be firm to be effective. Don't do the task yourself to avoid a confrontation. Be sure you are not expecting more than the child is capable of achieving. If the guidelines established include punishment, and they are violated, then punish. Remember that the value system you are trying to establish develops in their early years and must last their entire lives.

A simple rule of thumb in being fair with children is to remember that God is to the parents as the parents are to the children. Don't ever establish a harsher set of disciplines upon your children than

you would like God to put upon you. God does not expect us to be Spirit-controlled, mature Christians immediately upon salvation. To expect too much would only discourage us and drive us away from God. Apply the same loving patience with your children.

In addition to having rules and punishment, parents should develop a reward system. Just as God rewards us for our work and obedience, we should reward our children. To live in a home where everything is rules and punishment is not very conducive to spiritual growth. Parents who operate this way are actually selfish. They want everything their way, and children are considered an irritation rather than a blessing.

Children who are not old enough to work outside the home should have ways to earn extra money within the family. These jobs can range from actual work tasks, such as washing the car or mowing the lawn, to special projects, such as a Bible study or memorizing Scripture. The tasks should be oriented to the abilities of each child.

WHERE TO START

Decisions about developing financial discipline in children must be made by both husband and wife. Start with a conference on family goals. Set aside a weekend and place where you can be alone. Be willing to compromise on the areas where you disagree. It's the compromise that will balance the extremes. The next step is a family session where the children can input their ideas and objections. Show them your willingness to compromise without losing sight that your goal is to teach God's financial principles. Be sure the plan covers the following:

Savings. Savings should be tied to a future event or purchase, such as a bike or a summer trip. That allows the results of the savings to be seen and enjoyed.

Budget. From the earliest stage of a child's earned income he should be on a budget. In a very young child, the budget may just consist of a portion given to God and the rest rationed out for a week. By adolescence, the money is divided into normal categories, such as tithe, clothes, entertainment, college, and so on. By the teenage years, the budget should include a checking and savings account and the associated bookkeeping. By graduation, parents should have full confidence that their children can function in a paper-money society without borrowing to exist.

Tithe. Encourage, do not demand, tithing. Explain that giving is a blessing and a demonstration of surrender to God's authority. If possible, arrange for them to see the end use of the money they give. If possible, have the church give the money to a specific family or missionary and help them communicate with the recipient. Difficult? Yes. But rewarding? Yes—for a lifetime.

Borrowing. The vast majority of people will borrow money during their adult lives. Parents can teach their children the realities of debt by allowing them to borrow according to a rigid repayment plan with interest. The purpose is to demonstrate the realities of borrowing money. Remember that if you don't do this, eventually a creditor will.

"The rich rules over the poor, and the borrower becomes the lender's slave" (Proverbs 22:7).

Desires. Balance the discipline with love. God says that if we delight ourselves in Him, He will provide our heart's desires. As your children delight in you—honor and obey—be willing to bless them accordingly. That will demonstrate that your discipline is truly an act of obedience to God's Word.

Financial Discipline in Children

There are few events more uplifting for parents than to see their chidren develop into mature, disciplined adults. Conversely, there is nothing more frustrating and defeating than to see a son or daughter with great potential suffer and fail because of a lack of self-discipline. Many parents suffer additional grief because, seemingly without warning, their children get caught up in drugs or sex. Most outward signs are but symptoms of inner problems, and if the symptoms are not recognized and corrected, the problems persist and become more severe. Some symptoms are detectable at an early age and can be used as measures of spiritual problems. One of these early signs or symptoms is finances.

God's Word tells us that the way someone handles finances is a clear indication of whether or not he can handle greater things (Luke 16:19-11). That principle applies not only to adults but to children as well. Long before greater problems arise, parents can detect weaknesses that need to be dealt with by observing how their children handle money. (Obviously, money is not the sole indicator but should be used in conjunction with other signs.)

PERSONALITY TRAITS

Each child is a unique individual and is capable of exercising a free will. No amount of parental guidance or threats will change that. The mold has been made by God; parents are used by God to fill in the cracks. Nearly all parents find that each child is uniquely different about everything. One will be frugal, disciplined, and willing to accept directions about sharing, saving, and budgeting. Generally, these same characteristics will be found in other areas, such as school and work habits. Another child will spend nearly every penny available, borrow when possible, and defy all attempts at financial discipline. That attitude will also be observable in other areas, such as sloppiness, poor study habits, and disrespect.

DISCIPLINE VS. DESIRES

Scripture teaches that the relationship between God and parent is the same as between parents and children (Luke 11:11-13). God promises us the desires of our hearts (Psalms 37:4). But before we can achieve those desires, we must make His way our way (Psalm 37:5; Proverbs 3:6; Matthew 6:33). Just giving with no controls is not beneficial. You must be certain that their hearts are committed to God's way. Giving them the desires of *their* hearts will simply spoil them and develop greedy attitudes. A parent must help a child recognize that special gifts are rewards for correct attitudes (Proverbs 3:9-10; 8:21). Many parents give out of guilt or in hope that somehow they can bribe a child into being better. To do so does *not* help. It reinforces bad internal attitudes.

SHORT-TERM PEACE/LONG-TERM PROSPERITY

Often parents yield to the weaknesses of an undisciplined child to obtain some short-term peace. A disciplined child of any age expects very little and rarely demands anything, but an undisciplined child *forcefully* demands more and is rarely satisfied. Why? Possessions have little lasting value, and more is always required to satisfy. A parent must accept the responsibility of withholding in the short run in order for discipline to be ingrained in the long run.

"The rod and reproof give wisdom, but a child who gets his own way brings shame to his mother" (Proverbs 29:15).

VISIBLE SIGNS OF PROBLEMS

Most young children like to spend their available money. A few are self-disciplined and save for future needs with little or no encouragement. When you have one of these, just praise the Lord and help him to reach a good balance between hoarding and spending. A large number of children will spend if allowed or will save if required. Parents who establish early, routine discipline will achieve good results with these children if they are consistent. At the other end of the spectrum are those children who must spend everything they have quickly and often foolishly. Any attempt at control is usually met by resentment and, where allowed, blatant disobedience. These are outward, visible symptoms of much greater spiritual problems. A parent of such a child would be well advised to pay careful attention to other indicators of rebellion and insecurity.

These attitudes are correctable by parents if handled at an early age. However, it may well require a sacrifice. The biggest sacrifice will probably be short-range peace. A rebellious or simply strong-willed child is actually testing his boundaries. If the boundaries are movable, the child will push them back; if not, he will adjust to them.

Contrary to popular opinion, discipline does not retard a child's potential; it expands it. *"Whoever loves discipline loves knowledge, but he who hates reproof is stupid"* (Proverbs 12:1).

SHORT-TERM FINANCIAL GOALS

It is necessary for parents to establish some short-term goals for their children to help them see the purpose and logic of saving money. Initially, these goals should be very short-range, such as saving to buy a book, record, or game. Later the goals should be extended to cover things such as trips, vacations, and bicycles. It is also important to instill written goals. That means keeping a savings ledger and a written prayer goal.

"There is precious treasure and oil in the dwelling of the wise, but a foolish man swallows it up" (Proverbs 21:20).

Your goals and standards for handling money must be both fair and consistent. Both husband and wife should agree and be willing to live by the same standards they set for their children. Parents who never live on a budget will find it very difficult to teach their children to do so. A parent who continually borrows for cars, clothes, and vacations will have a difficult time convincing a son not to finance a car because it might preclude his going to college.

ALLOWANCES

In addition to having rules and punishment, parents should develop a reward system. Just as God rewards us for our work and obedience, we should reward our children. One method to do that is through an allowance. However, the traditional allowance is not scriptural, because it is usually given without any restrictions or controls. An allowance should be given only as a reward for completing assigned tasks.

GIVING

Giving should be established as an early discipline. Obviously, most young children won't fully understand why they are giving. But if a parent can help them see the *result* of their gifts, they will come to understand. An early habit of giving does not insure a commitment to the Lord, but an early habit of not giving usually instills a later attitude of not giving.

"Train up a child in the way he should go, even when he is old he will not depart from it" (Proverbs 22:6).

PARENTAL LOANS

Should a parent lend money to a child? I believe so. After all, eventually someone else will, and credit is not the problem; the misuse of credit is. If you lend money, do so only for specific projects, preferably those that will generate income, such as buying a lawn mower, materials for car washing, and a bicycle for a paper route. The contract to repay should be in writing, and interest should be charged and collected. The purpose is to establish a discipline and repayment under the same conditions as a creditor would operate. If he doesn't pay, repossess the bicycle.

"How blessed is the man who finds wisdom, and the man who gains understanding" (Proverbs 3:13).

However, if you won't actually enforce the terms of your agreement, it would be better not to lend. Otherwise, you may be instilling an attitude of indifference toward debts. Remember in enforcing your rules that debt is the number-one symptom that most often leads to divorce. If you love your children, you must teach them that all borrowing is potentially disastrous and should be used sparingly and wisely.

VOCATIONAL GOALS

No one is in a better position to give direction on vocational goals than you, as a parent. You will live with that child from birth through adulthood and should know his interests, desires, and personality. Therefore, it is important that, as basic abilities and desires be-come apparent, some vocational direction be suggested. It may not be possible to select the exact vocation, but it is possible to eliminate the wrong vocations. For instance, a parent will recognize whether or not a child is mechanically inclined, is outgoing, has a strong desire to serve, and so on. Early goal setting in this area will go a long way toward eliminating insecurities and frustration later in life.

"A plan in the heart of a man is like deep water, but a man of understanding draws it out" (Proverbs 20:5).

SUMMARY

The way anyone handles money is a visible indication of an inner spiritual condition. An observant parent can use this indicator to discern the inner needs of a child. At best, being a Christian parent is a learned rather than a taught skill, but by detecting character flaws early and applying consistent, loving, godly discipline, many deeper problems can be avoided. Use your child's attitudes toward money as a reliable indicator of later character. Fill in the mold according to God's plan rather than the world's.

"And, fathers, do not provoke your children to anger; but bring them up in the discipline and instruction of the Lord" (Ephesians 6:4).

Symptoms of Financial Problems

Without question, family financial problems seem to increase dramatically during an economic slump. Why do families experience more problems during economic down-turns? The truth is they *don't*. They suffer more symptoms. The symptom may be unpaid bills, and the consequence may be that their lights are turned off or their car is repossessed. But with rare exception, the problems that precipitated that began years earlier, perhaps even in childhood.

Many of the symptoms we see so abundantly today—business failures, massive bankruptcies, divorce, and two-job families—stem back to the same basic problem of ignoring God's Word and His warnings.

"Now it shall be, if you will diligently obey the Lord your God, being careful to do all His commandments which I command you today, the Lord your God will set you high above all the nations of the earth" (Deuteronomy 28:1).

God's instructions are neither complicated nor harsh. In fact, they are designed to free us, not bind us to a set of rigid dos and don'ts. The difficulty is that most American families have been duped into a life of "get rich quick" that includes the way we buy homes, cars, clothes, and food. God's principles in the area of finances have been largely ignored for the last forty years, and now we are reaping what has been sown.

I read an article in a business magazine that vividly brought this into focus. It seems that the largest mail order seed company in the country decided to go out of business, despite the fact that sales were higher than ever. Unfortunately, so were nonpayments by their mail order sales force. For nearly fifty years, the company had been supplying seeds to children who would sell them door-to-door, mostly in rural communities, to raise money. In recent years, the nonpayment rate to the company had risen steadily, until in 1981, it reached 70 percent. The average age of these delinquent salesmen was ten years! The final straw came when the company attempted to contact the parents, hoping they would help in collection, only to discover that the parents actually encouraged the kids.

The symptom described is nonpayment of a just debt, but the problem runs much deeper. It involves basic values that parents fail to instill in their children. It's an attitude that my rights come before others. The lack of integrity in the parents is reflected and amplified in the lives of their children.

It's unfortunate that later these parents probably won't understand why irresponsible children become irresponsible adults. *"A righteous man who walks in his integrity—how blessed are his sons after him"* (Proverbs 20:7).

EARLY SYMPTOMS

The symptoms seen today in family counseling are distressingly predictable. It seems obvious that the same basic errors in early family training are being made throughout our society. Before looking at the problems and solutions, it's necessary to identify the symptoms. Most young couples today come from middle-class families with nice homes, two cars each, color television sets, and a variety of credit sources used to purchase them. Their parents don't operate on a budget, and consequently the children aren't trained to do so either. The parents use credit readily and usually make buying decisions based on monthly payments rather than the initial price of the item. In more affluent families, the children are often provided with credit cards to buy clothes for themselves and gas for their cars. Many of these families dissolve over debt-related problems, but usually the children are buffered from the circumstances and never make the connection.

Once married and on their own, a young couple attempts to duplicate in three years what may have taken their parents twenty years to accumulate. The results are predictable. Within three years they have a lot of assets, but they're all tied up in liabilities. Many, if not most, experience the following symptoms:

Symptom 1: They can't pay the monthly bills. Once the maximum limits have been reached on credit cards and other readily available credit sources, the pressures begin to build. Creditors begin to harass, and each month it gets worse. Finally, in desperation, a bill consolidation loan is made. That lowers the overall monthly payments and stretches the debt out for a longer period of time. A resolution is made to avoid the credit trap, and the pressure is eased. Within a year the small debts return (the consolidation loan eats up all the available surplus), and the situation is worse than before.

Symptom 2: More income is needed. That conclusion seems logical at the time because they have already tried a consolidation loan, and more credit can't be the answer. So, usually the wife goes to work. If there are small children, the result is a break-even situation or less. But where no

children are involved, the end result is more money in and more money spent. Usually, within a year or less, the bills are larger rather than smaller, and the pressures are even greater, because now the extra income is necessary.

Symptom 3: Can't stand the pressure? Buy something new. Usually by this time the financed car and washing machine are breaking down, the house is beginning to need some repairs, and marital pressures are reaching a boiling point. The logical thing to do seems to be to buy a new car or take a vacation to "get away from it all." Unfortunately, it always gets worse later. Now desperation sets in, and loans are solicited from family and friends.

Many well-meaning Christians get involved with a bail-out program at this point, thinking they're helping without realizing they're only dealing with the symptoms rather than the problems. *"A man of great anger shall bear the penalty, for if you rescue him, you will only have to do it again"* (Proverbs 19:19).

Symptom 4: Divorce or bankruptcy. Once the financial pressures build, the marital pressures build as well. It's difficult to have much communication when all you ever talk about are problems. The wife may feel insecure, and the husband may get very defensive. For a few families, bankruptcy seems to be the solution, so they liquidate the debts and begin again. Since credit is easy to come by, they have no difficulty in borrowing again, particularly since they can't go bankrupt again for several years. Within a short period of time many of these couples face the same symptoms that promoted the bankruptcy.

Those who elect divorce find that the same symptoms appear in their next marriage. Fortunately, out of a feeling of panic, many seek immediate help. Many don't, however, and eventually find second and third marriages ruined by the lack of a sound spiritual and financial foundation.

It's bad enough that these symptoms occur over and over again in the non-Christian community. If we Christians were truly living by sound biblical principles, our lives would be lights to attract those who so desperately need help. In fact, nobody really *wants* to lose a marriage, to go bankrupt, or commit suicide. People do so because they have lost all hope. But even a greater crisis is that the same symptoms are occurring within Christian families and at about the same ratio. This crisis can be traced back to not teaching or applying the basic biblical principles God has established for us. Some principles are so fundamental it would seem all Christians would understand them. But unfortunately, they don't.

EARLY ATTITUDES

1. *Borrowing.* *"The wicked borrows and does not pay back, but the righteous is gracious and gives"* (Psalm 37:21).

Scripture clearly indicates that borrowing is not normal to God's plan and was never intended to be used as a routine part of our financial planning. Logically, it should be limited to appreciating assets, but Scripture does not say to borrow only for appreciating assets. It says, "Repay what is owed." Children should be encouraged to save for needs, not borrow to get them. Parental examples of trusting God to provide without borrowing are woefully lacking today.

2. *Saving.* *"There is precious treasure and oil in the dwelling of the wise, but a foolish man swallows it up"* (Proverbs 21:20).

In our upside-down inflationary economy, spending and borrowing are promoted as logical, and saving is discouraged. But let me assure you that those who borrow and spend always look for a saver in time of crises. Children should be taught that it is sounder, biblically *and* financially, to save for future needs than to rely on creditors. It's a sad indictment of how far we have strayed from God's truth when the average sixty-five-year-old man today has accumulated less than $100 in free and clear assets.

3. *Hasty decisions.* *"The plans of the diligent lead surely to advantage, but every one who is hasty comes surely to poverty"* (Proverbs 21:5).

Patience and consistency, rather than quick decisions and instant success, are the ways to financial security. Children should clearly understand that a firm financial foundation is built by taking small steps over a long period of time. They should also remember that God's plan is not the same for everyone. Children are not promised automatic affluence just because their parents have it. One of the best disciplines a parent can teach a child is to allow him to work to reach a goal. Too often everything is given without effort, and that can easily develop into a lifetime habit.

4. *Budget.* *"Poverty and shame will come to him who neglects discipline, but he who regards reproof will be honored"* (Proverbs 13:18).

Every one of our children should learn to live on a reasonable budget themselves. There is no greater financial asset that parents can leave their children than the knowledge of how to establish and live on a balanced budget. Overspending should be so discouraged in Christian homes that children wouldn't even consider it a possibility in their own homes later. Remember, at best the tug of worldly ways will tempt them down the wrong paths. At worst, our lack of training will send them down those paths without a way back.

HOW TO HELP

Obviously many more principles needed to steer our families and friends down the right path to God's plan are found in God's Word. I would encourage every couple to start a study of God's financial principles and begin to implement them in their own lives.

Once you have applied God's princi-ples in your own lives, begin a Bible study in your church or home, and share what you've learned with others. Help your church establish a regular teaching program on biblical finances and a coun-seling program to help families that have symptoms already. Every pastor's pre-marital counseling program should include a course on biblical principles of finance and a course on budgeting in which the couple actually establish their first year's budget.

Choosing the Right Vocation

A survey in *Business Week* magazine reported that only one out of six Americans is content with his job. That means nearly 83 percent are dissatisfied.

The most consistent complaint was a lack of fulfillment or long-term purpose. That is not surprising when you consider that the five most common factors expected by job seekers today are:

1. Long-term security
2. Advancement potential
3. Vacation and sick benefits
4. Pay (including automatic raises)
5. Limited authority over their work

The vast majority of Americans apparently believe a job should guarantee security against unseen perils. To accomplish that, they demand no-cut, no-layoff contracts, high-cost retirement plans, seniority rights, and new federal laws.

Certainly, many Christians also fall within this larger group of dissatisfied, fearful workers. Why? Because their value system has been altered by worldly standards to a great degree. Even within Christian schools and colleges, little or no attention is given to vocational planning on a spiritual rather than a material basis.

Well over half of the seniors in college have no specific vocation in mind. Why have they spent four years and thousands of dollars without actually finding a direction? Probably because they thought that somehow the system would settle that decision for them and also because parents consistently tell their children to "think of the future and get a good education." Unfortunately, the world says a success is someone with a good education, a secure position, and plenty of money. The Bible says a success is someone who serves God, is of service to other people, provides the needs of his family (spiritually, physically, and emotionally), and most of all is at peace. In other words, a success is someone with his priorities in order.

But just what are the priorities a Christian should consider in selecting a vocation, and how should Christian parents counsel their children?

GOD'S VOCATIONAL PLAN

Almost without exception, God's principles run contrary to prevailing worldly attitudes. For a Christian to accept non-Christian vocational goals is to invite future problems. *"But those who want to get rich fall into temptation and a snare and many foolish and harmful desires which plunge men into ruin and destruction"* (1 Timothy 6:9).

Most vocational principles are objective, such as those dealing with authority (Titus 3:1) or security (Hebrews 13:5), whereas others are subjective and require individual discernment by the Holy Spirit. Overwhelmingly such lifetime decisions fall into a scriptural priority system. Many alternatives can be eliminated because they conflict with these priorities. The remaining alternatives must be evaluated through prayer and Christian counsel.

GOD FIRST

One of the overwhelming characteristics of those who discern God's will for their lives is that they continually seek to put God first. Most Christians experience doubts and anxieties when faced with major decisions. However, most major decisions are actually a series of minor decisions that converge into a change direction. Consistently putting God first eliminates most decisions before they become crises.

"More than that, I count all things to be loss in view of the surpassing value of knowing Christ Jesus my Lord, for whom I have suffered the loss of all things, and count them but rubbish in order that I may gain Christ" (Philippians 3:8).

God has already endowed each Christian with unique abilities, desires, and gifts to accomplish His will through them. As a Christian seeks to truly serve God, the Holy Spirit will make known God's perfect vocation for him.

"But when He, the Spirit of truth, comes, He will guide you into all the truth; for He will not speak on His own initiative, but whatever He hears, He will speak; and He will disclose to you what is to come" (John 16:13).

Unfortunately, most Christians do not sense that direction because of worldly pressures, or they sense it and then lose it by failing to act upon it.

"And the one on whom seed was sown among the thorns, this is the man who hears the word, and the worry of the world, and the deceitfulness of riches choke the word, and it becomes unfruitful" (Matthew 13:22).

Quite often, putting God first in the area of vocation will necessitate choosing a vocation that has little or no retirement security or ego-building status. One example I often think of was a great college athlete who passed up a lucrative professional career to serve the Lord in a Mexican mission. Most of his friends and family urged him to go into the pros, but he knew what God called him to do.

FULFILLMENT

Regardless of the income, prestige, or security of a vocation, unless it truly merges with God's will, unrest will persist. Without exception, income is but a temporary satisfier. Most people who are trapped in a prestigious, well-paying job that does not meet their inner needs spend their lives envying the very people who are envying them.

"There is one who pretends to be rich, but has nothing; another pretends to be poor, but has great wealth" (Proverbs13:7).

INDICATORS

One of the best indicators of God's vocational direction is a spiritual gift (1 Corinthians 12). Our purpose on this earth is to serve God (Matthew 6:33). Thus, our vocation is simply an extension of our primary ministry. Many times we reverse the order and fail to recognize that the good salesman does not become a good teacher or exhorter; it is the other way around. Most often the helpful, kind secretary or housewife is the very one to whom people turn in time of distress. Why? Because she has a gift of mercy or help.

It is vital to seek discernment about God's plan and accept nothing less than the vocation that will complement and extend one's ministry.

Parents must play a vital role in vocational direction. That means teaching children to recognize and develop their gifts and talents and counseling them on God's value system.

"Train up a child in the way he should go, even when he is old he will not depart from it" (Proverbs 22:6).

PURPOSE

So often, at the end of a lifetime, a successful man states: "If only I had known forty years ago what I know now, I would not have wasted my life pursuing wealth."

In fact, the world's wisest man put it this way: *"Thus I considered all my activities which my hands had done and the labor which I had exerted, and behold all was vanity and striving after wind and there was no profit under the sun"* (Ecclesiastes 2:11).

As Christians, we have the advantage of knowing a certain future. Thus, we have the responsibility to orient our lives accordingly.

There is nothing wrong with a successful career; in fact, God promises great blessings. *"The reward of humility and the fear of the Lord are riches, honor and life"* (Proverbs 22:4). However, attitude is the key ingredient in any vocational decision.

Is the decision made by worldly standards—security, ego, income—or is it made to please and serve God and thus serve other people?

"He who loves money will not be satisfied with money, nor he who loves abundance with its income. This too is vanity" (Ecclesiastes 5:10).

As Christians, we have the advantage of being able to see life from God's perspective. We will spend eternity reaping the rewards of faithful service to God. Therefore, vocational planning for us and our children is based primarily on how we can best serve Him.

It is apparent that Solomon made nearly every human error possible concerning material things, and his assessment of vain pursuits could be summed up from Ecclesiastes 5:15 "As he has come naked from his mother's womb, so will he return as he came. He will take nothing from the fruit of his labor that he can carry in his hand."

Our Lord gives us some very sobering thoughts concerning how we invest our lives but none more convicting than in Matthew 16:26, *"For what will a man be profited, if he gains the whole world, and forfeits his soul? Or what will a man give in exchange for his soul?"*

What is Greater than God
Rich men

Poor men have it

~~without~~ If you eat it you will perish
die

Keeping Christ in Christmas

I t irritates me when I see Christ being taken out of Christmas. That is not limited to only non-Christians—even Christians have adjusted to the commercialism of the holiday season. Obviously not all of it is bad—in fact, the holiday season provides opportunities for families to reunite and also provides a pleasant break from our routines. I personally look forward to these days as an opportunity to visit with friends who are much too busy other times of the year to just stop and relax.

But we have become terribly imbalanced. We give a myriad of useless gifts at Christmas because it's expected of us, and we feel guilty if we don't. The commercialized world now makes a $100 toy seem perfectly normal. It's easy to observe the stress that our imbalanced society places on family members. Christian parents who cannot provide the latest indulgences to their children are often depressed and distraught. Obviously, no one person purposely makes them feel unworthy or insignificant, but the overwhelming emphasis we place on giving at Christmas certainly does.

So great is this social pressure that the closer we get toward Christmas Day, the more depressed and unworthy those who can't indulge feel. Unfortunately, the pressures don't end once Christmas is past, either. Those who can't afford to compete in their gift giving often dread congregating with their friends immediately after the holidays, because at "show and tell" time they don't have much to show. It is not a conscious act on the part of most people to openly display their pride. Rather, because we are in a competitive society we often determine a person's worth by his ability to buy things.

"For you have died and your life is hidden with Christ in God" (Colossians 3:3).

BALANCE

One extreme is not balanced by going to the opposite extreme. The distortion of Christmas won't be corrected by eliminating all gift giving and observing Christmas as a "religious" holiday. The fact is we *do* live in this world, and our families *are* greatly influenced by others. What we need to do is swing back toward the middle and eliminate the need to compete with others. Then we will have the freedom to develop God's plan for our families without the pressure from the commercial world.

In order to do so, I believe that, as Christians, we must first believe that God's plan is different from the world's and is more, not less, fulfilling. It is a deception to think that, by adopting a more disciplined life-style, we are somehow denied the "good life." It's like saying that by avoiding drugs we deny our children the euphoria that would make them feel "good." But to decide that all drugs are evil and absolutely refuse to use them makes for a painful experience if you have to have a broken leg set. The key, as always in God's plan, is balance. That always comes from following God's wisdom.

SHIFT OF ATTITUDES

Gift giving at Christmas is a relatively new idea. Until a couple of centuries ago, Christmas was reserved as a religious holiday on a noncommercial basis.

Most of our forefathers would have believed that trading presents on the day set aside to observe Christ's birthday was near blasphemy. However, gift giving became a generally accepted practice and was used primarily to show appreciation to loved ones. Gifts were usually simple regardless of the means of the giver so as not to embarrass those who couldn't afford to give very much. For a long while in most countries gifts were exchanged on New Years's Day (not a bad idea today—think of the great buys you could get!). Christmas gifts were limited to food for the poor or special gifts to pastors and missionaries.

As with most things that start out right, somewhere along the way the direction shifted. By the early twentieth century, families were exchanging simple gifts, usually handmade, on Christmas Day. Certainly there was really nothing wrong with that, except that under the growing influence of secularism it was a golden opportunity for Satan to divert our attention from Christ to Santa Claus. By post-World War II, Santa was the dominant figure at Christmas, and December was the calendar month for retail sales of all kinds.

How did it happen? It would seem apparent that Christians aren't as wise in the things of the Lord as non-Christians are in the things of the world. The secular world is always looking for ways to shift attention from God to material things, and we're naive enough to go along. By the time we realize that our whole direction has been diverted, as it has been at Christmas, we believe it's too late to change, so we give up.

"For all that is in the world, the lust of the flesh and the lust of the eyes and the boastful pride of life, is not from the Father, but is from the world" (1 John 2:16).

WHAT TO DO?

By anyone's standard, the way Christmas is celebrated today is a gross commercialism of the most important birth in history. But we don't need to preach to the unsaved world to put Christ back into Christmas. They shouldn't; we should. One thing I learned a long time ago in counseling is not to try to overcorrect too quickly. Not only are past habits, such as overindulging at Christmas, difficult to change, but quite often others around us don't see things just the way we do. If you attempt to stamp out all Christmas gifts suddenly, you'll end up with a revolt on your hands. The correct way is to make some positive steps to establish a better balance.

Step 1: Stamp out Santa Claus. Christian parents should let their children know that Santa is a fraud. Santa's harmless you say? Not so, when parents knowingly deceive their children about an apparently omnipotent being who travels the world in the wink of an eye and disburses presents on the basis of good and bad. It may be a small matter, but it is a place to start.

Step 2: Husband and wife should pray together and agree on a reasonable amount of gift giving. Once you have reached a decision that you feel is God's plan for your family, don't get caught by Satan's condemnation as Christmas approaches. The pressure to buy when everyone else is buying will be difficult to resist unless you *absolutely* agree. And again, I repeat, don't overreact. Develop a balanced attitude that will accomplish your goals in the next few years.

One method that has proved successful to many families is to commit an equal amount spent on gifts to feeding the truly needy. In many areas of the world, an amount equal to most of our gift purchases would feed and clothe a family for several months. By giving to a specific family through a Christian organization, your children can see the purpose and value of your sacrifice and theirs.

"And whoever in the name of a disciple gives to one of these little ones even a cup of cold water to drink, truly I say to you he shall not lose his reward" (Matthew 10:42).

Step 3. Stamp out credit. As bad as commercialized Christmas is, commercialized Christmas on credit cards is even worse. Many families literally indenture themselves to creditors for a whole year just to buy some useless junk at Christmas. As Christians, we need to decide if we *really* serve the God of the universe. If so, then He knows our needs and will meet them through His people, without indebtedness.

I know that some of the people reading this have some desperate needs. I also know that others sincerely want to help but don't know who has needs. The use of credit allows those who have needs to temporarily buffer themselves from God's real source. *"As it is written, 'He who gathered much did not have too much, and he who gathered little had no lack'"* (2 Corinthians 8:15). I believe Satan has used credit cards to cheat God's people out of blessings and to keep them in bondage.

WHY BOTHER?

With all the other important issues to deal with, such as crime, abortions, and drugs, a logical question would be, "Why bother with such a minor issue as gifts at Christmas?" Because gift giving is one area totally under our control, and, like the Easter bunny, it is a leaven that Satan sprinkles in the church. The practice of giving gifts is *not* the problem, just as the use of credit is not the problem. It is the misuse of these things that entangles us and diverts attention from Jesus Christ to material things.

We have enlisted in God's army and now find we can't identify the real enemy. *"No soldier in active service entangles himself in the affairs of everyday life, so that he may please the one who enlisted him as a soldier"* (2 Timothy 2:4).

Our problem is that we keep trying to negotiate a compromise with an enemy who is totally dedicated to destroying us. It's time that, as Christians, we decide to draw a battle line again. When it comes to commercializing Christ's birth or resurrection, we need to establish a balance.

"Instruct those who are rich in this present world not to be conceited or to fix their hope on the uncertainty of riches, but on God, who richly supplies us with all things to enjoy" (1 Timothy 6:17).

Setting Goals

Anyone who has done much counseling will attest to the fact that those who are successful in any field are the goal setters. They have a desire to achieve that is coupled with discipline. That combination is essential to being successful in anything, including Christianity. Clearly, this is evident in reading about the apostles, particularly Paul. He established goals and stuck to them, refusing to get side-tracked into nonministry related areas.

For instance, I'm sure Paul felt that pastoral work was important because he established it in the churches he started. But he also knew that he wasn't called to be a pastor. He could have settled down to teach at one of the churches he established—without criticism. After all, he had paid his "dues" and run his race. But Paul knew he was an evangelist, called to carry God's Word to the unsaved. That single-mindedness on Paul's part is what we would describe today as having firm goals.

FEW SET GOALS TODAY

With the emphasis on mass media over the past thirty years has come a group-decision mentality. It seems that most people want to find out what others are doing and emulate it.

Today, the lack of goal setting is approaching a crisis level. Our problem is that we don't have to set goals. Our level of affluence allows us to drift along in the group with relative ease and comfort. Christ said that condition would ultimately be the greatest threat to Christianity.

First, it would be a threat because it would cause us to drift away from God's path. *"For where your treasure is, there will your heart be also"* (Matthew 6:21). And second, it would be a threat because, when comforts are in jeopardy, many will choose to follow those comforts rather than Christ. *"Yet he has no firm root in himself, but is only temporary, and when affliction or persecution arises because of the word, immediately he falls away"* (Matthew 13:21).

That danger is directly related to the lack of godly goals or what might be called singleness of purpose. Without singleness of purpose we drift and get caught up in following the crowd. It is a condition that James described as "double-minded."

"For let not that man expect that he will receive anything from the Lord, being a double-minded man, unstable in all his ways" (James 1:7-8).

DANGEROUS GOALS

There are many miserable people with well-thought-out goals. Unfortunately, their goals are selfish, materialistic plans that attempt to fill a need that can be filled only by a personal relationship with Jesus Christ. Being single-minded of purpose about the wrong things is still wrong. In setting goals a simple priority system will help to avoid these problems:

First, be certain that whatever goals you're setting are compatible with God's Word. Success goals to soothe our fears or feed our egos are doomed to failure. God promised to meet our needs and provide an abundance to give to others but not when we intend to hoard it or squander it.

"You ask and do not receive, because you

ask with wrong motives, so that you may spend it on your pleasures" (James 4:3).

Second, husband and wife must establish goals together. If you find that you cannot do so because of your relationship, that should be your first goal. When that relationship is not right, it's time to be honest and correct it. For those who are single, it's important to seek counsel from a mature believer who is as different from you as possible. As in a marriage, if both of you agreed about everything, one of you would be unnecessary.

Third, when establishing financial goals related to income, growth, or success, make a written commitment to give either most or everything above an established level into God's work. Literally, your goal would be to make more to give, not to spend more. When husband and wife are working together on these goals, a good balance will be established. Usually one is tempted to keep too much, while the other wants to give it all away.

SCRIPTURAL CASE FOR SETTING GOALS

"The mind of man plans his way, but the Lord directs his steps" (Proverbs 16:9). God's Word says that we have been given both responsibility and authority on this earth. We are to plan our way, and God will provide the direction. Obviously, no one has a perfect insight into God's will for his life. It's a day-by-day process. But God promises us guidance to keep us on track if we're willing to listen. The prerequisite to receiving God's guidance is the willingness to accept it.

"Commit your works to the Lord, and your plans will be established" (Proverbs 16:3).

Most Christians sincerely want God's guidance, but they aren't willing to pay the price to get it. God's way is not one of several available alternatives. It is the only way. We must decide to either follow or reject God's way. Christ told us that we cannot serve two masters (Matthew 6:24). Until we decide to accept God's will for our lives, He is not going to reveal it. Unfortunately, that's why so many people will never find God's will; they want to try it on for size first. By "faith" we must accept that God's plan for us is best regardless of where it leads us.

"And without faith it is impossible to please Him, for he who comes to God must believe that He is, and that He is a rewarder of those who seek Him" (Hebrews 11:6).

SCRIPTURAL GOALS

1. _Bible study._ Before any financial goals can be established, the proper spiritual goals should be developed. The best place to start is with a study of God's Word. The Bible is like God's road map for us. It will take us wherever we want to go if we just know how to read it. God promises the wisdom to understand His Word if we'll spend the time to study it. When I was a new Christian, my first pastor started me out on a simple plan called 9:59. It was nine minutes and fifty-nine seconds set aside to study the Bible daily. This is a plan anyone can achieve.

2. _Prayer._ If the Bible is God's road map, then prayer is God's headlights. It keeps us on the road and out of ditches. You get to know about God by studying His Word, but you get to know God through prayer. Even Christ Himself needed to withdraw and pray to God, and certainly we need to pray as much or more. The one common characteristic of dry Christians seems to be the lack of consistent prayer life. Set a goal to pray

regularly and consistently, even if for only a few minutes a day.

3. *Church.* We are admonished not to forsake the assembling of ourselves together. *"Not forsaking our own assembling together, as is the habit of some, but encouraging one another;and all the more, as you see the day drawing near"* (Hebrews 10:25).

4. *Money.* Giving is the external evidence of an internal spiritual condition. But even more than that, giving is an objective, measurable commitment made to God. Few promises in God's Word are as clear as those related to giving. It is the principle of sowing and reaping found in 2 Corinthians 9:6.

"Now this I say, he who sows sparingly shall also reap sparingly; and he who sows bountifully shall also reap bountifully."

FAMILY GOALS

1. *Marriage.* Once the previous goals have been made individually, they must become a part of your partnership with your spouse. If your spouse is not a Christian, then you have an excellent goal to establish in your personal prayer life. Don't give up praying for your spouse. One Christian lady I know prayed for her husband twenty-two years before he accepted the Lord. It finally took the shock of three years in prison before he responded.

A minimum goal with which to start should be to read a few verses of Scripture together regularly and to pray for your family together.

2. *Children.* As Christian parents, we should teach our children God's principles. However, too much too soon will frustrate you and them. With very young children, study and prayer are relatively easy habits to develop in the family. Start with a good children's Bible guide, and pray for each other. With older children start where you can. Read a brief devotional at the breakfast or dinner table, and set aside a few minutes to pray together.

FINANCIAL GOALS

Woven in among every other area of goal setting and planning is the financial area. Unless some realistic spiritual goals are established in this area, the others are doomed to failure. The one overriding goal in the financial area must be that our life-styles are glorifying to God.

A minimum goal should be for husband and wife to set aside one full day to do some goal planning. From the goal-planning day, some minimums should be established.

1. *Yearly budget.* Perhaps you can't determine precisely what the entire year's budget will be, but some basics can be started.

2. *Study God's plan.* A good place to begin a long-range goal setting plan is by studying God's principles of finance.

The Issue of Inheritance

No generation of people has ever managed more material assets with less training to do so. In a single generation today, an individual can go from near poverty to an estate of millions of dollars. Unfortunately, the succeeding generation can just as quickly lose it all. We seem to be a people of extremes, and inheritance is no exception. One part of our society leaves enormous wealth to its generally untrained offspring, whereas another segment spends it all and leaves practically nothing.

I will delay discussing the latter group because that is really a discussion on current stewardship. It is sufficient to say that many Christians who spend all that they have without regard to their children are not good stewards. In fact, the legacy that many Christian parents leave today is one of debt.

"If a man fathers a hundred children and lives many years, however many they be, but his soul is not satisfied with good things, and he does not even have a proper burial, then I say, 'Better the miscarriage than he'" (Ecclesiastes 6:3).

Most of us have the ability to create an estate today. It may be land, businesses, homes, or an insurance policy payable upon our death, but nevertheless it is an estate. The common strategy with most people, including Christians, is to keep as much as possible while we're alive and leave it to our heirs upon our death. Unfortunately, quite often the heirs are poorly trained to manage the assets.

I recall one man I was counseling who had accumulated a sizable estate. When I asked him what he planned to do with it all, he said, "I'll leave it to my children, I guess." I asked him why he didn't just give it to them right then, and he replied, "Why, they don't know how to handle money; they'd just lose it all." When asked if he thought they wouldn't lose it after he died, his response was, "Well, I'll be gone then, so who cares?" Well, God cares because being a good steward doesn't stop with death.

Poor stewardship also means leaving an untrained wife to take over the management of the finances. Unfortunately, that is most often the case, and the results are anxiety, frustration, and dependence on unwise counselors. You would think that men would believe the statistics that tell us seven out of eight men die before their wives, but apparently they don't. Consequently, many women are forced into the role of estate manager with little or no knowledge in that area. To make matters worse, their husbands leave few guidelines for them to follow, and, in fact, in almost 70 percent of the cases they don't even leave a valid will. This leaves the asset distribution up to the state and its laws.

Further, the average man leaves about 20 percent of the minimum assets necessary to provide for his family. That includes total life insurance of about $20,000, or about the same average as in 1963. Why is this? Is it that the average American father doesn't care about his family? I don't think so. I believe it really boils down to two current flaws: ignorance and slothfulness—ignorance, because most of us haven't been taught good stewardship, which includes inheritance; and slothfulness, because many people know what they should do but procrastinate until it's too late.

Some Christians are superstitious

without realizing it and avoid discussing death for fear that it will happen. This I can say with certainty—unless the Lord comes first, it will happen for each of us. Talking about death neither hastens nor delays it; it only makes it easier for those left behind.

"The naive believes everything, but the prudent man considers his steps" (Proverbs 14:15).

BIBLICAL GUIDELINES

God leaves no subject untouched in His Word, and fortunately that includes the area called inheritance. Even a brief survey of the Bible reveals that God provided for each generation through inheritance. In biblical times, the sons inherited their father's properties and thus provided for the rest of their family. "A good man leaves an inheritance to his children's children, and the wealth of the sinner is stored up for the righteous" (Proverbs 13:22).

What is not so obvious is that in most instances, the sons received their inheritance while their fathers were still living. Thus, a father was able to oversee their stewardship while they were learning.

The parable of the prodigal son in Luke 15 reflects that principle. The father divided his inheritance between his two sons and lived to see the younger one restored. It would be interesting to see what money management training most children would receive if their parents knew they would turn over all the estate to them and depend upon them for their support. Of course, since the average sixty-five-year-old man's financial worth is only about $100 today, it wouldn't take a lot of management. It's rather obvious that fifty years ago their parents failed to teach them basic stewardship. The Bible says save, but the government says don't bother.

"House and wealth are an inheritance from fathers" (Proverbs 19:14a).

GODLY INHERITANCE

Obviously the most important inheritance we can offer our children is a Christian influence that leads to salvation. It's a good thing that most Christian parents don't leave that inheritance training until after death. Neither should we leave good materials training until after death—it's too late then. I would challenge every Christian to develop a godly approach to inheritance beginning right now. Establish a few fundamental absolutes about your inheritance.

1. *Training for wife.* Insure that the wife understands how to handle money well. If a woman has never actually managed the money, the training starts with basic budgeting. The wife should actually manage the home finances for at least the next year. Then, if something happens to her husband, she will know that she can manage the money.

2. *Create wills/trusts.* Every living American should have the basic legal document for after-death asset distribution—a will. Without a will, the state in which you live will distribute your assets according to their laws of intestacy. Rarely, if ever, will this be according to your wishes. Husband and wife both need wills, and each should understand the other's will. First, pray about how you wish your estate to be distributed, including the Lord's work. Then, write it out as clearly as possible and have a competent attorney write your plan into your will.

Some families will need a "trust" to manage their assets in order to reduce estate costs and/or save taxes. There are many varieties of trusts, and, contrary to most opinions, their use is not limited only to large estates. Almost any good bookstore or library will have several easy-to-read books on the use of wills and trusts. Several large Christian ministries, such as Campus Crusade for Christ, Billy Graham Crusades, and Christian Broadcast Network offer free estate planning services for those who support their ministry. All of them will provide good quality materials upon request.

3. *Develop a plan.* In addition to the legal instruments necessary to distribute and manage your estate, you must have a plan. For instance, at what age do you want to begin your children's training? How much will you entrust to their management? Who will help advise them? Obviously, each family's plan will be somewhat different, but the one common factor for Christians should be an understanding of God's principles for managing money.

Age. There is really no best age to start teaching children good money management, but the younger, the better. For very young children (two to four), start their training by helping them to understand the value of money. That can be started by associating money with work. Pay them small sums for tasks around the home, and then help them decide whether to spend it or save it. As they get older, you should begin to expand their training, including a good study of God's principles.

Practice. Nothing helps more to reinforce principle than problems. As your children approach the teen years, you need to put them into real-life money situations. That includes letting them open checking and savings accounts and doing the monthly balancing.

Borrowing. The principle of borrowing can best be demonstrated by lending money to them at interest and requiring that they repay the loan—totally. Many young couples would have been better served if their parents had taught them about debt while they were living at home, rather than waiting for a creditor to do it.

Investing. The risk-reward system of our economy can be clearly demonstrated to young people by entrusting to them a sum of money (small at first) to be invested. It is interesting to see how real the economy and money become to a teenager who has his money at risk. Sometime back, I helped each of our sons get involved in an area of investing to demonstrate how free enterprise really works. For one, it was a car to fix up and resell; for another, it was repairing a small rental house; and for another, it was a small coin investment. The cost to me was relatively small, but the reward was helping to develop three free-market enthusiasts.

Giving. Teach your children to give to God's work out of their earnings, and you have made what I personally believe is the most essential step in molding them into good money managers. *"Train up a child in the way he should go, and even when he is old he will not depart from it"* (Proverbs 22:6).

Rarely will you find a generous giver who manages money poorly. God promises wisdom to those who trust Him; giving is an evidence of that trust.

Part 7:

Ministries and Scriptural Highlights

Christian Fund-Raising

Fund raising would seem to be the national pastime of most non-profit organizations in America today. From the bulk of mail received by most Christian givers, there is little doubt that the competition for Christian support is acute. New organizations spring up every day, and as the number of organizations grows, the search for new funds grows more intense, as anyone who has donated money to one or more general appeal groups knows. Almost mystically, an unexpecting donor receives from scores of other organizations he never heard of. That is because many organizations either use a common fund-raising company or else they sell their donor lists to generate additional income.

Many well-meaning Christians get pressured into giving to groups they know little or nothing about because of emotional appeals or skilled manipulation.

Even many otherwise sound Christian ministries have turned to secular advertising and fund-raising companies to meet their growing demand for funds. Often they will pay up to 40 percent of all donations just to raise the money. Some promoters actually will be working on fund-raising campaigns for anti-Christian and Christian groups simultaneously. All of that is to say that each individual Christian must be responsible for how God's money is used, even in the most worthy of causes.

WHO? WHAT? HOW?

Before supporting any fund appeal, a Christian should ask some basic questions.

1. *Who is the group asking for the funds?* Get a list of references from the organization that can be easily verified through other well-known groups. It would be wise to drop a letter off to the Attorney General of the state of residence and also a letter to the head of a ministry or church nearby. Often the best method to do that is through your own pastor or church secretary.

2. *What are they going to use the funds for?* At least one good way to determine this is to ask for a projected budget. The lack of a budget is one reason why many organizations continually send out "crisis appeal" letters.

3. *How do they raise funds, and how do they manage them?* It is wise to ask if a fund-raising group is involved and what percentage of the funds go to them. Also, how much of the ministry's budget is dedicated to fund raising? Obviously, some media ministries (radio and TV) would normally have a higher ratio. A good indication of financial management is the debt-income ratio and the change in overhead expenses from year to year.

Once a Christian has asked these questions, the burden of making the decision based on common sense is satisfied. However, the burden of exercising spiritual wisdom can only be satisfied by the application of God's Word.

BIBLICAL PRINCIPLES

There must be a balance in a Christian's attitude toward ministry support. Too often a Christian will read a spectacular biography of how God used a particular individual, and he will use that as an absolute rule against everyone else. Personal testimonies are exciting and rewarding and can be of great value in providing alternatives. However, they are *not* to be used as yardsticks, unless confirmed in God's Word. As an example: many Christians have read the story of George Mueller's life and how he trusted God for everything without asking. They then concluded that no Christian should ever let a material need be known. That is noble and admirable but not scriptural. Paul admonished the Corinthians because they felt that he didn't have the right to ask them for support (2 Corinthians 11:7-9). In Exodus 25:1-3, the Lord told Moses to tell the people of Israel to raise a contribution for the Tabernacle.

However, just because asking is acceptable doesn't mean that it's God's plan for everyone or that every letter sent to supporters should ask for more money. Again, balance is the key principle. Nowhere in Scripture is there any indication that God's people went begging. It would appear evident that many more needs were met by praying than by asking. It also seems clear that once God's people are made aware of their responsibilities to give and support God's work, the need to ask goes down dramatically (Exodus 36:5-6).

WHICH GROUP TO SUPPORT

God does not intend for every Christian to give to every need. Attempting to do so will quickly result in frustration and, for most of us, poverty. Therefore, we must be able to sort out those we are to help from those we are not. That does not necessarily mean that the cause or the organization is not worthy—only that the need is meant for another to satisfy.

1. *God's work.* There are many worthy social organizations serving the needs of the poor, the sick, and the elderly. The vast majority make no pretense of going in the name of the Lord. That does not exclude them from receiving the portion set apart for God. It is abundantly clear throughout the Bible that gifts dedicated to God were to be distributed in His name. Since God obviously did not need the material goods, they were redistributed to satisfy those who had needs (Exodus 34:19; Leviticus 1:2; 27:30; Deuteronomy 12:6; 14:28).

2. *Deserving.* Just because a group has an emotional presentation for a seemingly worthy Christian cause does not mean they automatically qualify for support. It is important to determine that the funds will actually be used for the purpose they were given.

Above all else be certain about the doctrinal stand of the ministry. Many committed believers have been shocked to discover that they were contributing to an organization that was anti-Christian.

3. *Personal benefit.* Those organizations that have met needs in your life should be high on the support list. Obviously, those who should be most supportive of a ministry are those who were ministered to by it. If that organization is not a highly visible one (does not advertise or regularly appeal), then the support of those they minister to is essential.

"And let the one who is taught the word share all good things with him who teaches" (Galatians 6:6).

4. *Good stewards.* Just as in any other investment, a Christian should get the best benefit of his investment in God's work. Therefore, the organizations that manage their funds the best should be considered first. Obviously, the type of

ministry each group is involved in must also be considered. A rural church and a national television ministry will have vastly different budgets and should not be evaluated by total expenditures. If you have a desire to support a particular type of ministry, then locate the most efficient and productive one available.

The leaders of any ministry should have a clear, concise plan for accomplishing God's work and a reasonable idea of costs and time. The lack of written goals and objectives if usually a sign of slothfulness. There are other signs to look for, such as a heavy debt burden, a bad credit history, unfinished projects, significant staff turnover, and soliciting support from the unsaved.

"I passed by the field of the sluggard, and by the vineyard of the man lacking sense; and behold, it was completely overgrown with thistles" (Proverbs 24:30-31a; see also 1 Corinthians 9:14; Luke 16:13).

5. *God's leading.* The most important principle of all is to allow God to direct your giving. We are told to lean upon God's wisdom and not our own understanding (Proverbs 3:5), and that also applies to giving. Those people who have a problem in turning down anyone who asks must learn to wait and pray before giving. The others who have a problem sharing with anyone need to give more and wait less. *"But whoever has the world's goods, and beholds his brother in need and closes his heart against him, how does the love of God abide in him?"* (1 John 3:17).

An essential part of the balance system God has established is the husband and wife relationship. Almost without exception, one is prone to give too much and the other too little. Couples that can learn to communicate and accept each other's counsel will usually establish a reasonable balance.

CONCLUSION

It is impossible to lay down absolute guidelines for funding God's work, simply because God did not do so in His Word. However, there are some good guidelines available for both the askers and the givers. Any giver would be well advised to use biblical guidelines whenever possible to select those organizations that do or do not qualify. Then rely on God's inner direction to decide which groups to support. The biblical guidelines to be used are:

1. Adherence to sound biblical doctrine in the organization and ministry (Galatians 1:9)

2. Ministry in the name of the Lord Jesus Christ (Colossians 3:17)

3. Practice of good financial management within the organization (Luke 16:12)

4. Dependence on God's people for support (3 John 6-7)

5. Lives changed for Christ through the ministry (Galatians 5:22-23)

Give and It Will Be Given to You

"*Give, and it will be given to you; good measure, pressed down, shaken together, running over, they will pour into your lap. For by your standard of measure it will be measured to you in return*" (Luke 6:38).

Few Scripture verses are quoted more often Luke 6:38 regarding the principle of giving and receiving. When I first read this verse shortly after committing my life to Christ, I pondered it for many weeks. Did God really mean what that verse says? Do God's promises depend on our giving first? I read the previous and subsequent verses to see if perhaps it could be interpreted in another context. I then studied parallel and contrasting verses. After dedicating many hours of thoroughly enjoyable time to God's Word, I concluded that I really didn't understand the meaning of Luke 6:38. There were some seemingly obvious difficulties with the principle that receiving was a matter of giving first. What about those Christians I knew who gave but didn't receive much in return?

My first response was to assume the principle did not apply to all Christians. Perhaps it applied only to those with a gift of giving. I quickly eliminated the rationality of that. If Luke 6:38 applied to only a select few, Christ would not have delivered the message in Luke 6 to the masses. God may well select a few to receive and dispose of a large amount of His resources, but the principle described in Luke 6:38 is a promise to anyone who will apply it. I thought, *Perhaps the principle applies to spiritual, rather than material, rewards.* Indeed, further study confirmed that it does apply to spiritual rewards, as well as material. But there is no way to disassociate the material giving and receiving since in verses 30-35 Christ made direct reference to material things. The more I reviewed other Scripture dealing with the principle of giving and receiving, the more I realized there was no contradiction at all.

OBSERVATIONS

There were prerequisites that had to be met before even an understanding could be received. Once an understanding of God's promise is reached, then it is necessary to believe that promise. I determined to make a study of giving and receiving in the lives of Christians I knew, including myself, and match the result of my study to God's Word. Since all of God's principles are given as examples for living, an applied principle has to be verified in changed lives or else we either don't understand the principle or don't apply it. Before defining the scriptural principle, I would first like to share some observations of the study that started nine years ago and still continue.

1. Most Christians give far less than one-tenth of their incomes to work being done in the Lord's name.

2. Many Christians give at least a tenth of their incomes regularly but have not experienced what they assess as God's material or spiritual bounty.

3. Many Christians give at least a tenth of their incomes and can identify many instances of God's abundance, either materially, spiritually, or both.

4. A small percentage of Christians give far above a tenth of their incomes but cannot identify what they would describe as God's abundant return.

5. A very small percentage of Christians give far above a tenth of their incomes and can identify God's response, both generally and specifically.

Of course, there were other categories and instances in which Christians moved from one group to another. Many of these can be explained due to spiritual growth or withdrawal, which will obviously affect every area of our lives. A few can be classified as unique from a biblical perspective. That is most clear when a spiritually mature Christian gives in great abundance and outwardly appears to suffer materially. The apostle Paul would most assuredly identify with that group. God has a separate and unique plan for these people, and the depth of their commitment to Christ sets them apart in spiritual blessings.

I would like to make some observations about these groups without intending at all to be judgmental. I believe God has provided us with material indicators of spiritual condition. They are not for accusation; they are for admonition.

DON'T ROB GOD

Those who give less than even a tenth of their increase have limited what God can do for them according to His own Word. *"Will a man rob God? Yet you are robbing Me! But you say, 'How have we robbed Thee?' In tithes and offerings"* (Malachi 3:8). Lest we somehow believe this principle applies only to the Old Covenant, Paul amplifies it for us in 2 Corinthians 9:6. *"Now this I say, he who sows sparingly shall also reap sparingly; and he who sows bountifully shall also reap bountifully."* The lack of giving is an external material indicator that spiritual changes need to be made.

Those who give more than a tenth but not necessarily sacrificially and experience God's abundance (according to God's plan for them) are meeting God's prerequisites for where they are right then.

Many of those who give what we consider a material abundance and do not experience any particular spiritual or material reply may actually give for self-motivated reasons. Many are trying to bribe God into blessing them. They are much like Simon in Acts 8, who upon observing the benefits of God's power tried to acquire it without meeting the spiritual prerequisites. They require and even demand God's blessing because of what they consider their sacrifice. They are not in subjection to God but are trying to exercise control over Him. Paul addressed that attitude also in Romans 11:34-35.

"For who has known the mind of the Lord, or who became His counselor? Or who has first given to Him, that it might be paid back to him again?"

BELIEVE GOD

The last group is made up of those who give, expecting but never demanding. And although God often returns far beyond their expectations both materially and spiritually, their giving is out of a desire to please God, not to profit from the relationship. The evidence of that can be found in the fact that usually their sacrificial giving came long before the response from God, and their ratios of giving far exceed their accumulation regardless of the supply.

A Christian friend in Atlanta exemplifies that principle clearly. I met him several years ago during a particularly difficult time in his life financially. He was totally committed to giving sacrificially into God's kingdom, had experienced great blessings, and in fact was noted in Christian circles as a giver. Then for an extended period of time the bounty was withdrawn, and for all intents and purposes he was broke. His Christian "Job's friends" quickly pointed out every character flaw he had and advised him to repent and get straight with God. After some soul searching, prayer, and fasting, he was where God wanted him to be, doing what God wanted him to do. Consequently, he and his wife decided to give more, not less.

Mark 11:24 says, *"Therefore I say to you, all things for which you pray and ask, believe that you have received them, and they shall be granted to you."*

He concluded that to believe, he had to act. So they began to give furniture and other things they had collected during the abundance to others who had greater needs. Now he is being used by God to supply enormous sums of money into His work. His love for giving is matched by a deep sensitivity to the needs of others, and there is never a doubt who gets the glory for the abundance to give.

Several times he and his wife have saved to build a new home, and each time they have given the money away to meet a need in God's work. Every time I see him he has an excitement to make more money so they can give more away. The only caution I have ever given this kind of giver is not to give away all of the "seed corn."

SOWING AND REAPING

The spiritual principle behind Luke 6:38 is indeed giving and receiving, but it is not giving to receive. The prerequisites to receiving are found in Luke 6:27-37. A Christian who lives by these principles practices the surrendered life. Therefore, the giving is simply a material expression of the deeper spiritual obedience to Christ. Nearly every Christian desires to be obedient to God, and in many ways most are. However, Christ warned us that the greatest threat to our walk with God is the tug of our materialistic world.

"And the one on whom seed was sown among the thorns, this was the man who hears the word, and the worry of the world and the deceitfulness of riches choke the word, and it becomes unfruitful" (Matthew 13:22).

Seek the Kingdom of God

"*B*ut *seek first His kingdom and His righteousness; and all these things shall be added to you*" (Matthew 6:33).

The admonition to "seek first the kingdom of God" in Matthew 6:33 is given by the Lord as a contrast of worrying about material possessions. I believe there has never been a generation of Christians so caught up in worry about possessions as we are. We have a greater abundance available on a day by day basis than *any* previous generation. Most of us have machines that reduce the daily household labor required, our children are well-clothed and well-educated, and our life expectancy is more than God's promise of three score and ten. We have insurance plans, retirement plans, disability plans, and unemployment plans. Yet we are so caught up in making more money and buying bigger and better things that we have lost most of our thrust to reach the unsaved world. As I read through God's Word, it keeps asking the same fundamental question: "Are we seeking first the kingdom of God?"

WHAT DO YOU STAND FOR?

It would seem evident that if we are to spend an eternity in the presence of God and only seventy or so years on this earth that we should be more concerned about what we will receive then than what we are getting now. But when our priorities are reviewed it is apparent that most Christians live without real hope as Paul described it in Romans 8:24-25. We're willing to settle for what we can see, rather than what we cannot see. That is exactly the principle that Christ teaches in Matthew 6:19-33.

It's not the material things that cause the difficulties. God says that He will give us those things that the world cherishes so much. It is a matter of heart attitude. Are we more dedicated to accumulating material things than to serving God? Without a doubt the evidence of our lives shows that we are serving money—not God. *"For where your treasure is, there will your heart be also"* (Matthew 6:21).

The question is often asked, "What do Christians stand for?" The answer the world would give is, "Not much other than what we do." The sad part about it is that most people really want to know a personal God. They carve gods out of wood or rocks and worship idols, cows, demons, or whatever they can find. We have the only hope for a generation without hope, and yet we're spending the majority of our time pursuing vain things. Our energies are so depleted in accumulating bigger homes, businesses, cars, and retirement plans that we don't have much time to seek God's kingdom.

ONLY TWO CHOICES

Christ says that we have only two choices as disciples: to follow God or to follow money.

"No one can serve two masters; for either he will hate the one and love the other, or he will hold to one and despise the other. You cannot serve God and mammon" (Matthew 6:24).

The scriptural warning is clear, that we will be judged on the evidence of our material lives more than any other thing. The attraction of materialism is so great that Christ devoted two-thirds of His parables to warning His disciples about it. The writers of the epistles amplified that teaching as they observed the destructive force of materialism in the lives of believers.

"For the love of money is a root of all sorts of evil, and some by longing for it have wandered away from the faith, and pierced themselves with many a pang" (1 Timothy 6:10). *"Let your character be free from the love of money, being content with what you have; for He Himself has said, 'I will never desert you, nor will I ever forsake you'"* (Hebrews 13:5).

Again, it's not material things that are the problem, it's materialism. The alarming thing about our generation of Christians is that we have found a way of scripturally rationalizing our excesses. Many Christians actually believe that we can attract the unsaved by having the best. Let me assure you that those who are seriously seeking God in their lives are not attracted by the luxuries of Christians. They are attracted by an uncompromising commitment to God. If that commitment also yields material blessings, it's just an added benefit.

WHY CHRISTIANS STUMBLE

It's unfortunate that the zeal and dedication seen in new believers often fades as they get back into the old rut. Within a few months, or at best a few years, most have learned the Christian language and fall back in step with the world. They talk a lot about God's blessings—usually material blessings—but seldom experience real joy and peace. Even worse, lives aren't changed through contact with them. Why? They have become too busy to listen to God's voice.

Too busy to serve. When the Lord entered Martha and Mary's home, Mary sat at His feet to listen as He taught. That distressed Martha, who was apparently trying to impress Him with her activities. When Martha asked Jesus to rebuke Mary, His reply would fit most of us today.

"But the Lord answered and said to her, 'Martha, Martha, you are worried and bothered about so many things; but only a few things are necessary, really only one, for Mary has chosen the good part, which shall not be taken away from her'" (Luke 10:41-42).

Later Christ told His disciples a parable about being a part of the kingdom of God in Luke 14:16-26. Many will be called to serve in God's kingdom, but most will have excuses why they can't get involved.

At the conclusion of this parable we have one of the most convicting Scriptures of all Christ's teaching. *"If anyone comes to Me, and does not hate his own father and mother and wife and children and brothers and sisters, yes, and even his own life, he cannot be My disciple"* (Luke 14:26). Anyone who doubts the emphasis that God puts on placing His kingdom first should ponder that Scripture for a while.

Too many distractions. I find that the more things accumulate, the more distractions they cause. Two cars break down twice as often, two computers cause twice the errors, and so on. When most of us first began to work, our greatest concerns were a good job and a modest home. But as we make more, our expectations increase. Now we find ourselves distracted by buildings, cars, investments, and retirement plans for thirty years in the future. The very second that we cease to breathe, all of those concerns are going to be irrelevant. In counseling during the last few years, I have met several Christians who had learned they had terminal illnesses. Their perspective about the future and material things changed the instant they took on a short-range view of this world.

That is exactly what Christ is saying to us in Matthew 6:25: *"For this reason I say to you, do not be anxious for your life, as to what you shall eat, or what you shall drink, nor for your body, as to what you shall put on. Is not life more than food, and the body than clothing?"* Compared to eternity, we are all dying tomorrow. Don't be so distracted by the worries of this world.

KEYS TO THE KINGDOM

Over the last few years, I have read and reread Paul's letter to the Romans. It is obvious to me that somewhere between the seventh and tenth chapters, Paul describes a man (himself) who has found the keys to God's invisible kingdom. It becomes clear that what Paul is describing is a man who accepts God as the absolute authority in his life and is willing to surrender everything, if necessary, to serve Him—even to the point of death. Paul has learned, as he expressed in Philippians 1:21, that we live to serve Christ at any cost, even if death is what we must pay.

Several years ago I met a Chinese Christian who was saved as a member of the Red Brigade in Communist China. He was imprisoned, tortured, starved, and beaten in an effort to get him to renounce his faith. When he refused, his family was executed to "teach others a lesson." He said the thing that sustained him was an ever—deepening relationship with Christ and an unyielding commitment to serving God. When most of our commitments are weighed against his, it's easy to see why the keys to the kingdom elude us.

Perhaps God hasn't called us to the physical sacrifices that many Christian martyrs have suffered. But the admonition that Christ gives to all of us is abso-

lutely clear. *"Then Jesus said to His disciples, 'If anyone wishes to come after Me, let him deny himself, and take up his cross, and follow Me'"* (Matthew 16:24).

EVIDENCE OF OUR COMMITMENT

It's always good to have some standard of measure to compare where we are to where God wants us to be. The evidence given in God's Word is clear and simple. All we have to do is eliminate our ego and pride and consistently put the needs of others before our own, and we'll know we're on the right track. Is it difficult? No, it is impossible. But in Romans 7:24-25 Paul gives us God's solution—let go and *trust* God.

Humility. Christ is to be the most exalted being in the eternal kingdom of God. Knowing this to be true, He assumed the lowliest, most humbling position possible during His life. He not only served others, but He also assumed the position of a foot washer. In John 13:15 He says, *"For I gave you an example that you also should do as I did to you."* Perhaps to us this will mean giving up having the most and the best, and not just giving to someone else's need, but giving them the best.

"Self" denial. It is a contrast in human logic that by giving up something we can receive even more. But Christ taught this principle frequently; it's called sowing and reaping. We won't always reap the rewards immediately. In fact, I believe it is our choice whether to take what we want now or store it and receive it in God's eternal kingdom. When you compare the time to enjoy God's rewards to the time spent in this world, there is no contest.

"And He said to them, 'Truly I say to you, there is no one who has left house or wife or brothers or parents or children, for the sake

of the kingdom of God, who shall not receive many times as much at this time and in the age to come, eternal life'" (Luke 18:29-30).

Love for others. Last as we conclude this survey, God's Word tells us that an evidence of our commitment to His way will be shown in our concern for others.

In Matthew 25, the Lord describes the gleaning of the righteous servants from the unrighteous. The righteous servants were those through whom the love of God showed itself by sharing. *"And the King will answer and say to them, 'Truly I say to you, to the extent that you did it to one of these brothers of Mine, even the least of them, you did it to Me'"* (Matthew 25:40).

As we start each day we have a choice; to follow God or to follow this world. If we decide to totally follow God's path, it *will* cost us. We will be buffeted by Satan as never before. We'll doubt our decision and the wisdom of it. But on the sole authority of God's Word we can clearly know that our priorities are in order.

"I tell you that He will bring about justice for them speedily. However, when the Son of Man comes, will He find faith on the earth?" (Luke 18:8).